THEOLOGICAL INTERPRETATION OF THE NEW TESTAMENT

Theological Interpretation of the New Testament

A Book-by-Book Survey

Kevin J. Vanhoozer

General Editor

Daniel J. Treier
and N. T. Wright

Associate Editors

a division of Baker Publishing Group
Grand Rapids, Michigan

Published by Baker Academic
a division of Baker Publishing Group
P.O. Box 6287, Grand Rapids, MI 49516-6287
www.bakeracademic.com

Published in Great Britain by the Society for Promoting Christian Knowledge
36 Causton Street
London SW1P 4ST

Theological Interpretation of the New Testament first published in 2008. Chapters for this volume previously appeared in Kevin J. Vanhoozer et al., eds., *Dictionary for Theological Interpretation of the Bible* (Baker Academic/SPCK, 2005).

Printed in the United States of America

Library of Congress Cataloging-in-Publication Data
Theological interpretation of the New Testament : a book-by-book survey / Kevin J. Vanhoozer, general editor ; Daniel J. Treier and N. T. Wright, associate editors.
 p. cm.
 Includes bibliographical references and indexes.
 ISBN 978-0-8010-3623-1 (pbk.)
 1. Bible. N.T.—Theology. 2. Bible. N.T.—Criticism, interpretation, etc. I. Vanhoozer, Kevin J. II. Treier, Daniel J., 1972– III. Wright, N. T. (Nicholas Thomas)
 BS2397.T43 2008
 225.6—dc22   2008025593

British Library Cataloguing-in-Publication Data
A catalogue record for this book is available from the British Library.
UK ISBN 978-0-281-06102-0

Contents

Contributors

William R. Baker (PhD, University of Aberdeen) is professor of New Testament at Cincinnati Bible Seminary.

Christopher Bryan (PhD, University of Exeter) is C. K. Benedict Professor of New Testament at the University of the South, School of Theology.

S. A. Cummins (DPhil, University of Oxford) is associate professor of religious studies at Trinity Western University.

Peter H. Davids (PhD, University of Manchester) teaches New Testament theology at St. Stephens University.

David E. Garland (PhD, Southern Baptist Theological Seminary) is dean and William M. Hinson Professor of Christian Scriptures at Truett Theological Seminary.

Robert H. Gundry (PhD, Manchester University) is scholar-in-residence and professor emeritus at Westmont College.

Edith M. Humphrey (PhD, McGill University) is William F. Orr Professor of New Testament at Pittsburgh Theological Seminary.

Sylvia C. Keesmaat (DPhil, University of Oxford) is associate professor of biblical studies and hermeneutics at the Institute for Christian Studies.

Jon C. Laansma (PhD, University of Aberdeen) is associate professor of ancient languages and New Testament at Wheaton College.

I. Howard Marshall (PhD, University of Aberdeen) is professor emeritus and honorary research professor of New Testament at the University of Aberdeen.

Thorsten Moritz (PhD, London University) is professor of New Testament at Bethel Seminary.

Francesca Aran Murphy (PhD, King's College London) is a reader in systematic theology at the University of Aberdeen.

John K. Riches (MA, University of Cambridge) is honorary research professor in the department of theology and religious studies at the University of Glasgow.

Peter R. Rodgers (B.Litt, University of Oxford) is adjunct professor at Fuller Theological Seminary.

Daniel R. Streett (PhD candidate, Southeastern Baptist Theological Seminary) is assistant professor of New Testament at Criswell College.

Max Turner (PhD, University of Cambridge) is professor of New Testament studies at London School of Theology.

Kevin J. Vanhoozer (PhD, University of Cambridge) is research professor of systematic theology at Trinity Evangelical Divinity School.

Steve Walton (PhD, University of Sheffield) is senior lecturer in Greek and New Testament studies at London School of Theology.

Charles A. Wanamaker (PhD, University of Durham) is associate professor of Christian studies at the University of Cape Town.

N. T. Wright (DPhil, DD, University of Oxford) is bishop of Durham.

Stephen I. Wright (PhD, University of Durham) teaches biblical studies and practical theology at Spurgeon's College.

Abbreviations

Bible Texts and Versions

AT	Author's Translation
ESV	English Standard Version
ET	English Translation
KJV	King James Version
LXX	Septuagint
MT	Masoretic Text (Hebrew Bible)
NJB	The New Jerusalem Bible
NRSV	New Revised Standard Version
NT	New Testament
OT	Old Testament
Q	*Quelle*, hypothetical source of material common to Matthew and Luke but missing in Mark
RSV	Revised Standard Version

Old Testament Books

Gen.	Genesis	Neh.	Nehemiah
Exod.	Exodus	Esther	Esther
Lev.	Leviticus	Job	Job
Num.	Numbers	Ps. (Pss.)	Psalms
Deut.	Deuteronomy	Prov.	Proverbs
Josh.	Joshua	Eccles.	Ecclesiastes
Judg.	Judges	Song	Song of Songs
Ruth	Ruth	Isa.	Isaiah
1–2 Sam.	1–2 Samuel	Jer.	Jeremiah
1–2 Kings	1–2 Kings	Lam.	Lamentations
1–2 Chron.	1–2 Chronicles	Ezek.	Ezekiel
Ezra	Ezra	Dan.	Daniel

Hos.	Hosea	Nah.	Nahum
Joel	Joel	Hab.	Habakkuk
Amos	Amos	Zeph.	Zephaniah
Obad.	Obadiah	Hag.	Haggai
Jon.	Jonah	Zech.	Zechariah
Mic.	Micah	Mal.	Malachi

New Testament Books

Matt.	Matthew	1–2 Thess.	1–2 Thessalonians
Mark	Mark	1–2 Tim.	1–2 Timothy
Luke	Luke	Titus	Titus
John	John	Philem.	Philemon
Acts	Acts	Heb.	Hebrews
Rom.	Romans	James	James
1–2 Cor.	1–2 Corinthians	1–2 Pet.	1–2 Peter
Gal.	Galatians	1–3 John	1–3 John
Eph.	Ephesians	Jude	Jude
Phil.	Philippians	Rev.	Revelation
Col.	Colossians		

Apocrypha

Add. Dan.	Additions to Daniel	2 Esd.	2 Esdras (= 4 Ezra)
Bel.	Bel and the Dragon	Jdt.	Judith
Pr. Azar.	Prayer of Azariah	Let. Jer.	Letter of Jeremiah (Bar. 6)
Song of Thr.	Song of the Three Young Men	1–4 Macc.	1–4 Maccabees
		Pr. Man.	Prayer of Manasseh
Sus.	Susanna	Ps. 151	Psalm 151
Add. Esth.	Additions to Esther	Sir.	Sirach (Ecclesiasticus)
Bar.	Baruch	Tob.	Tobit
1 Esd.	1 Esdras	Wis.	Wisdom (of Solomon)

OT Pseudepigrapha

1 En. *1 Enoch (Ethiopic Apocalypse)*

Dead Sea Scrolls and Related Texts

1QS *Community Rule*

Other Jewish Works
Philo

Cher. De cherubim (On the Cherubim)

Other Early Christian Literature

Augustine of Hippo

Conf.   Confessionum libri XIII
(Confessions)

Clement of Alexandria

Paed.   Paedagogus (Christ the
Educator)

Eusebius

Hist. eccl.   Historia ecclesiastica (Ecclesiastical History)

John Chrysostom

Hom. 2 Cor.   Homilae in epistulam ii ad
Corinthios

Classical and Hellenistic Sources

Pliny the Younger

Ep.   Epistulae (Letters)

Seneca

Ep.   Epistulae morales (Letters)

Medieval Sources

Thomas Aquinas

ST   Summa theologiae/theologica

Additional Abbreviations

A1CS	The Book of Acts in Its First Century Setting
AB	Anchor Bible
ACCSNT	Ancient Christian Commentary on Scripture: New Testament
AnBib	Analecta biblica
BECNT	Baker Exegetical Commentary on the New Testament
BibInt	Biblical Interpretation
BNTC	Black's New Testament Commentaries
BSL	Biblical Studies Library
BU	Biblische Untersuchungen
CBQ	Catholic Biblical Quarterly
CJT	Canadian Journal of Theology
ÉBib	Études bibliques
ECC	Eerdmans Critical Commentary
EKKNT	Evangelisch-katholischer Kommentar zum Neuen Testament
ET	English translation/edition
EvQ	Evangelical Quarterly
FF	Foundations and Facets
HBT	Horizons in Biblical Theology
HTKNT	Herders theologischer Kommentar zum Neuen Testament
HTR	Harvard Theological Review
HUT	Hermeneutische Untersuchungen zur Theologie
ICC	International Critical Commentary
Inst.	John Calvin. Institutes of the Christian Religion. Edited by J. McNeill. Translated by F. L. Battles. 2 vols. Westminster, 1960

Int	*Interpretation*
JBL	*Journal of Biblical Literature*
JPTSup	Journal of Pentecostal Theology: Supplement Series
JSNT	*Journal for the Study of the New Testament*
JSNTSup	Journal for the Study of the New Testament: Supplement Series
JSOT	*Journal for the Study of the Old Testament*
KEK	Kritisch-exegetischer Kommentar über das Neue Testament (Meyer-Kommentar)
MTS	Marburger theologische Studien
NCB	New Century Bible
Neot	*Neotestamentica*
NIB	*The New Interpreter's Bible.* Edited by L. Keck. 12 vols. Abingdon, 1994–2002
NIBCNT	New International Biblical Commentary on the New Testament
NICNT	New International Commentary on the New Testament
NovTSup	Novum Testamentum Supplements
NPNF[1]	*Nicene and Post-Nicene Fathers,* Series 1. Edited by P. Schaff. 14 vols. 1886–90. Reprint, T&T Clark/Eerdmans, 1979–
NTC	New Testament in Context
NTG	New Testament Guides
NTS	*New Testament Studies*
NTT	New Testament Theology
RHPR	*Revue d'histoire et de philosophie religieuses*
RHR	*Revue de l'histoire des religions*
SBL	Society of Biblical Literature
SBLDS	Society of Biblical Literature Dissertation Series
SBLMS	Society of Biblical Literature Monograph Series
SBLSymS	Society of Biblical Literature Symposium Series
SBS	Stuttgarter Bibelstudien
SNTSMS	Society for New Testament Studies Monograph Series
TNTC	Tyndale New Testament Commentaries
TS	*Theological Studies*
TynBul	*Tyndale Bulletin*
TZTh	*Tübinger Zeitschrift für Theologie*
WA	*D. Martin Luthers Werke: Kritische Gesamtausgabe* (Weimarer Ausgabe). Edited by J. F. K. Knaake et al. 57 vols. H. Böhlau, 1883–
WBC	Word Biblical Commentary
WUNT	Wissenschaftliche Untersuchungen zum Neuen Testament
ZNW	*Zeitschrift für die neutestamentliche Wissenschaft und die Kunde der älteren Kirche*
ZTK	*Zeitschrift für Theologie und Kirche*

Introduction

What Is Theological Interpretation of the Bible?

Kevin J. Vanhoozer

Of the making of books commenting on biblical books there would seem to be no end. There are now more *series* of biblical commentaries than there are books in the Bible. What, then, could possibly justify adding one more item to an already well-stocked inventory? Neither the editors nor the contributors are under the illusion that a new secondary text will change the world. Nevertheless, we believe that the time is ripe for a new kind of interpretation of Scripture that combines an interest in the academic study of the Bible with a passionate commitment to making this scholarship of use to the church. And we are not alone. The "theological interpretation of the Bible" has become a growth industry of late, spawning new journals, academic conferences, and commentary series.[1]

The race to recover a compelling mode of theological interpretation recalls the Oklahoma Land Rush of 1893 when settlers rushed into virgin territory to stake a claim. That event was, in the words of an eyewitness, one of the most noteworthy events of Western civilization. At that time there was an economic depression that made finding a habitable dwelling place especially urgent. The situation at the end of the twentieth century was not so different: for two centuries, biblical interpreters had been wandering in

1. For a good overview of the challenges that continue to attend this project, as well as a typology of the various ways in which people are responding to them, see D. J. Treier, *Introducing Theological Interpretation of Scripture: Recovering a Christian Practice* (Baker, 2008).

what Paul Ricoeur called the "desert of criticism," unable to find spiritual nourishment in speculations about likely historical backgrounds, sources of composition, or etymological footnotes. The recovery of theological interpretation of Scripture is about emerging from the desert to settle in and inhabit the promised land.

Theological interpreters want to inhabit the text, but even more they want to dig. Perhaps the better analogy, then, would be the 1848 California gold rush. News spread slowly at first, but eventually that event drew prospectors from around the world. Textual prospectors are currently mining both Scripture and tradition for theological gold: the knowledge of God. The chapters in the present work display different sorts of gold recovery; more importantly, they display the nuggets discovered in the process.[2]

What Theological Interpretation Is *Not*

As to the process itself, however, initially it is easier to say what theological interpretation of the Bible is *not* rather than what it is.

Theological interpretation of the Bible is not an imposition of a theological system or confessional grid onto the biblical text. In speaking of theological interpretation, we do not mean to encourage readers merely to read their own theologies into the text. While it may be true that exegesis without theological presuppositions is not possible, it is not part of the present volume's remit to take sides with a specific confessional or denominational tradition. (On the other hand, we do affirm the ecumenical consensus of the church down through the ages and across confessional lines that the Bible should be read as a unity and as narrative testimony to the identities and actions of God and of Jesus Christ.)

Theological interpretation is not simply what dogmatic theologians do when they use the Bible to support their respective doctrinal positions. Although so-called precritical interpretations took biblical authority seriously and sought to read for the church's edification, they may be vulnerable at three points: They may fail to take the text seriously in its historical context. They may fail to integrate the text into the theology of the OT or NT as a whole. They may be insufficiently critical or aware of their own presuppositions and standpoints (Wright).

2. It should be noted that the chapters in the present work originally appeared (in alphabetical order) in K. J. Vanhoozer et al. eds., *Dictionary for Theological Interpretation of the Bible* (Baker, 2005).

Theological interpretation of the Bible is not an imposition of a general hermeneutic or theory of interpretation onto the biblical text. Theological interpretation is also not simply a matter of imposing a *general* hermeneutic on the Bible as if the Bible could be read "like any other book." There are properly theological questions, such as the relationship of the OT and NT, that require more than what is typically offered in a general hermeneutic (Watson). Stated more strongly, there are some interpretative questions that require theological, not hermeneutical, answers: "The turn to hermeneutics as a general discipline . . . has not so much offered a resolution of older theological questions, historically considered, as it has changed the subject" (Seitz 42). There is something left for interpreters to do after reading the Bible like any other book. At the same time, we believe that certain biblical and theological themes have implications not only for biblical interpretation, but for general hermeneutics as well.

Theological interpretation of the Bible is not a form of merely historical, literary, or sociological criticism preoccupied with (respectively) the world "behind," "of," or "in front of" the biblical text. Those who seek to renew biblical interpretation will incorporate whatever is true, noble, right, admirable, and useful in the various historical, literary, and sociological approaches used to describe the world "behind" the text (e.g., in the past), the world "of" the text (e.g., its plot and literary form), or the world "in front of" the text (e.g., the way in which readers receive and react to it). Theological interpretation may not be reduced to historical or to literary or to sociopolitical criticism, but it is not less than these either. For God has been active in history, in the composition of the biblical text, and in the formation of a people to reveal and redeem. Yet each of these disciplines, though ancillary to the project of interpreting the church's Scripture, stops short of a properly theological criticism to the extent that it brackets out a consideration of divine action.

Why "Theological" Interpretation of the Bible?

The present book of essays responds to two crises precipitated by Enlightenment and post-Enlightenment developments in biblical interpretation respectively: to the modern schism between biblical studies and theology, and to the postmodern proliferation of "advocacy" approaches to reading Scripture where each interpretative community does what is right in its own eyes. The primary purpose of the present volume is to provide biblical interpreters with examples of best interpretative practice: a display ranging across the canon of the state of the theological interpretative art. Our hope is that this work will encourage others to recover biblical studies as a properly theological discipline.

The "ugly ditch" in modern biblical interpretation: between exegesis and theology. The critical approach to biblical interpretation that has come to dominate the modern study of the Bible, especially in the university but also in seminaries, was developed in order to protect the Bible from what was thought to be its "dogmatic captivity" to confessional and theological traditions. For some two hundred years now, Christian faith has not been thought to be either necessary or relevant in the attempt to discover "what it meant." Theology thus came to be of only marginal importance for biblical studies as practiced in university and divinity school settings. Indeed, modern biblical studies has become a virtual "theology-free zone." Even scholars who identify themselves as Christians have to check their theological convictions at the door when they enter the academy (Fowl xii–xxx).

The divide separating biblical studies and theology was nothing less than Lessing's famous "ugly ditch": the gap between reason and faith, between publicly ascertainable history on the one hand and privately valued belief on the other. The goal of biblical studies for the typical modern scholar was to understand the texts by restoring them to their original historical contexts and by reading them on their own terms, namely, as (human) products of particular times and places, cultures and societies. In this interpretative framework, the Bible tended to be studied as evidence of a historically developing "religion," as evidence of how ancient Israelites—and later, Jesus and his followers—tended to think about God, the world, and themselves. To study "religion," however, is to study human beings and human history—in contrast to "theology" as the study of God and the mighty acts of God.

The problem was not so much with modern biblical scholarship's interest in reconstructing historical contexts and the history of the text's composition. The bigger problem was its tendency to treat the biblical texts as sources for reconstructing human history and religion rather than as texts that testify to God's presence and action in history. To treat the Bible as a source—as evidence for some natural phenomenon "behind" it—is to deflect attention away from what the texts are saying (as testimony) in favor of a hypothetical reconstruction of "what actually happened." History here trumps exegesis.

Further, it is likely that modern critics are working with an overly "thin" conception of history, as a self-enclosed, linear set of temporal events whose causal explanation is to be found in the relation of earlier to later events in the same horizontal space-time spectrum. The Bible, however, announces events that partake of the "fulness" of time, events that are the result of divine as well as human agency, events in which the future breaks in, as it were, from above. This way of viewing the ugly ditch posits a gap between thin (reductionist) descriptions of biblical history and thick descriptions that take account of the text's own appeals to divine agency.

Interpreted theologically, the ugly ditch may be nothing less than the perceived gap between "nature" and "grace." Reason, together with its many critical children—source, form, tradition, redaction criticism, and so on—is qualified to interpret the Bible as a historical and human text. But to read the Bible as the word of God is to make a leap into the realm of "grace" that either opposes, crowns, or outflanks reason (Wolters).

The "muddy ditch" in postmodern biblical interpretation: between exegesis and ideology. The Bible-theology relation in the late modern or postmodern era is less an ugly ditch, across which it is impossible to leap, than it is a "muddy ditch"—the quagmire of history, language, tradition, and culture—out of which it is impossible ever to extricate oneself. Postmoderns typically deny that we can escape our location in history, culture, class, and gender. Our readings of the biblical text will be shaped, perhaps decisively so, by our particular location and identity. The goal of interpretation is therefore to discover "what it means to my community, to those with my interpretative interest." Postmodern readers come to Scripture with a plurality of interpretative interests, including (perhaps) the theological, though no one interest may claim more authority than another. The postmodern situation of biblical interpretation gives rise to a pluralism of interpretative approaches and hence to a legitimation crisis: Whose interpretation of the Bible counts, and why?

Biblical interpretation in postmodernity means that independent standards and universal criteria for determining which of many rival interpretations is the "right" or "true" one will be met with no little suspicion. A host of postmodern thinkers has slain the giant assumption behind much modern biblical scholarship that there can be objective, neutral, and value-free reading of biblical texts. Postmodern thinkers have charged modernity's vaunted historical-critical method with being just one more example of an ideologically motivated approach. The critical approach only pretends to be objective, neutral, and value free. Modern biblical critics are as rooted in the contingencies of history and tradition as everyone else. Indeed, biblical criticism is itself a *confessional* tradition that begins with a faith in reason's unprejudiced ability to discover truth. The question postmoderns raise for historical critics is whether, in exorcising the spirit of faith from biblical studies, they have not inadvertently admitted even more ideological demons into the academic house.

Whereas the temptation of historical criticism is to offer only thin descriptions of the world behind the text or of the process of the text's composition, the temptation of ideological criticism is to offer only thinly veiled echoes of one's own voice. To be distracted by what is "behind" or "before" the text, however, is to miss its message; such nontheological biblical criticism is like music criticism by the deaf and art criticism by the blind.

What Is Theological Interpretation of the Bible?

Theological Interpretation of the New Testament and its companion *Theological Interpretation of the Old Testament* attempt to provide models for proceeding toward a more constructive engagement with Scripture. While the authors are not working from a single methodological template, three premises undergird the approaches represented herein.

The theological interpretation of the Bible is not the exclusive property of biblical scholars but the joint responsibility of all the theological disciplines and of the whole people of God, a peculiar fruit of the communion of the saints. It was Gerhard Ebeling who once declared that church history is essentially the history of biblical interpretation. To the extent that this is so, the present crisis in biblical interpretation—the confusion not only over what the Bible means but also over how to read it—is also a crisis for the church. The study of church history can itself be a theological discipline insofar as it helps the present church to learn from previous ways of interpreting Scripture. Indeed, one reason for the increased interest in theological interpretation of the Bible is the recent rehabilitation of the reputation of the church fathers as profound exegetes. Some have even touted "the superiority of pre-critical exegesis" (Steinmetz).

Is biblical studies a theological discipline? By and large, the resounding answer, at least in the setting of the modern university, has been *Nein!* Modern biblical scholars insist that biblical studies must be autonomous in order to be critical (Barr). Yet some degree of involvement with theology seems to be inevitable, for three reasons. First, biblical scholars must have recourse to theology in order to make sense of the Bible's main subject matter, God (Jeanrond). Readings that remain on the historical, literary, or sociological levels cannot ultimately do justice to what the texts are actually about. Second, biblical studies needs theology (especially the latter's analysis of contemporary culture) in order to be aware of the aims, intentions, and presuppositions that readers invariably bring to the biblical text (Wright). Third, biblical studies needs theology in order to provide a sufficient reason for the academy's continued engagement with the biblical text. Only the assumption that these texts say something of unique importance can ultimately justify the depth of the exegete's engagement (Levenson).

A word about biblical theology is in order, for on the surface this discipline seems a likely candidate to mediate the divide between biblical studies and theology. However, some (e.g., Barr; Fowl) see biblical theology as one more symptom of modern biblical scholarship's assumption that it is possible neutrally and objectively to describe the religious beliefs of the biblical writers. The results of this study—"what it meant" to *them*, back then—are of more antiquarian than ecclesial interest and are offered to the academy, not the church. Yet others (e.g., Watson; Rosner) view biblical theology as an activity that is practically identical with the theological interpretation of the Bible in its concern for hearing the word of God in the church today.

If exegesis without presuppositions is impossible, and if some of these presuppositions concern the nature and activity of God, then it would appear to go without saying that biblical interpretation is always/already theological. One's view of God, for instance, will influence which biblical statements about God one considers literal and which statements one takes as figurative. The inevitability of employing theological categories, however, does not automatically license a wholesale appropriation of any one theological system. Nevertheless, readers with a theological interest, whether in the academy or the church, will at least seek to go further than describing what *others* have said or thought about God. Theological interpreters want to know, on the basis of Scripture and in light of contemporary concerns, what *we* should say and think about God.

Finally, practical theology takes part in biblical interpretation when it inquires into how the people of God should respond to the biblical texts. The way in which the church witnesses, through its language and life, is perhaps the most important form of theological interpretation of the Bible.

The theological interpretation of the Bible is characterized by a governing interest in God, the word and works of God, and by a governing intention to engage in what we might call "theological criticism." Can theological interpretation be "critical," and if so, in what sense? Historical and literary criticism we know, but with regard to theological criticism, we may be tempted to ask, "Who are you?"

A theological interpretation of the Bible is more likely to be critical of readers than of biblical authors or biblical texts. It is not that text criticism and other forms of criticism have no role; it is rather a matter of the ultimate aim of reading. Those who seek to interpret Scripture theologically want to hear the word of God in Scripture and hence to be transformed by the renewing of their minds (Rom. 12:2). In this respect, it is important to note that God must not be an "afterthought" in biblical interpretation. God is not simply a function of a certain community's interpretative interest; instead, God is prior to both the community and the biblical texts themselves. A properly theological criticism will therefore seek to do justice to the priority of the living and active triune God. One way to do so is to guard against idols: images of God manufactured by the interpretative communities.

We believe that the principal interest of the Bible's authors, of the text itself, and of the original community of readers was theological: reading the Scriptures therefore meant coming to hear God's word and to know God better. Our aim therefore is not to impose yet another agenda or ideology onto the Bible, but rather to recover the Bible's original governing interest. On this view, biblical interpretation takes the form of a *confession* or acknowledgment of the work and word of God in and through Scripture.

One should not abandon scholarly tools and approaches in order to interpret the Bible theologically. On the contrary, modern and postmodern tools and methods may be usefully employed in theological interpretation to the extent that they are oriented to illumining the text rather than something that lay "behind" it (e.g., what actually happened) or "before" it (e.g., the ideological concerns of an interpretative community). At the same time, a theological vantage point calls into question the autonomy of the realm of "nature," and the autonomy of so-called critical approaches to reading the Bible, in the first place. Neither "nature" nor "knowledge" is ever religiously neutral; from the standpoint of Christian doctrine, "nature" is a divine creation, and "knowledge" is inseparable from some kind of faith. The challenge, therefore, is to employ critical methods, but not uncritically. Critical tools have a ministerial, not magisterial, function in biblical interpretation. The aim of a properly "confessional criticism" (Wolters) is to hear the word of God; theological criticism is governed by the conviction that God speaks in and through the biblical texts.

The strongest claim to be made for theological interpretation is that only such reading ultimately does justice to the subject matter of the text itself.

Because biblical texts are ultimately concerned with the reality of God, readers must have a similar theological interest (Jeanrond). Theological *text* genres (e.g., Gospels, prophecies, apocalyptic, etc.) call for theological *reading genres*, for styles of reading that proceed from faith and yet seek theological understanding. To read the biblical texts theologically is to read the texts as they wish to be read, and as they should be read in order to do them justice.

The theological interpretation of the Bible names a broad ecclesial concern that embraces a number of academic approaches. At present, no one model of theological interpretation of the Bible holds sway in the church.[3] The contributors to the present work recognize that there is more than one way of pursuing an interest in theological criticism. Because we are only in the initial stages of recovering a distinctly theological interpretation of Scripture, it would be unwise to preempt discussion of how best to read the Bible in the church. In choosing the various contributors, the editors were careful to invite representatives of different theological backgrounds, denominations, and interpretative approaches. Nevertheless, it is possible to discern at least three distinct emphases, more complementary than contradictory, that help us begin to distinguish types of theological interpretation.

Some interpreters have an interest in divine authorship, in the God-world relation "behind" the text as it were. This first type recognizes that our doctrine of God affects the way we interpret the Scriptures, while simultaneously acknowledging that our interpretation of Scripture affects our doctrine of God. Indeed, this two-sided problematic has been designated a matter of "first theology" (Vanhoozer). The focus here is less on establishing "what actually happened" than on reading the Bible in terms of divine authorship or as divinely appropriated human discourse (Wolterstorff). Interpreting Scripture as divine discourse opens up interesting possibilities for discerning the unity among the diversity of biblical books and for relating the two Testaments. Theological assumptions about God's involvement with the production of Scripture play an important role in how interpreters take or construe the text and in how they deal with thematic developments as well as apparent historical inconsistencies.

A second group of theological interpreters focuses on the final form of the text rather than on questions of human or divine authorship. For these interpreters, it is the text as a finished literary work or narrative that serves as the prime theological witness. One discovers who God is

3. See Davis and Hays pp. 1–5 for a statement of the Princeton Scripture Project's "Nine Theses on the Interpretation of Scripture."

by indwelling the symbolic world of the Bible. Proponents of this second approach seek to interpret the Bible on its own terms, whether these terms be literary (e.g., narrative) or properly religious (e.g., canon). Theology is a matter of "intratextual" reading (Lindbeck) that patiently unfolds the world of the text in order to learn what God was doing in Israel and in Jesus Christ. The God-world relation as depicted in the text thus becomes the framework for understanding today's world too.

Still other interpreters of Scripture identify the theologically significant moment with the reading and reception of the Bible in the believing community today. The divine action that counts for these interpreters is the work of the Holy Spirit, which they locate as much in the present as, if not more than, in the past. What makes biblical interpretation theological is a function of the aims and interests of the community of readers for which the Bible is "Scripture" (Fowl). The focus here is on the world of the Christian community and its members, who seek to live before God and to worship faithfully. The theological interpretation of Scripture is a distinct practice *of the church*, and hence it is regulated by the goods at which that practice aims. The primary concern with the *outcome* of biblical interpretation affords an interesting vantage point from which to assess the relative contribution of various types of biblical criticism and interpretative approaches.

The Purpose of a Book-by-Book Survey

Theological Interpretation of the New Testament and its companion *Theological Interpretation of the Old Testament* are intended as resources for all readers interested in the theological interpretation of Scripture, not merely for those who advocate a particular approach. The three emphases mentioned above are by no means mutually exclusive. One purpose of these books is to heal the debilitating breach that all too often prevents biblical scholars and theologians from talking to each other, or even from using the same reference books. If these books, together with their original host, the *Dictionary for Theological Interpretation of the Bible*, accomplish the purpose for which they were originally commissioned, they should appeal to biblical scholars, theologians, pastors, and laypeople alike.

The present work may prove an indispensable resource for any serious student of the Bible who also regards it as Scripture—a word from God about God. And this leads to the second purpose: to provide a resource for scholars in other disciplines to employ as they seek to promote biblical wisdom in and for their own disciplinary domains. The theological interpretation of Scripture is as important for scientists and sociologists as it is for exegetes and theologians proper—for all of us need a biblically and theologically informed framework for understanding God, the world, and ourselves.

The chapters of *Theological Interpretation of the Old Testament* and *Theological Interpretation of the New Testament* interpret every book of the Bible, focusing on the message rather than the historical background or process of composition that often make up the bulk of biblical commentaries. Each author was asked to discuss something of the history of interpretation, the theological message of the book, its relation to the whole canon, its unique contribution to the people of God, and to provide a brief bibliography for readers who may wish to probe further. Not all authors answered this editorial call in the same way. Some highlight special problems and/or contributions that particular books of the Bible make with regard to doctrine and theology. By and large, however, what is of special value in these pages is "canon sense" and "catholic sensibility." First, canon sense: authors are keen to discuss what each book contributes to Scripture as a whole and how its place in the canon affects its interpretation. Second, catholic sensibility: a bird's-eye view of the history of interpretation of a particular book provides a wealth of ecclesial wisdom in a nutshell.

Truth be told, our contributors are not representative of the whole width and breadth of the one true church. With some notable exceptions, they represent different shades of North American and British Protestant evangelicalism. It would therefore be interesting to read this book in conjunction with, say, the *Africa Bible Commentary* (Adeyemo).

Finally, let me repeat my initial point: the present volume is less a manifesto for a single way of interpreting the Bible theologically than it is a call to theological interpretation and a display of its best practice. Yet no single "best practice" is defined nor is one method mandated. Instead, the authors set about the various tasks of theological interpretation—tracing the history of interpretation, putting the text in canonical context, analyzing what the text says about God, reflecting on the text in light of the Rule of Faith—without saying which task is most important. Again, this is intentional; we are only at the beginning stages of recovering this complex practice. What this book presents is not a seamless garment, then, so much as a coat of many methodological colors.[4]

4. My reference to "seamless garment" alludes to M. J. Gorman's review of the *Dictionary for Theological Interpretation of the Bible* ("A 'Seamless Garment' Approach to Biblical Interpretation?" *Journal of Theological Interpretation* 1 [2007]: 117–28).

Conclusion: Reading to Know and Love God

Of the making of books about the Book there is no end. Quite so! Yet the "end" of the present work, its most important raison d'être, is to help promote the knowledge of God, the good, and the gospel via a recovery of the practice of theological interpretation. The ultimate justification for yet another book about the Bible is its utility in helping to promote the knowledge of what God has done in Israel and in Jesus Christ for the good of the world.

The principal thrust of theological interpretation is to direct the interpreter's attention to the subject matter of Scripture—God, the acts of God in history, the gospel—rather than to a particular theological tradition or, for that matter, to some other topic (e.g., the history of the text's composition, the secular history "behind" the text, the structure of the text, etc.). These other elements are included, however, to the extent that they help the reader grow in the knowledge of God.

Theological interpretation of the Bible, we suggest, is biblical interpretation oriented to the knowledge of God. For much of their history, biblical studies, theology, and spirituality were all aspects of a single enterprise, that of knowing God (McIntosh). Knowing God is more than a merely academic exercise. On the contrary, knowing God, like theological interpretation of the Bible itself, is at once an intellectual, imaginative, and spiritual exercise. To know God as the author and subject of Scripture requires more than intellectual acknowledgment. To know God is to love and obey him, for the knowledge of God is both restorative and transformative. The saving knowledge of God results in the transformation of the reader into the likeness of Jesus Christ. In the final analysis, theological interpretation of the Bible may be less a matter of knowing God than of engaging with the living God and being known by God (Gal. 4:9).

Theological interpretation of the Bible achieves its end when readers enter into the world of the biblical texts with faith, hope, and love. When we make God's thoughts become our thoughts and God's word become our word, we begin to participate in the world of the text, in the grand drama of divine redemption. This is perhaps the ultimate aim of theological interpretation of the Bible: to know the triune God by participating in the triune life, in the triune mission to creation.[5]

---

5. Matthew Levering is even more succinct: "the goal of exegesis is union with God" ("Principles of Exegesis: Toward a Participatory Biblical Exegesis," *Pro Ecclesia* 17 [2008]: 50).

No one denomination, school of interpretation, or hermeneutical approach has a monopoly on reading the Bible for the word of God. Insights from the whole body of Christ—a body animated and guided by the Spirit of Christ—are needed if Christians are to display the mind of Jesus Christ.

In sum, the aim of this book-by-book survey is to provide the resources necessary to respond to what for Johann Albrecht Bengel (1687–1752) was the biblical interpreter's prime directive: "Apply yourself wholly to the text; apply the text wholly to yourself." Interpreting Scripture theologically is the way to read the Bible "for a blessing" (Kierkegaard), for the sake of human flourishing, for the individual and social "good." Commentaries are not schools of sanctification, of course; yet the ultimate aim of the present work is to commend ways of reading Scripture that lead to the blessing of knowing God and of being formed unto godliness.

Bibliography

Adeyemo, T., ed. *Africa Bible Commentary*. Zondervan, 2006.

Barr, J. *The Bible in the Modern World*. SCM, 1973.

Davis, E. F. and Hays, R. B., eds. *The Art of Reading Scripture*. Eerdmans, 2003.

Fowl, S., ed. *The Theological Interpretation of Scripture*. Blackwell, 1997.

Jeanrond, W. *Text and Interpretation as Categories of Theological Thinking*. Crossroad, 1988.

Levenson, J. *The Hebrew Bible, the Old Testament, and Historical Criticism*. Westminster John Knox, 1993.

Levering, M. *Participatory Biblical Exegesis: A Theology of Biblical Interpretation*. University of Notre Dame Press, 2008.

Lindbeck, G. "Postcritical Canonical Interpretation: Three Modes of Retrieval." Pages 26–51 in *Theological Exegesis*, ed. C. Seitz and K. Greene-McCreight. Eerdmans, 1999.

McGrath, A. *The Genesis of Doctrine*. Eerdmans, 1990.

McIntosh, M. *Mystical Theology*. Blackwell, 2000.

Rosner, B. "Biblical Theology." Pages 3–11 in *New Dictionary of Biblical Theology*, ed. T. D. Alexander and B. Rosner. InterVarsity, 2000.

Seitz, C. "The Theological Crisis of Serious Biblical Interpretation." Pages 40–65 in *Renewing Biblical Interpretation*, ed. C. Bartholomew et al. SHS. Zondervan/Paternoster, 2000.

Steinmetz, D. "The Superiority of Pre-Critical Exegesis." Pages 26–38 in *The Theological Interpretation of Scripture*, ed. S. Fowl. Blackwell, 1997.

Treier, D. J., *Introducing Theological Interpretation of Scripture: Recovering a Christian Practice*. Baker, 2008.

Vanhoozer, K. *First Theology.* InterVarsity, 2002.

Watson, F. *Text, Church, and World.* T&T Clark, 1994.

Wolters, A. "Confessional Criticism and the Night Visions of Zechariah." Pages 90–117 in *Renewing Biblical Interpretation,* ed. C. Bartholomew et al. SHS. Zondervan/Paternoster, 2000.

Wolterstorff, N. *Divine Discourse.* Cambridge University Press, 1995.

Wright, N. T. *The New Testament and the People of God.* SPCK, 1993.

1

Matthew

ROBERT H. GUNDRY

The popularity of the Gospel of Matthew enhanced its influence on the theology of the early church and made it an important object of early Christian theologizing. Its Jewish slant combined with its interest in the discipling of "all the nations" to give it universal appeal (28:19 [all ET by author]). Its systematic organization lent it to heavy liturgical use. (To this day, its version of the Lord's Prayer is regularly used instead of Luke's.) And its featuring the ethical teaching of Jesus made it especially suitable for catechetical instruction.

Historical Examples of Interplay between Matthew and Theology

Without evaluation, here are some of the more important instances of interplay between Matthew and theology. The doctrine of the Immaculate Conception grew out of the story of Jesus' virgin birth (1:18–25; also in Luke). The doctrine of Mary's perpetual virginity marked a further development. John the Baptist's saying he needs Jesus to baptize him has played into the doctrine of Jesus' sinlessness, and Jesus' insisting on baptism by John "to fulfill all righteousness" despite his (Jesus') sinlessness played into the doctrine of Christ's imputed righteousness (3:14–17).

The designation of Jesus as God's Son at the baptism contributed to adoptionism, and the temptation of Jesus (4:1–11) raised the theological question whether he was able not to sin or was not able to sin. His affirmation of every jot and tittle of the Law and the Prophets (5:18) has been used to undergird belief in the verbal, plenary inspiration and inerrancy of Scripture. The nonabolishment of the Law and demand that it be taught and kept (5:17–20) have posed a theological confrontation with Paul's rejection of law-righteousness. Jesus' escalation of the law's demands (5:21–48) led to perfectionism (as in the monastic and Anabaptist traditions), ethical idealism (as in the two-kingdoms doctrine of Lutheranism), the social gospel (as in Protestant liberalism), and limitation to a future millennium (as in dispensationalism).

Matthew's pervasive stress on the kingdom of heaven has gone in the theological directions of consistent eschatology (Jesus thought the end was about to come), ecclesiology (the church represents the kingdom), and millenarianism (Jesus offered the kingdom to the Jewish nation—"the gospel of the kingdom" differing from the Christian gospel—and most Jews refused it, so that the kingdom will arrive in a future millennium only after the interim of the church age). Consistent eschatology produced interim ethics (ethics for only the brief period before the expected end). An ecclesiastical kingdom put emphasis on the visible church as an institution, a mixture of the true and false, a mixture that also raised questions of church discipline. A millennial kingdom led to belief in a restoration of the Jewish nation, complete with a reinstitution of the OT law as interpreted by Matthew's Jesus. Indeed, dispensationalists have often regarded the Gospel of Matthew as not addressed to the church. Parables of the kingdom, such as those of the mustard seed and leaven (13:31–33), have been thought to support the dominance of the church in society at large (as in the Middle Ages), the eventual conversion of the whole world (as in postmillennialism), and the corruption of the institutional church (according to the dispensational understanding of leaven as symbolizing evil, and the birds that nest in mustard branches as symbolizing false teachers).

The prominence of Peter in Matthew, especially in the beatitude pronounced on him by Jesus (16:17–19), has been used to support the Roman Catholic doctrine of the papacy. Nevertheless, "the rock" on which Jesus said he would build his church has also been identified, not with Peter either as the first in a line of popes or by himself, but with his confession of Jesus as the Christ, with Jesus himself, and with Jesus' "words" (cf. 7:24–27). Peter's denying Jesus "before . . . all" (26:70) combines with Jesus' denying before his Father those who have denied him before others

(10:33) and with Matthew's omission of Peter's name from the story of Jesus' resurrection (contrast 28:7 with Mark 16:7) to suggest in Matthew's portrayal of Peter the symbolism of a false disciple.

The eschatological discourse in chs. 24–25 has been referred to the Jewish War of 66–70 CE, to a future tribulation, and to a following return of Christ. The judgmental separation of the nations into sheep and goats has been theologically geared to general humanitarianism on the part of individuals, to true Christians' treatment of their persecuted fellows, and to treatment of the Jewish people by nations qua nations.

Matthew's Christology and Soteriology

A survey of Matthew's Christology and soteriology, with hamartiological, ecclesiological, and eschatological entailments, reveals the extent to which this Gospel and theology can contribute to each other.

Christology

Historic Christology speaks of humanity and deity in the one person Jesus and helps readers of Matthew to see in it just such a Christology, while a reading of Matthew contributes to its construction. Jesus' humanity appears clearly in the genealogy with which Matthew starts. In contrast with Luke's genealogy of Jesus, which goes back to God (Luke 3:38), Matthew's starts with the human being Abraham, gives prominence to David, and prepares for emphasis on Jesus' Davidic ancestry (1:1–2, 6, 17, 20; 9:27; 12:23; 15:22; 20:30–31; 21:9, 15). Apparently written for a Jewish audience, however, Matthew's Gospel lays at least equal emphasis on Jesus' deity, for to Jews this was more unbelievable and objectionable (cf. 26:63–66).

The designation of Jesus as "God-with-us" (1:23) is matched by the replacement of "God" with Jesus' "I" in the promise, "And behold, I am with you all the days till the consummation of the age" (28:20). This designation is also supported in the middle of Matthew's Gospel with Jesus' assurance that where two or three are gathered in his name, there he is "in their midst" (18:20). Because of his reference to "every word coming out through the mouth of God" (4:4, but lacking in the parallel, Luke 4:4), the opening of his mouth to teach (5:2) makes his teaching consist of the very words of God, in consonance with Jesus' being "God-with-us."

God the Father is the first to pronounce Jesus his Son (already in the OT; cf. 2:15 with Hos. 11:1), and in further such pronouncements adds both "beloved" to the designation and the command, "Hear him." This distinguishes Jesus from other sons of God (3:17; 17:5; contrast 5:9, 45), so that the relation between the Father and the Son is unique (11:27). Matthew's changing the baptismal voice from "*You are* my beloved Son" (Mark 1:11//Luke 3:22) to "*This is* my beloved Son" turns an assurance to Jesus into a pronouncement about him. Accordingly, his disciples prostrate themselves before him, even while they are in a boat, and say, "Truly you are God's Son" (14:33). Peter adds to his confession of Jesus as "the Christ" the further identification, "the Son of the living God" (16:16; lacking in Mark 8:29//Luke 9:20). Not as in Mark 15:39 and Luke 23:47, the guards at Jesus' crucifixion join their centurion to declare, "Truly this one was God's Son," upon seeing among other things "the earthquake" that occurred when Jesus "let go" his spirit, an earthquake being typical of theophanies in the OT. Likewise, Jesus has angels just as God does (13:41; 16:27; 24:31), and the kingdom is his as well as the Father's (13:41; 16:28).

At the climactic close of his Gospel, Matthew puts emphasis on Jesus' deity in an incipiently trinitarian passage by sandwiching Jesus as "the Son" between God "the Father" and "the Holy Spirit" in a baptismal formula that features "the name" (singular!) of the three. Even if "the name" were meant to be repeatedly supplied before "of the Son" and before "of the Holy Spirit," the very ellipses would draw the three closely together. The participation of the Father and the Holy Spirit at Jesus' baptism previewed this trinitarian climax.

Matthew does not mention Jesus' preexistence as God's Son, as John, Paul, and Hebrews do. But Matthew does narrate the virginal conception and birth of Jesus (1:18–25), as John, Paul, and Hebrews do not. Considering the whole of the NT canon, then, systematic theologians may legitimately interpret the virginal conception and birth of Jesus as the means by which the preexistent Second Person of the Trinity became incarnate. Thus, both Matthew on the one hand and John, Paul, and Hebrews on the other hand contribute to a larger theological picture. And though Luke mentions Jesus' preexistence no more than Matthew does, perhaps we have the beginnings of this picture already in Luke's tracing of Jesus' genealogy back to God, designating Jesus as God's Son at the annunciation to Mary, and attributing the virginal conception of Jesus to the work of the Holy Spirit (Luke 1:26–38).

Soteriology

Right after presenting Jesus himself, Matthew introduces the topic of salvation, and his first mention of it indicates that salvation consists of deliverance from sins (1:21). The plural "sins" implies that Matthew does not conceive of sin as an external power that has enslaved its victims so as to make them sin against their will (contrast esp. Rom. 7:7–23). By modifying "sins," "their" fixes the blame for sinning on the sinners themselves, so that deliverance from sins means deliverance from punishment for sinful acts, such as those listed in 15:19: "evil designs, murders, adulteries, fornications, thefts, false testimonies, blasphemies" (all plurals in this list). With this view of salvation agree Matthew's references to forgiveness of moral debts (release from having to pay them—6:12; cf. 18:27, 32, 35), forgiveness of trespasses (6:14–15), and forgiveness of sins (9:2, 5–6; 26:28), even every sin and blasphemy except for blasphemy against the Spirit (12:31–32). The plural of "debts," "trespasses," and "sins" is again notable, as is also the modifier "every" when "sin" and "blasphemy" occur in the singular.

On the other hand, salvation consists in rescue from "evil" (neuter) or "the evil one" (masculine, 6:13). The use of the masculine in 13:19 for the "evil one" who snatches the word of the kingdom out of hearers' hearts favors a reference to Satan in both passages (cf. also 5:37, where "the evil one" stands opposite "the Lord," "God," and "the Great King" in the preceding verses; and 13:38–39, where "the evil one" equates with "the devil"). So rescue from the evil one means rescue from the devil, Satan, as the one who tempts people to commit sins (4:1–11; 16:23).

Thus, Matthew portrays human beings as responsible for their sins rather than victimized by sin as a dominating force, as Paul does. But just as Paul does not negate human responsibility, so Matthew does not negate the satanic power of temptation. Systematic theology must take into account the tension between human responsibility and external influences in the matter of sin just as in the matter of repentance and faith.

To the woman who has an issue of blood, Jesus pronounces salvation (9:22); and at his crucifixion chief priests, scribes, and elders say, "He saved others; he cannot save himself!" (27:42). Since the supposed inability of Jesus to save himself has to do with physical deliverance from crucifixion, his antithetically parallel saving of others had to do with deliverance from the physical effects of their sins, just as the woman's salvation had to do with stopping her issue of blood (cf. 4:23–24; 8:16–17; 11:4–5; and other stories of healings, exorcisms, and the raising of a dead person). Perhaps it is relief from these physical effects of sinning to which Jesus refers in promising rest to the weary and heavy laden who come to him (11:28–30; cf. his miracles mentioned in the earlier part of ch. 11). Such relief raises the question of "healing in the atonement" (as in Pentecostal theology; cf. 8:17) and links up with Paul's description of a better body at the resurrection (1 Cor. 15:42–55; 2 Cor. 5:1–5; Phil. 3:21) and with John the Seer's description of believers' eternal state (Rev. 7:17; 21:4).

For Matthew, however, salvation goes beyond deliverance from the physical effects of sin. It extends to deliverance from condemnation (11:22–24), from being lost and perishing (18:14), from wrath (3:7), from being thrown into a furnace of unquenchable, eternal fire and thus from weeping and gnashing of teeth (3:10–12; 7:19; 13:30, 42, 50; 18:8–9). Positively, salvation extends to justification, being pronounced righteous because of one's words (12:36–37), to entrance into life (18:8–9; 19:17) with the result of having life that is eternal (19:16). This entrance into life comes by way of entrance into the kingdom of heaven (18:3)—through bodily resurrection, if necessitated by prior death (12:41–42; 22:23–33; 27:51b–53). The result is participation in God's heavenly rule on earth, a participation that brings with itself comfort in place of mourning, property in place of poverty, vindication in place of shame, mercy in place of judgment, a vision of God, acknowledgment as God's sons and daughters, and great reward in place of persecution (5:3–12). The links with Johannine soteriology (e.g., John 3:16, 36; Rev. 20:11–15) are obvious, as also the link with Pauline justification. Yet, systematic theologians must forge an accommodation between justification by the quality of the words one speaks and justification by faith, just as they have to forge an accommodation between justification by the quality of one's works (James 2:14–26) and justification by faith. Presumably this accommodation rests on the distinction between an inward state of faith and the outward evidence of faith.

Jesus saves, as his very name indicates (1:21; cf. Peter's outcry in 14:30, "Lord, save me," though he was asking Jesus to save him from drowning). Since salvation includes forgiveness of sins, salvation by Jesus naturally includes *his* forgiveness of sins (9:1–7). And since he acts always in consort with God, salvation naturally includes forgiveness by the Father in heaven as well (6:12 with 6:9). Furthermore, since Jesus' baptizing of people in the Holy Spirit and fire appears in its Matthean context to consist of his Spirit-endowed ministry, the Holy Spirit joins Jesus and God the Father in the act of salvation (3:11–17). This trinitarian cast accords with Matthew's trinitarian formula for baptism, discussed above (28:19; cf. the trinitarian cast of salvation in Eph. 1:3–14).

That Jesus, God the Father, and the Holy Spirit do the saving presents a vertical axis of salvation. But a horizontal axis appears, too. For disciples' restoration of a sinning fellow disciple counts as gaining that fellow disciple so that the straying one does not perish (18:12–18). Thus, we can say that in Matthew disciples save each other. Not only "the Son of Man" but also "human beings" (plural) have "authority" to forgive sins (9:8 with 9:1–7; cf. 18:21–35). Since salvation includes forgiveness, as already noted, and since the authority of human beings to forgive sins parallels the Son of Man's authority to do so, we can say once again that in Matthew disciples save each other.

Matthew does not stop with trinitarian and ecclesial salvation, however. His soteriology proceeds to self-salvation. Those who lose their lives for Jesus' sake will find—save—their lives (16:24–26). Such a losing of life counts as "one's own doing" (16:27), so that you save yourself (cf. Phil. 2:12–13, "With fear and trembling work out your own salvation," though Matthew has nothing corresponding to Paul's addition, "for God is the one working in you"; also John 6:29, where believing is "the work" that God requires). Again, a systematic theological distinction between inward state and outward evidence is required to avoid synergism.

It is Jesus' "people" who are saved (1:21; cf. "my church" in 16:18). They are those who "call his name 'Immanuel,'" those who confess that in him "God [is] with us" (1:23), and who make this confession in public despite the threat of persecution (10:32–33). The third person plural of "they will call" in Matthew's quotation of Isa. 7:14 is text-critically unique. No other known text of the OT passage has the third person plural. Most likely, then, Matthew himself produced this reading by altering a different one so as to define the people whom Jesus saves as those who call his name Immanuel. They are a sinful people; at least they were sinning prior to his saving them from their sins. But he came to call sinners, not the righteous (9:9–13).

For the saved, Matt. 21:43 uses another collective term, "nation." Jesus' having saved them as a people from their sins, they are now a nation that produces the fruits of God's kingdom: good deeds, righteous conduct (see, e.g., 5:16; 21:32). Comprising this nation are people of faith in Jesus, and of discipleship to him, from all nations (8:10–11; 28:19), plus holy ones, saints, from the past (27:51b–53). This makes an international nation of little people, social nobodies, and mental infants as to human wisdom and prudence (10:42; 11:25; 18:6, 10, 14; 25:40, 45). But the saved are few, the Monaco of nations as far as population is concerned (7:13–14), so few as to be a family (5:22–24, 47; 7:3–5; 10:21; 12:46–50; 18:15, 21, 35; 25:40; 28:10). These are the saved.

Because of their mental infantilism, Jesus' people have to be saved by divine revelation (11:25–26), by God's giving them to know the mysteries of the kingdom of heaven (13:11). Because of their sins, Jesus' people have to be saved by divine mercy (5:7) and generosity (19:30–20:16), and by the service of Jesus in giving his life as a ransom in substitution for them (20:28), by the shedding of his covenantal blood "for the forgiveness of sins" (26:28; contrast the taunt, "Save yourself . . . and come down from the cross" [27:40–42], and Elijah's not coming to save Jesus from death by crucifixion [27:49]). Thence comes the doctrine of substitutionary atonement. So much for what is done on behalf of Jesus' people for salvation.

What do they need to do for themselves? They need to repent of their sins by being baptized, confessing their sins during baptism, and producing fruit worthy of repentance—speaking and acting in a way that shows their baptism in water to have been prompted by genuine repentance (3:6–10; 7:16–20; 12:33–35; 21:43; 28:19–20). They produce such fruit by learning and keeping the law as explained, commanded, and exemplified by Jesus (5:20–48; 11:29; 13:1–23, 51–52; 19:16–19; 28:19–20). Such learning and obedience mean leaving the way of wickedness and going the way of righteousness (21:28–32), speaking good words (12:33–35), doing good deeds (5:16; 16:27; 25:14–30), converting themselves into the lowly position of little children (18:3–4), not causing others to stumble into sin (18:6–7), and not stumbling into sin themselves (18:8–9). The list of specifics goes on and on: meekness, mercy, purity of heart, peacemaking, conciliation, avoidance of lust, maintenance of marriage, truthfulness, love of enemies, prayer for persecutors, secret charity, secret fasting, secret praying, forgiveness of debtors, forgiveness of those who have sinned against you, renunciation of earthly wealth, self-criticism, practice of the Golden Rule (see the whole of the Sermon on the Mount [chs. 5–7] and passages such as 18:21–35; 19:21–30, among others). Matthew will not present salvation apart from these and other evidence—for example, the absence of vices opposite to the foregoing virtues—that repentance was genuine.

Repentance from sins and the practice of virtue do not suffice for salvation, however. One must also believe in Jesus (18:6; cf. 8:25–26; 9:2, 22; 14:31; 16:8; 28:17). Believing in him entails confessing him in public (10:32–33); calling him "Immanuel" (1:23); loving him more than one loves father, mother, son, or daughter (10:37); taking one's cross and following him, which means risking persecution by open discipleship (10:38–39; 16:24–27); persevering under persecution (10:16–23; 24:9–13; cf. 13:18–23; and contrast the denials of Jesus by Peter [26:69–75] and Judas Iscariot's betrayal of Jesus [26:47–57]). Because of double mention by Matthew, it bears emphasis that under persecution one must persevere to be saved: "But the one persevering to the end—this one will be saved" (10:22; 24:13). In contrast is the one who hears the word and receives it immediately and joyfully, but because of tribulation and persecution turns out to be "temporary" and stumbles into sin rather than bearing the fruit of good deeds (13:20–21). Matthew's stress on the necessity of perseverance is not balanced by an equal stress on the comfort of eternal security, so that a systematic theology must supplement Matthew with John and Paul.

Belief in Jesus shows itself not only through perseverance under persecution, but also through endangering oneself by extending hospitality and charity to fellow disciples who are fleeing persecution (cf. 10:41–42; 25:31–46 with 10:11–13, 23, most of this material being unique to Matthew). More generally, genuineness of repentance and belief shows itself in faithful, prudent, and kind treatment of fellow disciples; otherwise, there awaits dichotomization, a fate shared with the hypocrites, and weeping and gnashing of teeth (24:45–51).

Negatively, Matthew takes pains to note that salvation does not come by baptism as such (3:7). To drive this point home, he shifts the phrase "for the forgiveness of sins" from John's baptism (so Mark 1:4//Luke 3:3) to the words of institution (Matt. 26:28). Again negatively, Matthew notes twice that salvation does not come by virtue of Abrahamic ancestry (3:9; 8:11–12).

Forgiveness of sins takes place in the present. "Your sins are being forgiven," Jesus says to a paralytic (9:2). Then he heals the paralytic to prove that as the Son of Man "on the earth," he has authority to be forgiving sins (9:6). Inversely, blasphemy against the Holy Spirit will not be forgiven "in this age" (12:31–32). But neither will it be forgiven "in the coming [age]." Since forgiveness of sins equates with salvation, then, salvation occurs both now and hereafter. By virtue of repentance and coming to hear the wisdom of Solomon, respectively, the men of Nineveh and the queen of the South will rise up "in the judgment" and condemn Jesus' generation. Corresponding to the condemnation of Jesus' generation, then, the salvation of the men of Nineveh and the queen of the South must take place in the day of judgment, which is also the day of resurrection. Since those who do not turn and become like little children "will by no means enter the kingdom of heaven" (18:3), the entrance of those who do convert will likewise occur in the future. And the going away of the righteous into eternal life (25:46) will occur "when the Son of Man comes in his glory, and all the angels with him," at which time "he will sit on his throne of glory" and judge "all the nations."

Notably, Matthew presents a catchall doctrine of salvation (cf. his catchall Christology: Jesus as the Christ, Immanuel, the Son of God, the Son of Man, Lord, and Wisdom). His is the soteriology of both-and rather than this-but-not-that. In 19:16–30, for example, having eternal life, inheriting eternal life, entering life, entering the kingdom, having treasure in heaven, and being saved—all carry the same soteriological meaning. Fine distinctions mean little to Matthew. Though he distinguishes between repentance and belief on the one hand and evidence ("fruit") on the other hand, he does not distinguish cleanly between salvation as a gift and salvation as a reward, or clearly deny the latter in favor of the former, as Paul does. And it remains unclear what relationship, if any, exists between the covenant in which Jesus' blood is shed for the forgiveness of sins (26:28) and the various covenants that the OT talks about. For answers to these questions, systematic theology requires the letters of Paul and Hebrews.

Within Matthew's soteriological potpourri, however, we can discern certain emphases. For him, salvation consists primarily of forgiveness of sins (though this element is expressed in a variety of terms). But stress falls not so much on God's forgiving mercy, accepted through faith, as on human beings' saving themselves in the sense of demonstrating that they have truly repented of their sins. Thus, it is the righteous who are saved, and they are saved by persevering in the superiorly righteous conduct they have learned from Jesus' teaching and example. Because they must persevere to the end, their salvation occurs mainly in the future.

Matthew's soteriological emphases seem to have grown out of circumstances in which he perceived Jewish Christians to be suffering persecution from fellow Jews who had not become Christians. As a result, and as always happens in times of persecution, some were falling away to save their necks. Matthew saw Christians, Judas-like, betraying other Christians to their persecutors (24:10). He saw Christians, Peter-like, falsifying their earlier profession with public denials of Christ (10:33). He saw their distinctively Christian conduct lapsing in such a way as to make them indistinguishable from their fellow Jews who made no Christian profession (24:12). He saw them failing to evangelize those fellow Jews and failing to make disciples of Gentiles as well, for such evangelistic efforts would mark them for persecution.

Warning! Your salvation depends on perseverance in the Christian life and witness. Otherwise you will be lost along with those who make no profession, many of them your very persecutors. Prove yourselves true. Do not let persecution lead you to hide your connection with Jesus. Flee if you must, but preach the gospel of the kingdom wherever you go. And do your good works as Christians in the full gaze of the public, even to the extent of endangering yourselves by openly ministering to persecuted fellow Christians. The day of judgment is coming. Show yourselves salty, not saltless; wise builders, not foolish ones; wheat, not tares; good fish, not bad; wearing a wedding garment, not lacking one; useful in service, not slothful and useless; wise virgins, not foolish ones. Do not slip into the category of goats rather than sheep. Your salvation is at stake. Make sure you are one of the few that will be saved.

If Matthew's emphasis on salvation by works of righteousness arises out of a need for persecuted Christians to prove the genuineness of their profession, we might ask whether a similar emphasis in the Letter of James arises out of the same need, or out of a different one. If out of a different one, has the difference in need made a difference in the emphasis? In James, the emphasis arises out of a need to quell contentiousness within local assemblies; hence, the works of righteousness have to do with the gaining, or regaining, of harmony in those assemblies. In Matthew, however, the emphasis arises out of a need to prove genuineness of Christian profession under persecution; hence, the works of righteousness have to do with the risks of open discipleship and Christian evangelism in the larger society.

If Matthew's emphasis arises out of a need for persecuted Christians to prove the genuineness of their profession, we might also ask whether the emphasis has a purpose of combating Paul's doctrine of salvation—or, as he prefers to say, justification—by faith apart from works, or of combating an antinomian aberration of Paul's doctrine. To ask the question in terms of *persecution* is to cast doubt on an affirmative answer. The same is true if we ask whether Matthew's emphasis has the purpose of combating, or competing with, the rabbinic Judaism that was evolving in the last quarter of the first century. For it is one thing to claim superiority over that Judaism for the purpose of keeping persecuted Christians true to the faith, but it would be quite another thing to claim superiority over that Judaism for the purpose of taking command of Jewish religious life. And to suppose a synergy of both purposes founders on the unlikelihood that a persecuted minority thought of taking over the large, persecuting body. On the contrary and as already noted, Matthew underlines the fewness of those who will be saved: "For the gate is small, and the way is narrow that leads to life, and few are those who find it" (7:14):

> These emphases pose the danger of legalism and need balancing by the doctrine of the indwelling Spirit, through whose life and power alone Jesus' disciples can fulfill the righteous requirement of the law (Rom. 8:1–4). But it is good to have Matthew's emphases without that balance; for in some situations to introduce the doctrine of the Spirit quickly is to dull the edge of the demands made on Jesus' disciples. They might fail to feel the pain caused by the sharp edge of those demands. Only when that pain is felt will

37

the Spirit's enablement amount to more than a comfortable sanctification open to the incursion of antinomianism. Wherever the church has grown large and mixed, wherever the church is polarized between the extremes of latitudinarianism and sectarianism, wherever the church feels drawn to accommodation with forces that oppose the gospel, wherever the church loses its vision of worldwide evangelism, wherever the church lapses into smug religiosity with its attendant vices of ostentation, hypocrisy, and haughty disdain for its underprivileged and correspondingly zealous members—there the Gospel of Matthew speaks with power and pertinence. (Gundry 9–10)

Bibliography

Blomberg, C. *Matthew*. Broadman, 1992.

Burgess, J. *A History of the Exegesis of Matthew 6:17–19 from 1781 to 1965*. Edwards Brothers, 1976.

Carlston, C. "Christology and Church in Matthew." Pages 1283–1304 in *The Four Gospels 1992*, ed. F. Van Segbroeck et al. Leuven University Press, 1992.

English, E. *Studies in the Gospel according to Matthew*. F. H. Revell, 1935.

Green, H. *The Gospel according to Matthew*. Oxford University Press, 1975.

Guelich, R. *The Sermon on the Mount*. Word, 1982.

Gundry, R. *Matthew*. 2nd ed. Eerdmans, 1994.

Hagner, D. "Apocalyptic Motifs in the Gospel of Matthew: Continuity and Discontinuity." *HBT* 7 (1985): 53–82.

———. *Matthew 1–13*. Word, 1993.

Luz, U. *Matthew 1–7*. Augsburg, 1989.

———. *Matthew 8–20*. Fortress, 2001.

———. *Matthew in History*. Fortress, 1994.

———. *The Theology of the Gospel of Matthew*. Cambridge University Press, 1995.

Meier, J. P. *The Vision of Matthew*. Paulist, 1979.

Przybylski, B. *Righteousness in Matthew and His World of Thought*. Cambridge University Press, 1980.

Simonetti, M., ed. *Matthew 1–13*. ACCSNT 1a. InterVarsity, 2001.

———. *Matthew 14–28*. ACCSNT 1b. InterVarsity, 2002.

Suggs, M. J. *Wisdom, Christology, and Law in Matthew's Gospel*. Harvard University Press, 1970.

2

Mark

THORSTEN MORITZ

Mark's Gospel is generally thought to be the earliest. Mainstream opinion is somewhat divided between assuming a date of origin just before the Jewish War or in its immediate aftermath. There is broad agreement that this Gospel became the literary basis for at least two others, Matthew and Luke, and possibly a third (John). Matthew and Luke have considerable overlap with Mark; John's Gospel does not. This is often explained on the assumption that the author wanted to avoid significant overlap with other Gospels, which already enjoyed wide circulation by the time John wrote. The language and the narrative architecture of Mark's Gospel is less sophisticated than those of the other Gospels, but in recent decades there has been a growing appreciation of the theological use of narrative techniques by this author as well. Clearly, Mark was as serious a theologian as any other NT author; characterizing his literary and theological awareness as that of a mere collector of early Christian tradition is no longer a viable option. His linguistic (Greek) capabilities may be limited at times, but his narrative-theological contribution is immense. Mark's significance for the Christian church becomes apparent when it is realized that this Gospel represents the move from oral Jesus tradition (gospel) to a written "Life of Jesus" (Gospel). The likeliest option for genre is that the canonical Gospels should be treated as ancient *bioi*. If so, the recent view that the Gospels did not have specific audiences in mind (Bauckham) ought to be viewed with some caution. There is little doubt that most ancient *bioi* were written to be read or "performed" orally (Bryan) and in specific contexts.

Interpretation and Approaches

Mark's history of reception is by far the least substantial compared to those of the other Gospels, to some extent lingering for centuries in the shadows, particularly of Matthew and John. The situation eventually changed, but not before the last decades of the eighteenth century with the emerging interest in historical questions. Markan priority began to be explored as a real possibility, for it was noticed that Luke and Matthew agree the most in their respective structures where they overlap with Mark. Ironically, this happened at around the same time (1835) when "Q" first emerged as a viable hypothesis. Along with Q, Mark came to be received as a crucial tool needed to rebut Strauss's evaluation of the Gospels as mythical accounts of Jesus. Later, the assumption that Mark preserves some kind of *Urevangelium*, or at least the basis for a definitive historical answer to Strauss, was challenged, but in the nineteenth century it helped propel the Gospel from relative anonymity to the center stage it still commands today.

With hindsight, this rise to prominence toward the end of the nineteenth century was based on positivistic assumptions and motivations that now appear questionable. Mark's Gospel was seen as a historical antidote to the "speculative" nature of John's. But from the perspective of those who enlisted Mark's help in reconstructing a solid "life of Jesus," it was unfortunate that this Gospel proportionally placed more emphasis on miracle stories than any other did. The two-source theory named Mark and Q as the main sources behind Matthew and Luke, with Q denoting the overlap between Matthew and Luke against Mark. Part of this theory's attraction was that Q, with its emphasis on Jesus' teachings, could balance Mark's preoccupation with the miraculous, which was regarded as incompatible with notions of historicity.

It is still against this background of Strauss's challenge to Mark's historical value and the attempt by others to find solid historical ground that Wrede developed his theory of the "messianic secret." According to that theory, the early church attempted to legitimize its understanding of

Jesus as Messiah by projecting the secrecy motif back into Jesus' ministry. Historically, Wrede argued, Jesus did not regard himself as Messiah. The disciples' alleged lack of understanding and Jesus' reported enjoinders to them to keep his messianic role and status secret are said to have no historical basis. Instead, they supposedly were introduced into the pre-Markan tradition to explain why belief in Jesus' messiahship only came about as a consequence of the resurrection kerygma. If judged successful, Wrede's argument would undermine the historical value of Mark for reconstructing the life of Jesus, for it was the early church that introduced some of the most theologically significant aspects of this Gospel into the pre-Markan tradition.

In Germany, Wrede's historical skepticism was largely received with approval. Increasingly, Mark's Gospel was viewed as a theological reflection of the early church's perception of Jesus, not Jesus himself. Its role as a historically verifiable source to be used for legitimizing the church's modern christological consciousness began to wane. Form criticism thus tacitly threatened the predominance of Mark in Gospels studies, but then a renewed interest in Mark accompanied the emergence of redaction criticism (Marxsen), though it soon became clear that Matthew and Luke proved more fertile for such studies. Mark's redaction-critical potential was subordinated by some to the continuing interest in the historical Jesus.

Marxsen's assumption that there was substantial continuity between Mark and the earliest days of Christianity meant for some that it would be compelling to compare Mark's theology with that of the early letters of Paul, especially if those letters are the oldest documents in the NT. As such, they present us with a so-called primitive eschatology, not far removed from that of Jesus himself. In addition, there are now significant efforts to reclaim "biography" as a valid category for exploring Mark's genre (Dihle; Hengel). Having said that, few would now want to reduce the theological contribution of Mark to matters of either historicity or "primitive eschatology."

In recent German scholarship the theological focus on the role of the suffering righteous one in the Gospel as a whole (as opposed to just being a component of the passion narrative) is noteworthy (Ruppert; Steichele). In contrast to diachronic and theological concerns, synchronic approaches seek to connect the world in the text with that in front of it and emphasize the likely impact of the text upon the reader. At the postmodern end the interpretative weight tends to be shifted so far in the direction of the reader that stability in interpretation becomes impossible and is perceived as largely undesirable.

Probably the most promising avenue into a theological reading of Mark's Gospel is one that takes its cue from the OT allusions in the opening three verses of the Gospel itself (Watts). At least some recent commentators have recognized the importance of Mark's OT allusions as interpretative keys to unlocking his theology (France; Marcus). The following section demonstrates the importance of this line of inquiry.

Text and Message

Given the relative simplicity of Mark's Gospel, it is ironic to note the sheer diversity of attempts at defining its core theological objectives. Among the obvious main candidates are the kingdom of God, Christology, and discipleship. They are self-evident to the extent that Mark emphasizes all three topics in his opening twenty verses. Form-critical as well as sociologically inclined scholars often focus on community instruction as an underlying theme (Kee). Gundry reads Mark as an apology for the cross. The list could easily be extended. The difficulty, however, is that none of these topics or approaches are wide enough to cover all of Mark, yet distinct enough to explain Mark's specific purpose. The best approach may well be that chosen by Watts. The starting point of this line of argument is the frequency with which Mark employs Exodus motifs such as the wilderness in the prologue, the two feeding stories, and the mount of transfiguration episode (cloud, dwellings), with its reference to Moses and the sea crossings. Once this is combined with the striking editorial combination of Isa. 40:3 with Mal. 3:1 and Exod. 23:20 in Mark's opening verses, what emerges is an important hermeneutical key to this Gospel. In its original context Isa. 40 is about the inauguration of the long-awaited new exodus (NE), including Yahweh's return. Malachi 3 and Exod. 23:30 are about Yahweh's threat that accompanies his coming at the culmination of the NE.

Isaiah 40 is a word of comfort about the nearing end of Israel's exile (cf. ch. 6, which is partially quoted in Mark 4:10–12), and Isaiah's message is inherently good: Yahweh will return to his people and be enthroned in a restored Jerusalem. Isaiah's comfort culminates in a messenger announcing to Jerusalem the good news (40:9–11) of her redemption and rebuilding (44:26; 45:13; 54:11–12). The link between Mark's prologue and Isaiah is further strengthened by the parallel acclamation of the son in whom God is well pleased (Isa. 42:1//Mark 1:11), for Jesus takes the place of true Israel, the "son."

Malachi 3:1–3 gives the other side of the coin: The coming of the Lord to the temple also means judgment. The reasons are clear: "You are ignoring me" (Mal. 3:7–9). Malachi's setting is the disappointment following the return from the exile; Isaiah's grand promises have still not fully eventuated (cf. Isa. 40–55 and 66). The delay of the Isaianic NE would necessitate the preparation of "the way" in the desert by a messenger. Malachi puts the blame for the delay at the door of both the priests and the people, certainly not God (chs. 1–2), for God is faithful and will eventually return (2:17–3:5).

The middle ground between Isaiah's and Malachi's respective emphases is covered by the third OT component of Mark's prologue, Exod. 23:20: The way of the Lord is being prepared, and Israel must make sure she is ready for it (vv. 21–31). The Exodus text belongs to the Book of the Covenant (20:22–23:33), which is set in the context of Israel's account of her founding moment. The context of v. 20 has the classic covenantal duality of blessings for the obedient (vv. 25–26) and a threat for the disobedient (v. 33). Also, the sins listed in Mal. 3:5 are in breach of either the Decalogue or Exod. 23. In short: Mark quotes the very OT verse that links back to the prototype of the NE, the original exodus, and that emphasizes the duality of God's redemptive faithfulness as opposed to Israel's faithlessness. But there are also close parallels of warnings and promises between Isa. 40:3 and Mal. 3:1 and their respective contexts.

The major advantage of reading Mark in light of his use of OT motifs is that it does justice both to the prologue as well as numerous aspects that are otherwise difficult to fit into an overall purpose. Examples include Mark's emphasis on Jesus' wanderings around Galilee and Judea, which may well have the purpose of reliving the desert wanderings of Israel. The transfiguration is now linked to Sinai, Jesus being the eschatological equivalent of the giver of the law. To be sure, it is not that Mark appeals to the OT a lot. The only time he does so explicitly *as narrator* is in chapter 1. But his allusions to the covenant, the temple, the "way," and the wilderness, along with the symbolism of story elements—such as "by the sea," the point of Israel's deliverance (1:16; 3:7); "on the mountain," Sinai reflection on the renewal of the community (3:13–35); "at home," the golden calf incident (6:1–6); "in the wilderness," Israel's place of rebellion (6:7–31)—all fit well with the exodus/NE scheme. The combination of quotations, allusions, and fragments of OT material (details in Watts) makes the case a strong one.

Mark consciously sets the appearance and ministry of Jesus in the context of the NE. For him, this is the story of the beginning of the renewal of God's covenant people, and Jesus is revealed not just as a protagonist in the NE story, but as Israel's returning God. Once it is set in this theological framework, it becomes clear that Jesus is the embodiment of Israel's returning God, in terms both of good news and ominous threat. Astonishingly, the messenger figure of Malachi is from Mark's perspective not just a prototype of John, but an anticipatory icon of Jesus as the bringer of the NE. Jesus embodies the very presence of Israel's Lord.

For Isaiah, the NE motif involves three main stages: Yahweh's deliverance of his exiled people, the journey along the "way" (away from captivity), and arrival in Jerusalem, resulting in Yahweh's enthronement. In light of Isaiah's and Mark's deliberate use of the "way" motif, it seems possible that Mark's threefold geographical progression (Galilee, journey, Jerusalem) is designed as a symbolic allusion to Isaiah's NE motif. This itself does not deny the historicity of his account, but it certainly provides a plausible and even powerful theological explanation of the evangelist's selectivity and narrative arrangement. More importantly, it gives the reader a much-needed framework for making sense of Jesus' death and resurrection. Paradoxically, the cross was "the way" of launching the long-promised NE of God's people—a way of seeming defeat but actual vindication.

Mark and Canon

Given the previous section, we are well on the way to situating Mark's Gospel within the biblical canon. It remains to explore its place within the NT. On grounds of probable dating, Mark's relationship with Paul's letters is especially intriguing. If John Mark is the historical author of the Gospel, a view accepted by most, it is interesting that he and Paul both experienced some tension with the Jerusalem church. The main bone of contention for both Paul and Mark was the initial lack of enthusiasm of the "pillars" toward subordinating Jewish tradition to the exalted Jesus (Mark 7:1–23), thus potentially hindering the progress of the gospel among the Gentiles. Together with Paul's letters, it gives us an excellent insight into the early days of Christianity.

The importance of Mark alongside Matthew's and Luke's Q material has been mentioned. Without the evidence of Mark, our appreciation of Jesus' miracles as signs of Israel's eschatological restoration would be significantly poorer, though Luke makes the same theological point. Both Matthew and Luke are deeply indebted to Mark, though Luke in particular replicates Mark's basic outline, possibly because he recognized Mark's allusion to Isaiah's NE. John seems to have taken care not to duplicate Mark's account, for even where he twice presents the same episode as Mark ("feeding" and "sea" episodes—Mark 6 and John 6), he offers different historical details and theological angles. It appears that he took the widespread existence of Mark's Gospel for granted.

Acts begins with what looks like an alternative to Mark's ending, and the theological rationale for the differences appears straightforward. Acts is the second volume of Luke's Gospel and as such connects with Israel's eschatological expectations (such as spiritual restoration) in ways that are replete with Jewish allusions and themes that Mark considered too specific for his Gentile audience. However, both Mark (Isaiah's NE) and Luke-Acts (death-resurrection-ascension-Pentecost cycle) do share an emphasis on the present realization of the kingdom. Even Mark 13 is no exception to the evangelist's interest in pre-70 CE events. It is perfectly plausible to interpret the entire chapter with a first-century referent in mind (France gets close to this).

Peter's greetings in 1 Pet. 5:13 have given rise to speculations about connections between the historical Mark and the author of 1 Peter, even though most literary parallels link 1 Peter to Matthew, not Mark. Perceived ecclesiological (in the general sense of "God's people") differences between Mark and 1 Peter go beyond our purview, for they depend more on exegetical and historical assessments of 1 Peter than Mark's Gospel. Perhaps the most significant overlap between the two documents consists of their common emphasis on Jesus as Isaiah's Suffering Servant (Mark 9:35; 10:45) and their preoccupation with the relationship of faith and suffering.

This last point also closely connects Mark (10:29–30; 13:9–13) to Hebrews. Other common trajectories are their "interior" understanding of purity (Mark 7:1–23), their spiritualized Christian understanding of sacrifice (12:32–34), and their assessment of the Jerusalem temple as a human construction (14:58).

It was implied above that Mark 13 is in its entirety a discourse about the procession toward and climax of the Jewish War. The war and impending fall of the city and temple are presented as another "return" of Jesus, this time as judge (Son of Man; cf. Dan. 7:13). In light of Isaiah's NE motif, Jesus' entry into Jerusalem (Mark 11:1–19) was nothing less than God's return to his people to sacrificially complete Israel's failed mission on her behalf (10:45). The Son of Man's further return to the city as judge (70 CE) brought the negative side of Isaiah's NE to partial fulfillment. In recent scholarship the parousia-oriented eschatology of

Revelation has increasingly been interpreted with reference to the first-century experience of the persecuted church, and to that extent Mark's eschatological concern with the first century and the suffering community seems compatible with and similar to that of Revelation.

Mark and Theology

In general terms, Mark's theological agenda can be described as a combination of affirming the faithfulness of Israel's God and the relevance of this for Gentiles. Jesus is the embodiment of Israel's returning God, and as such he enters the city and takes Israel's fate upon himself by becoming the sacrifice for the many (10:45). In the process he pronounces judgment on the corrupt establishment as represented by the temple (11:12–26) and is set to execute the judgment himself, as the Danielic Son of Man, by allowing Jerusalem and the temple to be reduced to rubble (Mark 13). This apparent paradox makes perfect sense once Mark's understanding of Isaiah's NE is taken seriously. Israel is redefined as the renewal movement of those committed to him: The remnant (= disciples) should be able to understand this, Jesus explains. Those outside of this christocentrically defined group, however, experience temporary hardness of heart, thus ensuring that they become subject to the Son of Man's imminent judgment (4:10–12; cf. ch. 13). The Isa. 6 quotation in Mark 4 lays the foundation for the more explicit judgment call of chapter 13. Neither of these texts is about the physical end of the world, yet both are about the end of the (Mosaic) age as humanity knew it. Jesus inaugurated his kingdom decisively, both in self-sacrifice and in judgment, and the clear implication is that his followers should live accordingly. This means readiness for suffering and unfailing loyalty to the One who alone is the defining center of Israel's—and in fact humanity's—renewal. The promise to Abraham is being fulfilled, despite Israel's failure. Jesus and those around him are Israel restored. The responsibility to model authentic creational humanity rests squarely on those who, despite their continuing failures, recognize Jesus as king of Israel and Son of God (15:32–39). Humanity is thus defined christocentrically; ethnicity, social standing, and so forth are transcended in Jesus.

In terms of contemporary relevance, the following selection is suggestive rather than complete (for more discussion, see Telford 214–41). (1) Mark's theology of the cross and self-denial in the name of Jesus stands in stark contrast to modern and postmodern definitions of success in life. Mark's first half (1:1–8:21), which concentrates on glory and success, is followed by an account of the disciples' bitter learning experience in the face of Jesus' self-sacrifice. (2) Jesus' repeated emphasis on the new wine's need for new skins (not always in these words) challenges us to examine and reconfigure the role of religious tradition in our understanding of God's people following the Christ event. Yet, the debates about what was permissible on the Sabbath remind our 24/7 society of the important interplay between covenantal demands and creational values. (3) Politically, Mark's Gospel teaches us a healthy skepticism toward ethnically centered or even nationalistic understandings of God's people. Israel's task was not to overthrow the Roman Empire ("Give to Caesar what belongs to Caesar"), but to reform itself by rendering to God what belongs to him. The one who urges his hearers to pay attention (13:14) also informs us that Jesus' political stance seriously raised some eyebrows in Israel (12:17).

Our final question relates to the contribution Mark has to make in the arena of systematic theology. The most significant challenge falls in the areas of Christology and the Trinity. Traditionally, both have been approached in terms of Aristotelian-inspired substance metaphysics. The issue has often been compounded in NT scholarship by subjecting Mark's christological titles rather exclusively to a history-of-religions approach. It would be anachronistic to expect Mark to frame his theological concerns in this way. From his first-century perspective the most pertinent claim is that somehow Christ embodies the returning God of Israel. Along with his fellow writers, he stops far short of ontological speculations about either the natures of Christ or the inner-trinitarian position of Christ. More importantly for him, Christ is the sole definer of the remnant, the true people of God, for he alone is both the returning God of Israel and the fulfiller of Israel's true destiny. It is at this convergence of *Christ as God* and *true man* throughout Jesus' life that Mark anchors his implied incarnational Jesus theology. For him, this is not an end in itself, but the crucial component in redefining the centerpiece of the Abrahamic project: humanity—that is God's people—in light of the Son of Man's journey to the cross and beyond. Mark's christological titles should not be interpreted as substance-metaphysical indicators, but as powerful narrative ways of connecting *Jesus as God* with the remnant people (Son of Man), whose salvific mission he accomplishes on the cross and in resurrection.

Salvation for Mark is not strictly a concern for the future. In his "already/not yet" scheme, the focus is firmly on the "already." People are rehabilitated spiritually, physically, socially, and emotionally—clear indications that the kingdom has arrived. Life after death starts at the transforming encounter with Jesus, not after physical death. The latter is but a stepping-stone along the way. The disciples experience Israel's eagerly awaited restoration. Mark may not be as interested as Luke in linking Jesus' miracles to the power of the eschatologically awaited Spirit, but he is equally clear that the salvation Jesus brings to repentant sinners is nothing less than Israel's restoration. Consequently, for Mark eschatology is a matter of interpreting the present realization of the kingdom as the climactic renewal of Israel. The future matters primarily in its impact on the present, not as a "not yet" reality. Sinners repent not to await salvation, but to enjoy it by living authentically among God's people. Any systematic-theological correlation of eschatology and soteriology focused on a chronologically final sequence of events will do little justice to Mark's theology.

Mark bases his theological confidence squarely on his reading of the OT, especially the NE motif. His other main source for theological reflection on Christ and his people is the disciples' religious experience of Jesus' divine presence. The two are intimately connected throughout his narrative, for it is God's presence through Jesus with the disciples that, more than anything else, illustrates the arrival of the NE. Instead of walking away from his covenant with an unfaithful people, God through Jesus brings to successful completion the mission of Israel as the model people in the world. God is justified after all. For Mark, the communion meal is not only a powerful reminder of this, but a crucial and appropriate speech-act that re-creates among God's people and in creation this divine faithfulness manifested in Jesus. The Abrahamic recovery project of humanity is alive and well—indeed, it has reached a crucial climax, for "the Son of Man . . . [has given] his life as a ransom for many" (10:45).

Bibliography

Bauckham, R. "For Whom Were Gospels Written?" In *The Gospels for All Christians,* ed. R. Bauckham. Eerdmans, 1997.

Bryan, C. *A Preface to Mark*. Oxford University Press, 1993.

Dihle, A. "Die Evangelien und die biographische Tradition der Antike." *ZTK* 80 (1983): 33–49.

France, R. T. *The Gospel of Mark*. NIGTC. Eerdmans, 2002.

Gundry, R. *Mark*. Eerdmans, 1993.

Hengel, M. *Studies in the Gospel of Mark,* trans. J. Bowden. SCM, 1985.

Marcus, J. *Mark 1–8*. AB. Doubleday, 2000.

Marxsen, W. *Mark the Evangelist,* trans. J. Boyce et al. Abingdon, 1969.

Ruppert, L. *Jesus als der leidende Gerechte?* SBS. Katholisches Bibelwerk, 1972.

Steichele, H.-J. *Der leidende Sohn Gottes*. BU 14. F. Pustet, 1980.

Strauss, D. F. *The Life of Jesus Critically Examined*. Translated from the 4th German ed. by G. Eliot. Fortress, 1972.

Telford, W. *The Theology of the Gospel of Mark*. NTT. Cambridge University Press, 1999.

Watts, R. *Isaiah's New Exodus in Mark*. BSL. Baker, 2000.

Wrede, W. *The Messianic Secret*, trans. J. C. G. Greig. J. Clarke, 1971.

3

Luke

STEPHEN I. WRIGHT

History of Interpretation

Early interpretation of Luke included meditation on its significance as one strand of the fourfold Gospel. Each Gospel was assigned a unique purpose, sometimes linked with a traditional symbol—in Luke's case, the ox. Thus in Ambrose, Augustine, and Bede, a connection is made between the symbol of the ox and the Evangelist's emphasis on the temple, the place of animal sacrifice (1:5–25; 2:22–52; 13:35; 24:53). This is seen as reflecting the truth of Christ's mediation as sacrificial victim and high priest (Wright 68–69).

The discernment of pattern and purpose in Scripture, attributed to divine authorship, reached new sophistication in medieval times and is well represented by Bonaventure's commentary on Luke. His reading of 4:18–21 treats Jesus' "sermon" in Nazareth as not only programmatic for his ministry, but also descriptive of Luke's purpose in writing. Thus, Luke's Gospel itself is read as offering "good news to the poor." Luke's purpose is construed as manifesting truth, healing infirmity, and pointing to eternity. These three are interwoven: it is through knowledge of the truth that we find healing, a healing that will only be complete hereafter. Jesus' ministry is thus represented as being recapitulated by Luke for a far wider public, whose eternal benefit, conversely, finds symbolic expression in the transformations wrought by Jesus while on earth. The traditional identification of the Evangelist with the "beloved physician" of Col. 4:14 assists this rich reading of the many-layered significance of the Gospel (Wright 71).

The historical interest of Luke, clearly stated in 1:1–4 and exemplified in his careful (if not completely accurate) dating statements of 2:1–2 and 3:1–2, naturally started to claim greater attention with the advent of modern historical sensibilities. Some conservative scholars have used this historical interest as an argument for Luke's historical accuracy. Scholars who recognize Luke's careful artistry, however, have tended to see the heavy hand of the theological interpreter in Luke's "historiography." Thus, Luke and its companion volume, Acts, have sometimes been taken as evidence for an "early Catholicism" that supposedly departed from the radical gospel of Paul, accommodating itself to the nonappearance of Christ in glory, and putting greater emphasis on the institution of the church and its organic relation to Judaism.

So Luke's "history" could be seen not so much as a sober record of the facts but as a placement of Jesus and the early church within a framework of "salvation history." This was the position of Rudolf Bultmann and Hans Conzelmann. Conzelmann read in Luke the portrayal of a Jesus who stood "in the middle of time" as the fulfillment of Israel's history and the seed of the church's.

More recently, both "conservative" and "liberal" approaches have given way to more nuanced appreciations of Luke's historical, literary, and theological achievements. The contours of "salvation history," which Conzelmann and others saw as Luke's artifice, Oscar Cullmann saw as, in essence, common to the perspective of early Christianity generally and indeed Jesus himself (Marshall 81–83). It is recognized that theological purposes do not necessarily conflict with historical ones: indeed, the "facts" of Jesus are of fundamental importance for theology, according to Luke. But neither does historical purpose necessarily imply complete accuracy according to modern canons. With literary skill (see esp. Tannehill) Luke weaves together the story as he has received it and its meaning as he believes it to be.

The Message of Luke

Luke's "message" is a story, an "orderly account" of events to give its recipients a secure basis for faith (1:1–4). "For Luke, . . . narration is proclamation" (Green, *Theology*, 19).

The core of Luke's narrative is shared with Matthew and Mark, and its basic shape with John. Jesus of Nazareth proclaimed God's kingdom, called and taught disciples, restored the victims of spiritual, physical, and social dysfunction, encountered opposition, was crucified, and rose from death. We will concentrate on Luke's particular emphasis in telling this story.

The Setting: Jewish and World History

After the elegant Hellenistic prologue in 1:1–4, we are transported back into the world of the Jewish Scriptures. Chapters 1 and 2 recount the births of Jesus and his precursor John in a manner reminiscent of marvelous OT birth stories (e.g., Judg. 13:2–25; 1 Sam. 1:1–2:10; Drury 46–66). Throughout the Gospel scriptural echoes underscore the continuity between Jesus' story and that of Israel, as well as contrasts (Jesus' virgin birth, for instance, is unique; Green, *Theology*, 24–28).

Luke 2:1–3 and 3:1–3 remind us of the contemporary political context in which these boys were born, that of Roman rule over Palestine. The genealogy (3:23–38), in which the "ancestry" of Jesus (via his foster father, Joseph) is traced all the way back not just to Abraham but to Adam, seals this emphasis. Jesus is the heir to human destiny as well as Jewish hopes (cf. 2:32).

The Anointed One

Like the other Evangelists, Luke testifies that Jesus is Israel's Messiah. In common with Matthew and Mark, he records Jesus' extreme reticence to claim this title for himself before his death, but acceptance of it on the lips of Peter (9:20–21) and of the closely related title "Son of God" from the Sanhedrin (22:70). Unique to Luke are the angels' announcement that "Christ the Lord" is born (2:11), the revelation to Simeon that he would not die before he had seen "the Lord's Christ" (2:25–38), and the explanation by the risen Jesus of how he has fulfilled the true destiny of the Messiah (24:25–27, 45–47). Jesus' coming is the occasion for joyous celebration, the first taste of the longed-for messianic feast (2:10; 13:17; 15:1–2, 7, 10; 19:6, 37; 24:41).

The Vocation of a Prophet

For Luke, Jesus' *prophetic* anointing and calling are central to his messiahship (Tuckett 61–62). By contrast, although Gabriel tells Mary that her child will have an everlasting throne (1:33), Luke's portrayal of Jesus as *King* is ironic. The crowds cry, "Blessed is the *king* who comes in the name of the Lord!" (19:38), but Jesus is on a donkey, not a royal charger. Before Pilate, Jesus is accused of claiming "to be Christ, a king" (23:2)—just before he is led out to die.

But there is no irony in the portrayal of Jesus as the prophet par excellence. His link with the prophetic outpourings of the past is emphasized by the "prophecy" of Zechariah before his birth (1:67–79) and his own implicit self-comparison with Elijah and Elisha (4:25–27). His sense of uniqueness is seen in 4:21, where he declares that Isa. 61:1–2 is fulfilled "today" in his own Spirit-inspired proclamation. After his death he is recalled as "a prophet, powerful in word and deed" (24:19; cf. 7:16).

"Powerful in Word"

Jesus comes to "declare good news," "proclaim freedom," "proclaim the year of the Lord's favor" (4:18–19). This "word" ministry is evident throughout the Gospel. Jesus' announcements of what God is doing in salvation and judgment are combined with challenges to join in with God's work.

Luke gives us the largest number of Jesus' narrative parables. These sound a subversive note of both hope and warning. God is pictured at work in surprising ways, to vindicate those who cry out to him in their need for justice and mercy, and disturb those who think they are secure (e.g., 18:1–14). Like Second Isaiah, Jesus discerned light where many saw only gloom. He also, like Jeremiah, discerned judgment impending in the place where many pinned their hopes—the holy city and especially the temple (13:34–35; 19:41–44; cf. Jer. 7:1–11).

Jesus' prophetic words not only concern God's activity. They also contain an immediate challenge for radical generosity and forgivingness, going right against the grain of entrenched social positions and attitudes (Green, *Theology*, 16), as especially seen in 14:7–24.

"Powerful in Deed"

Jesus comes "to release the oppressed" (4:18). To reassure John's messengers, he performed many cures there and then (7:21). A typical act was release of a crippled woman from her bondage—physical, social, and spiritual (13:10–17).

Jesus acts as Savior (2:11). Here there are overtones of the leadership and protection that God provided and promised to his people in OT times (cf. 1:69–71). But his "salvation" does not come through military prowess.

It occurs as the physically weak, socially ostracized, and morally degraded find a new dignity and place in the community through relating to Jesus. "Your faith has saved you," he says to the "sinful woman" who anoints his feet (7:50). In Jesus, "salvation" comes to Abraham's children, even immoral folk like Zacchaeus, resulting in new justice and generosity (19:1–8).

The forgiveness of sins, especially evident in Luke as central to Jesus' ministry (in particular see 7:41–49; 15:1–32), is much more than restoration of inward peace with God, though it is not less than that. It involves the establishment of a new state of fellowship in the community and signals Israel's renewal. It is not "cheap grace" that demands no repentance, but a forgiveness propelled by a new "economy of grace, inspiring repentance" (Barton). This work of Jesus is to continue, as "repentance and forgiveness of sins" are preached to all nations (24:47).

The Way to and of the Cross

Jesus' calling is that of the *lonely* prophet. He meets rejection among his own countryfolk (4:28–30). In 9:51 he "set[s] his face to go to Jerusalem" (KJV)—for, as he wryly remarks, "no prophet can die outside Jerusalem!" (13:33).

There he will, indeed, meet a lonely death, fulfilling his "exodus" (9:31 Greek) and liberating his people. But Jesus' literal "way *to* the cross" is mirrored in "the way *of* the cross," which he calls *the disciples* to travel. Luke's narrative of the journey to Jerusalem (9:51–19:27) includes much teaching on the nature of discipleship. Jesus takes his people *with him* out of bondage to a new promised land. The travels of Paul in Acts, and especially his final journey to Rome (chs. 27–28), recapitulate Jesus' own journeying and suffering, suggesting the oneness of Christian disciples with their Master.

The disciples are presented in a positive light when compared to Mark and Matthew. Luke does not even mention Peter's objection to Jesus' talk of his death and Jesus' rebuke (cf. 9:18–27 with Mark 8:27–38//Matt. 16:13–18, 20–23). To some extent, therefore, disciples in Luke are exemplary figures for the church. They are those who are traveling the way of Jesus. According to Luke, discipleship means giving up "all" in a quite literal sense (5:11, 28; 14:33; 18:22; Tuckett 96–97). Jesus' way is lonely, but there are others who were at least beginning to accompany him, and Luke wants his readers to join in the journey, taking up the cross "daily" (9:23).

Luke's portrayal of Jesus' suffering and death is well summed up by the centurion's comment: "Surely this was a righteous man" (23:47). Luke accents not so much the anguish of the cross as the innocence and compassion of its victim (23:4, 15, 22, 28, 34). In his dying moments Jesus entrusts himself to the one he had always known as "Father" (23:46; cf. 2:49; Ps. 31:5). Like the other Evangelists, Luke is understated concerning the significance of Jesus' death. But he makes clear that it was utterly undeserved. Therein lies Luke's clue to the resurrection and all that would ensue (cf. Acts 3:14–15).

Luke in the Canon

The Biography of Jesus

To Luke we owe the stories of Jesus' birth in a manger and childhood (ch. 2), his meeting with two disciples on the Emmaus road (24:13–35), and his ascension (24:51). The inclusion of these events gives narrative completeness to his Gospel. It also grounds theological conviction about Jesus in the circumstances of his human life. It is true that belief in the incarnation does not depend on the story of the virgin birth, and that belief in the universal rule of Jesus does not depend on the story of the ascension. Yet these stories remain appropriate and enduring symbols of these truths, and are told with a lack of mythological elaboration that suggests they are based on faithful tradition.

Women

The prominent part played by women throughout the story is one of Luke's unique contributions to our vision of Christian discipleship.

Mary, Jesus' mother, is favored with an angelic visit (1:26–38), actively cooperates (1:38), and praises God (1:46–56). Women make an important contribution to the mission of Jesus and the Twelve (8:1–3). Jesus affirms the (normally male) role Mary of Bethany has chosen as a learner (10:42). A story of a woman is often paired with one of a man (e.g., 7:1–10, 11–17; 15:3–7, 8–10; Donahue 135).

Israel and Church: Continuity and Transformation

Luke's portrayal of the Jewish people and their leaders is in some ways more sympathetic than that of the other Gospels. Some Pharisees are friendly to Jesus (13:31), and he eats with them, even though he also castigates them (7:36–50; 11:37–54; 14:1–24). The disciples' worship in the temple is seen as continuous with that of godly Israelites before Jesus appears (1:8–10; 24:53). Jesus is viewed as respectful of traditions, bringing fulfillment and development rather than an overthrow of old ways (Thielman 135–67).

Nevertheless, Jesus' words and acts in Luke subvert any limitation of God's purposes, or God's people, to the Jewish race. Luke does not read back a full-blown "mission to the Gentiles" into Jesus' ministry. But Jesus suggests that a Samaritan might keep the law (10:30–37; cf. 17:15–18) and forbids the disciples to call down punishment on an unwelcoming Samaritan village (9:51–55). He welcomes those on the margins of Jewish society, tainted by their regular contact with Gentiles, in table fellowship (5:27–32; 15:1–2; 19:1–10) and in narrative (e.g., 15:11–32; 16:1–8; 18:9–14).

A Kingdom of Reversals

Luke's Jesus proclaims "the good news of the kingdom of God" (4:43). Luke, with his accounts of the "acts of Jesus" in both his earthly ministry and his Spirit-filled church, has been seen as toning down the austere apocalyptic expectation evident in Mark. He points to the reality of the kingdom in the present and supposedly makes its future consummation a far-distant event (Conzelmann 101–25; critiqued in Marshall 130–31).

But the difference is simply one of degree. Luke indeed has the saying "the kingdom of God is within you" (or "among you," 17:21 NRSV). But he also has apocalyptic passages (17:22–37; 21:5–38), and as in Matthew and Mark, these have a clear first focus in the disaster that Jesus foresees coming on Jerusalem. Probably Luke's readers, unlike Mark's, would know that this prophecy had been fulfilled—so Luke could place more emphasis on the present evidence of the kingdom, in both judgment and grace. But the kingdom, Luke knew, had not yet come in final fullness (21:9), and in his own day he would have been well aware of the persecutions and temptations that signaled the urgency of the times (12:35–59).

So the distinctive Lukan insights concerning the kingdom of God lie not so much in the issue of the kingdom's *timing*. Rather, Luke particularly stresses the *reversals* entailed in the establishment of the kingdom (1:52–53).

Jesus' blessings and woes (6:20–26) starkly express these reversals: the kingdom belongs to the poor, while the rich have received their comfort. A new perspective on the present is offered in light of certain justice in the future. The parables of 12:16–21 and 16:19–31 warn that reversal may not be far off. Death itself is the first great leveler, and it may strike suddenly.

The kingdom's presence can leave none complacent. Prostitute and Pharisee alike need forgiveness (7:36–50). Yet if that presence is realized, repentance and reconciliation are possible. The rich man's brothers may obey the law, reach out to the poor at their gates, and stay with them on the right side of the great gulf (16:27–31).

Luke and Paul

The relationship between the theologies of Luke and Paul has been much debated. Undoubtedly the two have distinct perspectives. But we may note a fundamental connection.

Luke's emphasis on Jesus' welcome for those whom Israel's moral policemen pushed to the margins is, in Rom. 15:7, linked with Paul's exhortation, on the basis of the grace given to Jew and Gentile alike: "Welcome one another . . . as Christ has welcomed you" (NRSV). The "New Perspective on Paul," by highlighting the social context and implications of Paul's doctrine of justification by faith, has shown that Paul is much closer to the thrust of the Gospels, and especially Luke, than has often been thought.

Luke and Theology

Narrative, History, and Theology

As an early "narrative theologian," Luke raised to new sophistication a genre with which Mark (and maybe Matthew) had already experimented. He does his "theology" through the story he tells of Jesus, carefully linked with that of Israel and the church (Green, *Theology*, 21). The fact that this narrative approach preceded the theological systematizing of later generations should not be lost on us.

Luke's skillful storytelling is not mere spinning of yarns to edify or entertain. His story centers on historical events. It is based on tradition from eyewitnesses and his own careful investigation (1:2–3). More than any other biblical book, Luke reminds us that theology not anchored in history is sub-Christian and docetic.

Supremely among the Evangelists, Luke shows us that *Jesus' own* "theologizing" was done largely in story. Unlike the Gospel itself, his parables do not depend for their force on any claim to represent actual events. But though they are often surprising and shocking, they depict realistic scenes from the world of Jesus' hearers, inviting them to reconfigure that world in mind and behavior (Wright 182–226). In fictional microcosm they have a similar purpose to Luke's historiographical macrocosm: to enable people to recognize God's activity in the world, and then fall in step with it.

The Plan of God

Luke's concern for the continuity of the story of Jesus and the church with that of Israel warns us to avoid preaching an individualistic gospel of "Jesus and me." Luke summons us to point to the great tradition into which disciples enter. By the grace of God, anyone may become part of his universal purpose, revealed and accomplished through Christ.

While this forbids the marginalization of the OT and/or the Jewish people in Christian theology, it equally forbids interpretations of the OT that regard its prophecies as fulfilled in present-day developments in Israel or elsewhere. With John the Baptist, "the Law and the Prophets" came to an end (cf. 16:16). What was glimpsed in the ministry of Jesus was to be made plain after the resurrection: God's gospel was for "all nations" (24:47).

The immediate prospect for Jerusalem was terrible punishment (21:20–24). The Gentile aggressors would have their "times . . . fulfilled" (21:24)—God would punish them also, as he had promised to punish Israel's aggressors in OT times—but the center of gravity of his plan was shifting. Jerusalem would be the starting point of the disciples' mission (24:47, 52–53). Nevertheless, from now on God's plan would be centered not on a land, a city, a temple, and a nation, but on a message going everywhere, in the name of Christ, through a new multinational people empowered from on high—and all this as "it is written" (24:45–49 NRSV).

Luke does not allow us to underplay the uniqueness of Christ, his pivotal role in God's plan, or the fact that he and all he set in train are the true fulfillment of the OT.

The Scope of the Gospel: The Whole Person and the Whole of Society

Luke does not merely state the universal thrust of the gospel in general terms. He grounds it in vivid portrayals of humans. He demonstrates in narrative that the gospel is for all kinds of people, in the longings, needs, and opportunities of their physical everyday lives, not merely for their "souls" or "spirits." This is especially symbolized by Jesus' coming to people in their homes (7:36; 10:38; 14:1; 19:5–6; 24:29).

So good news comes to an aged couple still bearing the stigma of childlessness (1:5–25), to a fisherman after a fruitless night's fishing (5:4–6), to a bereaved mother (7:11–17), to a harassed cook (10:38–42), to a dying terrorist (23:40–43). But in addressing people where they are, the gospel lifts them far beyond the situation that preoccupies them. Above all, this is seen on the Emmaus road, where far from being merely comforted in their loss, Cleopas and his friend are fired with a new sense of the meaning of the Scriptures and of the one they thought they had lost (24:32).

Moreover, the gospel is for humans *in relationship with each other*. The vision communicated by Jesus in parable, miracle, and table fellowship is not merely of new persons, but of a new society.

Luke's good news remains oriented to the future and offers no easy promises about the certainty of societal transformation in the present (16:19–31). Testing times are to come; ultimate "redemption" is not yet (21:5–36). But the gospel refuses to let the signs of the kingdom be indefinitely postponed. "*Today* this Scripture is fulfilled in your hearing" (4:21). "*Today* salvation has come to this house" (19:9). For Christian theology that seeks to articulate sensitively a gospel of future hope and present opportunity, Luke must surely be the primary resource.

Bibliography

Barton, S. "Parables on God's Love and Forgiveness." Pages 199–216 in *The Challenge of Jesus's Parables*, ed. R. Longenecker. Eerdmans, 2000.

Conzelmann, H. *The Theology of St Luke*. Faber & Faber, 1960.

Craddock, F. *Luke*. Interpretation. John Knox, 1990.

Donahue, J. *The Gospel in Parable*. Fortress, 1988.

Drury, J. *Tradition and Design in Luke's Gospel*. Darton, Longman & Todd, 1976.

Evans, C., and J. Sanders. *Luke and Scripture*. Fortress, 1993.

Green, J. *The Gospel of Luke*. Eerdmans, 1997.

———. *The Theology of the Gospel of Luke*. NTT. Cambridge University Press, 1995.

Johnson, L. T. *The Literary Function of Possessions in Luke-Acts*. SBLDS 39. Scholars Press, 1977.

Marshall, I. H. *Luke: Historian and Theologian*. Paternoster, 1970.

Squires, J. *The Plan of God in Luke-Acts*. SNTSMS 76. Cambridge University Press, 1993.

Tannehill, R. *The Narrative Unity of Luke-Acts*. 2 vols. Fortress, 1986.

Thielman, F. *The Law and the New Testament*. Herder & Herder, 1999.

Tuckett, C. *Luke*. NTG. Sheffield Academic Press, 1996.

Wright, S. *The Voice of Jesus*. Paternoster, 2000.

4

John

S. A. CUMMINS

Traditionally, the church has viewed Holy Scripture as divinely inspired and authoritative, read it communally within the context of ecclesial faith and practice, and sought coherence and common ground amid exegetical diversity and disagreement (cf. Hall 7–42). It is in relation to this rich heritage that we must view the interpretation and influence of the Gospel of John, its message and motifs, its role within the canon, and within the church its ongoing reception as the word of God.

History of Interpretation: John's Role in Church and Scholarship

In the Early Church

Today it is often argued that the earliest interpretations of the Gospel of John are now embedded within the final form of the text, having occurred during the several stages of its composition within a rather isolated and evolving late-first-century "Johannine community." During this process notable contributions would have included those of a "beloved disciple" (13:23; etc.), an "evangelist," and editors and/or "elders" ("we," 21:24), who together sought to shape and safeguard John from secessionist factions and their unorthodox interpretations (cf. 1 John 2:18–19; 4:1). Moreover, it is claimed that the outcome of all such orthodox efforts remained in doubt until well into the second century. Then, early and enthusiastic gnostic use of John, and concomitant wariness and neglect by mainstream Christians, was only finally reversed through the strenuous efforts of Irenaeus (ca. 130–200; esp. *Against Heresies*, ca. 185). In this view, Irenaeus rescued and restored John to the great church (cf. Sanders; Culpepper 107–38).

However, it is likely that such estimations would have puzzled second-century readers themselves, who normally associated the Gospel's origin with the apostle John and the church in Ephesus and Asia Minor. Certainly there was gnostic, more particularly Valentinian, interest in John. This is shown by allusions in writings such as the *Apocryphon of John*, *Gospel of Truth*, *Gospel of Thomas*, and others; citation by Basilides; a commentary on the prologue by Ptolemy; the first complete commentary by Heracleon; and interpretations by Theodotus (all ca. 130–80). Yet, inasmuch as John was clearly inimical to gnostic positions on creation, Christology, and salvation, such interest did not signify ringing endorsement but rather regularly entailed polemic and rejection (see Hill 205–93). Similarly self-serving were Montanist appeals to John in support of their unorthodox views on the Holy Spirit.

Moreover, there is considerable underestimated evidence that together indicates the widespread ecclesial ownership of John during the first half of the second century. This is shown in the writings and teachings of Ignatius, Polycarp, the longer ending of Mark, (John) the Elder, Aristides, Papias, the Shepherd of Hermas, and the *Epistula Apostolorum*. In the later decades John's broad influence and repute is attested by early extant papyri, Justin, Tatian, Apollinarius, Melito, Theophilus, Athenagoras, the *Epistle of Vienne and Lyons*, Hegesippus, Polycrates, the *Muratorian Fragment*, Appollonius, and Tertullian. In sum, familiar and habitual use of John reveals the authoritative, indeed scriptural, role it played within the early church at large, with any dissenting voices (purportedly Gaius of Rome) clearly the exception that proved the rule (on all this, see Braun; Hengel; and now esp. Hill).

In subsequent centuries the church continued to plumb John's theological depths for both pastoral and apologetical purposes. Clement of Alexandria (d. ca. 215), linking John to the Synoptic Gospels and recalling its inspired apostolic and communal context of origin, memorably encapsulated its unique nature: "John, last of all, conscious that the outward facts had been set forth in the Gospels, was urged on by his disciples, and, divinely moved by the Spirit, composed a spiritual Gospel" (in Eusebius, *Hist. eccl.*

6.14.7). Similarly Origen (ca. 185–254), who emphasized John's originality and extolled it as the choicest of the four Gospels, wrote a *Commentary on John,* which attended to both literal and allegorical aspects in seeking to discern its intellectual and spiritual sense. He critiqued Gnostics such as Heracleon for private and arbitrary interpretations, which lacked the church's testimony. For Origen, inasmuch as John disclosed the very Word dwelling with the Father, it exhausted all human interpretation (Schnackenburg 202–3).

John played a significant role in the christological and trinitarian debates of the third and fourth centuries, as attested in the writings of Athanasius, Eusebius of Caesarea, Gregory of Nyssa, and others (Pollard). So, for example, Athanasius countered Arius's subordination of Jesus to God by regarding John 1:1 and 1:14 as complementary rather than contradictory, insisting on both Christ's humanity (incarnation) and divinity, held together in mysterious union. Chrysostom (ca. 347–407) also refuted the Arians in his *Homilies on the Gospel of John,* a quite influential series of pastoral and polemical expositions that stressed the revelatory, theological, and spiritual dimensions of John in service of the practical needs of the church. Commentaries by Theodore of Mopsuestia (d. 428) and Cyril of Alexandria (376–444) also drew much upon John in support of both the divinity of Christ and the distinction between his divine and human natures as upheld by the Nicene Creed (Schnackenburg 204; Wiles 129–47).

Such emphases are also evident in Augustine's important *Tractates on the Gospel of John,* 124 sermons that pastorally appropriate the great mystery of the divinity and incarnation of Christ. Augustine attributes the source of John's profound theology to its author's privileged proximity to Christ (John 13:23), reclining and receiving all his secrets, and issuing in a Gospel that refines the mind so that it may contemplate God. Compared to his Synoptic counterparts, "the Evangelist John, like an eagle, takes a loftier flight, and soars above the dark mist of earth to gaze with steadier eyes upon the light of truth" (*Tractate* 15.1).

From the Middle Ages to the Reformation

Patristic exegesis of John dominated its interpretation during the Middle Ages, with Chrysostom's *Homilies* and Augustine's *Tractates* especially influential in the East and West respectively. While much medieval commentary took the form of sample collections and epitomes of the patristic materials, we know of a number of notable works devoted to John (Kealy 1). The Venerable Bede (ca. 673–735) wrote a homily on the prologue; Alcuin (ca. 740–804) produced a widely circulated and much revised commentary; John Scotus Eriugena (ca. 810–77) also left a homily on the prologue ("The Voice of an Eagle") and an unfinished commentary. Later the Byzantine exegete Theophylactus (ca. 1050–1125) wrote a commentary. So too did the Benedictine Rupert of Deutz (ca. 1075–1129); his 800-page work was designed to reconsider and supplement Augustine's efforts, refute all ancient christological heresies, and meditate upon the divinity of Christ. Bonaventure (1217–74) also wrote in response to heresy, with his very popular *Postilla* (a brief commentary and questions) *on the Gospel of John* reflecting upon this "sublime" Gospel in terms of the divine Word in itself (1:1–6) and as joined to human nature (1:7–21:25).

The commentary by Thomas Aquinas (ca. 1225–74) on John is a supreme example of scholastic medieval exegesis. It cites extensively from Origen, Chrysostom, and Augustine; aims to refute all error from the Arians to the Pelagians; and attends carefully to the literal (intended) meaning of the text, while also explicating its threefold spiritual sense. Major themes drawn from John include the all-surpassing love of God; the incarnation, redemption, resurrection, and return of Christ; and the great truth, authority, and contemplative weight of this Gospel, written so that the faithful might be built up into the temple of God. A later commentary by the medieval mystic Meister Eckhart (ca. 1260–1328) employed the now-familiar image of the eagle to portray John the Evangelist as scrutinizing, pondering, and preaching from above, his Gospel of the Word become flesh countering the pretentiousness of a needy humanity (on above, Kealy 1:115–84).

The Gospel of John also played a prominent role in the Reformation period. From 1516 to 1555 alone, some thirty or more authors published works on John in more than 125 separate printings, many of them notable in various respects. Erasmus (1469?–1536), who produced a popular *Paraphrase on John*, caused an uproar with his 1519 Latin version of John 1:1 as "*In principio erat sermo* [in the beginning was the Speech/Discourse]," rather than employing the Vulgate's "*Verbum* [Word]." The also popular first Protestant commentary on John by Philipp Melanchthon (1497–1560) then developed this in the direction of Jesus as the "*oratio* [oration]" of God. An interesting blend of influences, Melanchthon followed Chrysostom and Augustine in his christological and trinitarian readings of certain passages. Yet he was also significantly shaped by Aquinas's scholastic commentary. As a man of his own day, he regarded John as something of a Renaissance historian and Jesus as a divine rhetorician. Other important works included those of Martin Bucer (1491–1551), François Titelmans

(Franciscus Titelmann, 1502–37), and Wolfgang Musculus (1497–1563; see Farmer).

Martin Luther (1483–1546) never wrote a commentary on John, but he did give it an honored place among NT texts, observing how its focus on the preaching of Jesus served to highlight his divinity and saving significance. Similarly, John Calvin (1509–64) viewed John as the key to understanding the other Gospels, preferring its rich Christology; typically, his commentary attended to the divine intent and transformative impact of the text (Kealy 1:203–74; cf. Larsson).

From the Enlightenment to the Present Day

The increasingly rational, historical, and often skeptical approach toward biblical studies in the centuries succeeding the Enlightenment, not least in relation to Jesus and the Gospels, was also directed toward John in ways that puzzled prejudicially over its historical value and distinctive theological nature. To the extent that a Gospel such as Mark could be seen as taking us closer to the original environment and eyewitnessed activities of a Jewish Jesus, the very different Gospel of John was deemed all the more remote and Hellenistic. Its Jesus was counted as a theologically laden construct of later "Catholic Christianity." Such an outlook was evident in the influential 1820 commentary of K. G. Bretschneider (1776–1848), and more broadly in the wider work of the Tübingen School under F. C. Baur (1792–1860) and D. F. Strauss (1808–74). It resulted in the proliferation of skeptical positions on the authorship, date, purpose, unity, and significance of John.

There were, however, more moderate voices. In his 1832 lectures F. Schleiermacher (1768–1834) regarded John as a trustworthy and realistic eyewitness to a Jesus of "depth and substance." A 1,500-page commentary by Friedrich Lücke (1791–1855) upheld it as an authentic, apostolic Gospel, which combined historical content and spiritual understanding. An 1881 commentary by B. F. Westcott (1825–1901) also defended its apostolic origins and provided a deeply theological analysis of its focus upon Christ's self-revelation to the world (1:19–12:50) and to his disciples (13:1–21:25). Even so, by the beginning of the twentieth century, scholars widely regarded John as a largely second-century Hellenistic presentation of the gospel, theological rather than historical, portraying an "idea" rather than an "actual" Jesus (cf. Kealy 1:357–471).

Over the last century scholarly interpretations of John have often focused on competing and nuanced claims regarding a certain set of interrelated issues: principally, its background, relation to the Synoptic Gospels, sources, composition, and community context. R. Bultmann's influential commentary (1941; ET, 1971; see Ashton) did develop the history-of-religions and Hellenistic approach by arguing for a background in Mandaean Gnosticism. However, most scholars now rightly recognize that the evidence instead points to John's decidedly Jewish setting and traditions. John is far too familiar with the geography, customs, and culture of first-century Palestine; its language and imagery find closer parallels in strands of Judaism such as represented by the Dead Sea Scrolls. Moreover, this same evidence may well indicate that John actually preserves its own early and genuine Jesus materials, and thus can also be seen as emerging reliably and independently of the Synoptic Gospels (e.g., Dodd). While this "new look" at John may reopen basic considerations—such as on dating, apostolic authorship, witness to the historical Jesus (Robinson)—it has largely been taken as clearing the ground for additional proposals. Rather than drawing upon the Synoptics, John may be using common traditions and/or "signs," "discourse," and other sources, all put together by one or more redactors (cf. Fortna). Indeed, as intimated at the outset of this review, rather than requiring the primary eyewitness of an apostolic author, it is usually argued that John unfolded over a multistage compositional and communal process, whether construed as a Johannine community, circle, or school (e.g., Martyn; Brown).

Without depreciating or dismissing any genuine gains arising from these ever-expanding and increasingly nuanced hypotheses, I observe that too often they deflect and defer the essentially theological concerns that earlier commentators regarded as intrinsic to the message of the Gospel of John. Happily, more recent interest in the narrative, symbolic, theological, and spiritual dimensions of John is beginning to redress the oversight and imbalance (e.g., Kelly and Moloney; Schneiders; Thompson; and others).

Message and Motifs: John and the Drama of the Divine Life

The Gospel of John narrates a two-act divine drama that reveals and enacts the redemption and re-creation of humanity and the world. The prologue unveils the divine life and the entrance into the world of the Word, Jesus the Messiah and Son of God. In the first act the divine will unfolds in the works and words of an obedient if much misunderstood Jesus. The second act displays God's glorification in the departure, death, and resurrection of

Jesus. The epilogue charges Jesus' followers with the ongoing embodiment of the divine life in the world (cf. Smalley 141–54).

Prologue: God, Word, and World (1:1–18)

The prologue raises the curtain on the divine drama. The opening transcendent and primordial scene discloses the preexistent Word in eternal communion with and as God (1:1–2). This is the divine life, which we later learn also includes the Spirit (1:32). Out of this triune communion has issued the created order, with the co-Creator Word bringing into being all things, including humanity, who thus have in him the divine life and light that sustains and illuminates (1:3–4). Yet, with all this, the Word is also identified as "he/this one" (1:2) (Kelly and Moloney 34–35). In a startling shift in scenes from the heavenly to the earthly realm, we find that in order to overcome a now darkened world (1:5), the co-Creator has entered into creation and history as a human person: the Word has become flesh (1:14). The first witness to this astounding event is John the Baptist, sent by God to testify to the divine light now present so that all might believe through him (1:6–7, 15). However, equally remarkably, the world does not recognize the Word as its Maker; "his own people" do not see that they are his own (1:8–11 NRSV) and that in rejecting him they are denying their true selves.

Yet some do indeed believe in his name—accepting the Word's divine origin, identity, and saving mission—and thus no longer live as those merely "of man" but as "children of God" (1:12–13 NRSV). The manner in which the Word has incarnated the fullness of divine glory and truth is further specified both in relation to God and to the world: he comes as the only Son of the Father and as Jesus Christ (1:18). The prologue thus attests to the primary purpose of the Gospel of John, that its recipients believe Jesus to be Israel's Messiah and the Son of God (20:31). In this way they may be the beneficiaries of "grace upon grace" (1:16 NRSV): the outworking of divine redemption traceable from the giving of the torah to the self-giving of God in Jesus Christ. Given the magnitude of all that is taking place, it is discernible only as disclosure, witness, and confession of faith ("we have seen," 1:14).

Act I: God the Father Revealed in the Works and Words of Jesus the Son (1:19–12:50)

The prologue's divine pattern and purpose materializes with the advent and unfolding of Jesus' public ministry within first-century Israel. The first act is focused upon his revelatory and regenerative works and words (signs and discourses). This involves a series of encounters with a range of representative figures and groups, who gradually divide into those who reject or follow him. In the course of these highly charged events, the main issues and themes come into view.

At the outset John the Baptist openly announces the identity and mission of Jesus: "Here is the Lamb of God who takes away the sin of the world!" (1:29 NRSV). The divine life strides onto the earthly stage and will rescue its entire cast by rewriting their script in a wholly unexpected and self-sacrificial way. After calling the first enthusiastic but as yet unenlightened members of his new company (1:35–51), Jesus challenges Israel's usual players and practices in a series of provocative and pregnant episodes. At Cana the Jewish ritual of purification is transformed into the new wine of divine glory (2:1–12). The Jerusalem temple incident foreshadows the replacement of a bankrupt and closed Jewish establishment by a Jesus-centered and Spirit-enriched inclusive community (2:13–22). A representative and too self-assured Nicodemus ("we know," 3:2) has yet to recognize the love of God and receive the eternal life that comes only "from above" in the form of Jesus and the Spirit (3:1–21). The Samaritan woman learns that salvation does indeed come from the Jews, but climactically in Messiah Jesus, who reaches out and includes all faithful worshippers within the divine design (4:1–42). This startling scenario is extended even further in Jesus' ensuing encounter with a believing Gentile official (4:46–54) (cf. Kelly and Moloney 61–114).

There follows a more extensive series of works and words from Jesus, all significantly set against the backdrop of various highly symbolic Jewish festivals. Jesus' healing on the Sabbath critiques "the Jews'" constraint of the holy day and its Lord, and instead enables him as Son to reveal the Father in new, authoritative, and life-giving ways (5:1–47). (In view of later unconscionable anti-Semitic readings of "the Jews," it must be stressed that in John this phrase is a cipher for *all* who are closed and opposed to the divine economy operative in Jesus.) With the Passover in view, the feeding of the five thousand, walking on the water, and accompanying "bread of heaven" discourse—these together display Jesus' divine origin ("I am," 6:35) and limitless provision for his people (6:1–71). The Festival of Tabernacles (or Booths) is the setting for Jesus' ensuing temple teaching and failed arrest; his discourses on the light of the world, coming death, discipleship, and Abraham; and the incident of the man born blind (7:1–9:41). In all these events it is Messiah Jesus (not the temple) who is associated with true and living water, light, and the glorious divine presence (again, "I am," 8:12, etc.), and God's saving action ("lifted up," 8:28). Jesus' divine work effects true freedom, sight, witness, and worship; this gives rise to children of God, who are characterized by their life, love, and truth.

On either side of a reference to the Festival of Dedication (or Hanukkah, 10:22), we find Jesus' discourse on the Good Shepherd and an account of his rejection by "the Jews" (10:1–42). The latter are aligned with former false leaders in Israel (e.g., Ezek. 34) and contrasted with the selfless outpouring of the Father's love in the Son's atoning self-sacrifice, which overcomes all human pretense and issues in abundant eternal life. Indeed, all this arises out of a divine life in which "the Father and I [Jesus] are one" (10:30 NRSV). This claim incurs charges of blasphemy from those purportedly concerned to safeguard the glory of God and yet failing to recognize that it is revealed only insofar as (says Jesus) "the Father is in me, and I am in the Father" (10:38).

Two complementary scenes—the raising of Lazarus (11:1–57) and Mary's anointing of Jesus (12:1–8)—anticipate his paradoxical death and resurrection, the subject of Act II. But first the current act closes with Jesus' dramatic entrance into Jerusalem, dialogue with both Gentiles and Jews, and his summary reflections upon his much misconstrued mission to date (12:12–50).

Act II: God the Father Glorified in the Death and Resurrection of Jesus the Son (13:1–20:31)

The second act finds Jesus focused upon preparing his disciples for his forthcoming departure and their own role thereafter (13:1–17:26). This is immediately followed by a climactic rendering of the events involved in his crucifixion and resurrection (18:1–20:31). Herein the revelation of the Father in the works and words of the incarnate Son is ultimately realized through their shared glorification in Jesus' shameful death, astonishing vindication, and return to the eternal divine life. Again, a rich tapestry of motifs is discernible throughout.

With both the Passover and "his hour" at hand, God's very own Lamb prefigures his self-sacrifice and prepares the disciples for their own share in his servanthood by humbly washing their feet. Attended by Judas's betrayal and the other disciples' lack of understanding, this act expresses Jesus' exemplary and enduring love (13:1–38). It is also a sign of the divine hospitality that will ultimately be given to his followers ("in my Father's house," 14:2). This will be made possible by Jesus' departure and the sending of the Spirit, who in the interim will abide, guide, teach, and comfort the people of God (14:1–31). With all this in view, Jesus, himself "the way and the truth and the life" (14:6), exhorts his disciples to expand their limited horizons ("Rise, let us be on our way," 14:31 NRSV). He thus summons them to follow him homeward into the Father's glorious realm—albeit via the cross and thence the resurrection (Kelly and Moloney 270–306).

Union with Jesus ("the true vine") and his sent Spirit enables his followers to have communion with God and hence a fruitful life of love and joy in one another; this will overcome the barren existence of a hateful and degenerate world (15:1–16:3). Jesus develops these themes as he accounts for his divinely designed yet disturbing death and anticipates its advantages for his disciples. The cross will expose and eradicate the world's sin and injustice, and the Spirit will bring forth the Father's abundant new covenant life in the form of love, joy, and peace (16:4–33). Then in a prayer Jesus binds together all his hopes and fears for himself, his disciples, and all believers, drawing them up into his own eternal communion with the Father. Once again, many interrelated motifs recur, gathered around God's limitless grace, love, holiness, truth, authority, knowledge, protection, unity, and eternal life. All this is found in Jesus' obedient mission, which climaxes in the coming "hour" with the mutual glorification of the Father and the Son (17:1–26) (Kelly and Moloney 307–51).

Paradoxically, in the betrayal, arrest, trial, and death of Jesus, humanity's self-destructive schemes are taken up into God's gracious grand design. At Gethsemane, a remarkably assured Jesus discloses his divine identity ("I am he," 18:6) to the startled authorities and surrenders himself to "the cup the Father has given [him]" (18:11). He is abandoned by his disciples and even denied by Peter ("I am not," 18:17). Behind closed doors Jesus reminds the high priest, Caiaphas, that he has always spoken openly and rightly—of God and of himself in relation with his Father—in the synagogues, the temple, the world (18:19–24). Then a puzzled Roman governor, Pilate ("I am not a Jew, am I?" 18:35 NRSV), also finds himself caught up in this climactic conflict with a strange but seemingly innocent Jewish "Messiah," who pointedly informs him: "My kingdom is not from this world" (18:28–38a NRSV).

The divine logic, which escapes and subverts all concerned, unfolds inexorably: "The Jews" falsely acclaim Caesar as their king; Pilate ironically returns the compliment, calling Jesus "King of the Jews" (19:19–22); and on the cross Jesus truly reveals his identity and destiny, thus also disclosing and glorifying God. Therefore, although the situation seems disastrous to the bereft disciples, the reverse is actually the case. The empty tomb attests to a risen Jesus, who reappears, is acknowledged as "Lord and God," and bequeaths the Spirit, in whose form he will continue to be present with his disciples (20:1–29). From thence he will ascend "to my Father and your Father, to my God and your God" (20:17), to the glory to be enjoyed by all those who believe and receive the divine life given in Jesus, the Messiah and Son of God (20:30–31).

Epilogue: Embodying the Divine Life (21:1–25)

In an epilogue, perhaps added later, Jesus again appears and exhorts his gathered disciples, including Peter and "the disciple whom Jesus loved," to remain faithful witnesses and to care for the people of God. This, we are now informed, the beloved disciple has done, not least with the provision of this spiritual Gospel, which invites and enables its audience to join Jesus, the apostles, and all the saints in the divine life.

The Canon: John and the Divine Company

The Gospel of John offers itself as a revelatory and inspired new-covenant document generated by the teaching and deeds of Jesus as recalled through the operation of his Spirit within the witnessing community of faith (cf. 14:25; 20:21–23, 30–31; 21:24–25). On this basis its author (known early on as the apostle John) and its initial audience preserved, transmitted, and proclaimed this divinely authoritative Scripture (cf. 2:22; 19:36–37; 20:31). Despite scholarly claims that this Gospel struggled for acceptance, there is every indication that it was widely received and revered by the early church, and that it played a distinctive, prominent, and indeed canonical role (see Hill). Among the most important elements in this are John's use of the OT and its early associations with both a Johannine corpus of literature and the Synoptic Gospels.

It is according to the OT that John views its own witness to the fulfillment of God's purposes for Israel and the world in Jesus and his Spirit-empowered disciples (5:39, 45–47). This is immediately evident from a range of OT citations, particularly from the Pentateuch, Isaiah, and Psalms, variously quoted by Jesus (1:51; 6:45; 10:34; 13:18; 15:25), his Jewish contemporaries (1:23; 2:17; 6:31; 12:13), and the author (12:15, 38, 40; 19:24, 36–37). Even more impressive is the extent to which John's account of Jesus' message and mission includes a typological and polemical reworking of various OT elements. These include symbols (torah, temple, Sabbath), figures (Moses, Isaiah's Servant, the Psalms' righteous sufferer, Ezekiel's Davidic shepherd), imagery (vine, water, light), and festivals (Passover, Tabernacles). Thus, what John says of the prophet is true of the entire OT: "Isaiah said this because he saw [Jesus'] glory and spoke about him" (12:41). From John's postresurrection perspective, what Isaiah foresaw and the OT prefigured and promised was the startling glory of a cruciform Christ, the very self-expression of God. Above all, this is what lies at the heart of the collective witness of the OT, Jesus, and the Gospel of John.

Yet, not the Gospel of John alone; this document invites comparison with its NT counterparts, not least the Letters and Revelation of John. The well-recognized collocation of so many striking verbal, conceptual, and thematic similarities between the Gospel and especially 1 John is unlikely to be incidental. We may cite, for example, Jesus as Messiah and Son of God; the Paraclete and "S/spirit of Truth"; believers as "children of God"; the love commandment; light and darkness imagery; a stress on truth, witnessing, eternal life; and the exhortation to know, remain in, and love God. All this the recipients of the Letters of John have heard and seen from the beginning, perhaps via the Gospel itself (cf. 1 John 1:1; 2:7, 24; 3:11; 2 John 5, 6). While Revelation is an apocalyptic prophecy in the form of a letter, rather than a Gospel, it too bears notable christological (e.g., Lamb, Logos) and eschatological affinities; it emphasizes similar significant themes (witnessing, commandment-keeping, overcoming, glorification); it also draws extensively and evocatively upon OT language and imagery (cf. Bauckham, *Revelation*; Keener 1:122–39; Köstenberger 203–5). Moreover, while scholarship has usually considered the origin and identity of the Gospel, Letters, and Revelation of John individually, there is strong evidence from the early second century of an ecclesial awareness that they belonged to an authoritative (even scriptural) corpus. Mention may be made of the common and often intertextual exegesis of two or more Johannine documents; their implicit and explicit attribution to the same author, the apostle John; and the possible existence of codices containing these Johannine works (Hill 451–64).

As noted earlier, the patently distinctive Gospel of John has caused many contemporary scholars to conclude that it emerged independently of and sits rather awkwardly alongside Matthew, Mark, and Luke. Yet, from its outset John presupposes much concerning Jesus, not least as the Word who was Messiah and Son of God, which would only have made sense in the light of the sort of information supplied in documents such as the Synoptic Gospels (Smith). Given the extensive networking between the early and expanding Christian communities, and the probability that each of the Gospels was intended for all Christians (so Bauckham, *Gospel*), it is all the more likely that they were correlated with one another. Indeed, second-century evidence (such as from Tatian and Clement) suggests that the church regarded John as written in the full knowledge of Matthew,

Mark, and Luke; that it soon circulated in their company; and that it was strategically located last because it could clarify, amplify, supplement, and provide a broader and deeper theological framework for its Synoptic counterparts. In sum, then as now, the reader is invited to read John as a Gospel among the Gospels; and, by extension, to regard it as an integral document within a two-Testament witness to the triune God.

John and Theology: God, Church, and World

From the foregoing it is evident that the Gospel of John is entirely "of God"—in its emanation from Jesus, the Word made flesh, as first witnessed to within its own apostolic and communal context of origin; in its expeditious and widespread reception within an increasingly inclusive and ever-expanding early church; in the mutually interpretative canonical company it has kept from its earliest days as Spirit-shaped Scripture; and in its continued profound effect, explication, and enactment throughout the church historic and universal.

As such, John cannot be constrained by mere human conjecture and self-serving sectarian readings, but must always be embodied ecclesially and thence manifest publicly as a rich and resonant witness to the triune God's self-giving and limitless love for the whole world (3:16; 21:24–25). In God the Father this gracious love precedes and exceeds, creates and generates, sustains and consummates all things. In God the Son this love is incarnate and cruciform as it unmasks and overcomes sin and death, and is vindicated and glorified as it opens up and enables a transformed way of life. In God the Spirit, the continuing presence of the Son, this love also establishes, indwells, abides, witnesses to, and guides all the people of God (cf. Kelly and Moloney 388–94).

It is this all-encompassing divine love and life that governs and authenticates the church and its mission in the world. The church is to be present, faithful, and giving. It is to help, heal, endure, question, confront, and transform. It is to reach out, invite, gather, welcome, and include. Certainly such a calling must not be distorted in the direction of religious pluralism and syncretism (or, conversely, recoil into a peevish parochialism); it is at all times the church of *this* God. Thus, the church must personify God's glory in all its grandeur, with a love and faithfulness that is both vital and vulnerable, disclosing the heavenly horizon and economy within which humanity can know its true identity and destiny. In this way a world that is otherwise enslaved by often unspeakable evil may be providentially rescued and relocated within a new heaven and earth, and so enjoy eternally the divine life.

Bibliography

Ashton, J. *Understanding the Fourth Gospel*. Clarendon, 1991.

Bauckham, R. *The Theology of the Book of Revelation*. Cambridge University Press, 1993.

———, ed. *The Gospel for All Christians*. Eerdmans, 1998.

Braun, F.-M. *Jean le théologian et son évangile dans l'église ancienne*. 3 vols. J. Gabalda, 1959.

Brown, R. *The Community of the Beloved Disciple*. Paulist, 1979.

———. *The Gospel according to John*. 2 vols. AB 29–29A. Doubleday, 1966–70.

Bultmann, R. *The Gospel of John*, trans. G. R. Beasley-Murray. Blackwell, 1971.

Culpepper, R. A. *John, the Son of Zebedee*. University of South Carolina Press, 1994.

Dodd, C. H. *Historical Tradition in the Fourth Gospel*. Cambridge University Press, 1963.

Farmer, C. S. *The Gospel of John in the Sixteenth Century*. Oxford University Press, 1997.

Fortna, R. *The Fourth Gospel and Its Predecessor*. Polebridge, 1988.

Hall, C. A. *Reading Scripture with the Church Fathers*. InterVarsity, 1998.

Hengel, M. *The Johannine Question*, trans. J. Bowden. Trinity, 1989.

Hill, C. E. *The Johannine Corpus in the Early Church*. Oxford University Press, 2004.

Kealy, S. P. *John's Gospel and the History of Biblical Interpretation*. 2 vols. E. Mellen, 2002.

Keener, C. *The Gospel of John*. 2 vols. Hendrickson, 2003 (esp. bibliography at 2:1251–1409).

Kelly, A. J., and F. J. Moloney. *Experiencing God in the Gospel of John*. Paulist, 2003.

Köstenberger, A. J. *John*. BECNT. Baker, 1999.

Larsson, T. *God in the Fourth Gospel*. Almqvist, 2001.

Martyn, J. L. *History and Theology in the Fourth Gospel*. 2nd ed. Abingdon, 1979.

Pollard, T. E. *Johannine Christology and the Early Church*. SNTSMS 13. Cambridge University Press, 1970.

Robinson, J. A. T. *The Priority of John*, ed. J. F. Coakley. SCM, 1985.

———. *Twelve New Testament Studies*. SCM, 1962.

Sanders, J. N. *The Fourth Gospel in the Early Church*. Cambridge University Press, 1943.

Schnackenburg, R. *The Gospel according to St. John*. Vol. 1, trans. K. Smyth. Crossroad, 1982.

Schneiders, S. *Written That You May Believe*. 2nd ed. Crossroad, 2003.

Smalley, S. S. *John, Evangelist and Interpreter*. 2nd ed. InterVarsity, 1998.

Smith, D. M. "Prolegomena to a Canonical Reading of the Fourth Gospel." Pages 169–82 in *"What Is John?"* ed. F. Segovia. Scholars Press, 1996.

———. *The Theology of the Gospel of John*. Cambridge University Press, 1995.

Thompson, M. M. *The God of the Gospel of John*. Eerdmans, 2001.

Wiles, M. *The Spiritual Gospel*. Cambridge University Press, 1960.

5

Acts

Steve Walton

History of Interpretation

Acts is arguably one of the most complex books of Scripture for the interpreter because of its multiple dimensions. It is a narrative that locates the growth of the early Christian movement in particular geographical and historical settings. As Luke's second volume (Acts 1:1), it is unique in the NT in continuing the story of Jesus into the story of the church. But in it Luke also presents a portrait of the church designed to persuade (the purpose enunciated in Luke 1:1–4 covers both volumes), so students of Acts need to ask what Luke seeks to persuade his readers about. Hence, for a book so full of references to God and the Spirit, that necessarily involves asking about the book's theology. Because of its multiple layers, Acts has been a laboratory for most types of critical study, although many are theologically disappointing.

The earliest full commentary on Acts is that of John Chrysostom, a series of sermons displaying a strong concern to relate Acts to Christian life and faith in his day—at times to the exclusion of the historical focus of twentieth-century scholarship. Similar concerns can be seen in the sixteenth-century commentaries of Luther and Calvin, who regard Acts as speaking to the issues of their day.

However, it took the nineteenth-century missionary movement for Acts to become seen as a resource for the church's *mission* in the contemporary world. Most notably, Roland Allen, a High Church Anglican, challenged the burgeoning missionary societies of the early twentieth century to adopt a strategy more like that portrayed of Paul in Acts, developing indigenous leadership for nascent churches and handing responsibility over to local leaders. It was only in the later twentieth century—with honorable exceptions—that Allen's plea began to be heard.

Mainstream academic study of Acts, meanwhile, was strongly focused on historical criticism. Three German scholars are pivotal: Dibelius, Conzelmann, and Haenchen. Their studies focus on Luke's theology, in the sense that they believe that Luke put his own stamp on his material, in both his selection and shaping of the stories. They combine studying Acts by using the tools of redaction criticism with a thoroughgoing historical skepticism, assuming that many parts of the story did not take place as Luke described them. In large measure, they do so because they believe that Luke was reinterpreting early Christian history to come to terms with the "delay of the parousia"—the collapse of the expectation that Jesus would return soon.

Conzelmann, in particular, develops a view of Luke-Acts that centers on a threefold division of time into the time before Jesus' coming, the time of his ministry (called "the middle of time," the German title of his seminal work *The Theology of St. Luke*), and the time of the church; he sees this threefold division in Luke 16:16. Conzelmann proposes that Luke replaced the imminent expectation of the earliest generation with a theological interpretation of continuing history, which Conzelmann calls "salvation history" (German: *Heilsgeschichte*), including moving the return of Jesus into the remote future.

The debate over the "delay of the parousia" dominated Lukan scholarship for most of the second half of the twentieth century, with the result that historical questions were foreground in debate and theological questions tended to be sidelined. Thus, O'Neill's *The Theology of Acts* is subtitled *In Its Historical Setting*; it begins with a chapter on the date of Acts, and then reads the book against O'Neill's reconstructed historical setting in the first third of the second century. A shining exception to this trend is Marshall, *Luke*, who argues cogently that salvation is a, if not the, central theme of Luke-Acts.

In the 1980s narrative criticism grew in prominence, applied to Luke-Acts first by Johnson and later by Tannehill. Their work reset the agenda of Acts scholarship and led to more theological readings of Acts. Notably, narrative criticism's emphasis on studying the "final form" of texts, rather than hypothetical sources, means that Acts is seen holistically. Of course, analyzing Luke's presentation in Acts does not compel a scholar to agree with Luke's view (e.g., Tannehill [3] disagrees with what he understands to be Luke's view, that Christians should call Jewish people to become followers of Jesus). But it does produce a "level playing field," where scholars can discuss together what Luke's theology is. Thus, in more recent times there are stimulating and helpful studies of the theology of Acts (not all from a narrative-critical perspective).

The Message of Acts

There are numerous proposals for the theological center of Acts; in particular, "salvation" is widely seen as Luke's major theme across his two volumes (Marshall, *Historian*; Green 19–22). Here is a typical statement: "Salvation is the principal theme of Acts, its narrative centrally concerned with the realization of God's purposes to bring salvation in its fullness to all people" (Green 19). Although salvation is very important, and the book of Acts is the story of salvation spreading "to the ends of the earth" (1:8), a careful reading shows that God is the one who drives the story along and takes the initiatives that lead to the expansion of the believing community. And so we consider the message of Acts from this perspective.

In Acts, God is *purposeful*. Luke presents the church's growth as fulfilling Scripture, with a particular stress on Isaiah and the Psalms (e.g., "fulfillment" language is prominent in the key speech in 13:27, 29, 33–35, 41, citing Psalms, Isaiah, and Habakkuk; see Pao). God is now bringing about these purposes (Peterson; Squires), manages events to his own ends, and directs his servants to be in the right place at the right time to bring others to know God (e.g., 8:26, 29, 39).

Acts portrays God as *a missionary God*, seeking first Jewish people to come to know him through Jesus the Messiah, and then drawing in Gentiles too, carrying out the program of 1:8. In the earlier sections Acts focuses on evangelism among Jews (e.g., 2:5–11; 3:11–26), and throughout the book the mission goes to Jewish people first, whether in synagogue (e.g., 17:1–3; 18:4) or a (Jewish) place of prayer (16:13–16). At the end, Paul is seeking to persuade Jewish people in Rome to become followers of Jesus (28:17–23). This shows that Acts should not be read as the story of God abandoning the Jewish people, but rather as God redefining the nature of his people (Jervell, esp. 18–25, 34–43).

As the book progresses, God pushes the believing community out among the Gentiles. At crucial points, God intervenes to direct the believers. Thus, it is God's initiative that creates and progresses Philip's encounter with the Ethiopian eunuch (8:26, 29)—a man whose castration would not permit him to take a full part in Jewish worship (Deut. 23:1). God engineers Peter's meeting with the Roman centurion Cornelius, sending an angel to Cornelius's house, using a vision to overcome Peter's reluctance to go to the home of a Gentile, and speaking by the Spirit to Peter (10:1–8, 9–16, 17–21). Then God pours the Spirit on the Gentiles, thus overcoming any outstanding hesitancy from both Peter and the Jerusalem believers (10:44–48; 11:15–18). When Barnabas and Saul leave the pioneering Jew-Gentile community in Antioch, it is God who calls them to do this by the Spirit (13:1–3, presumably speaking through a prophet in the gathering). When Paul and his colleagues cannot find the right way to go, God is actively preventing them from going in wrong directions (16:6–8), and God then communicates the right direction by a vision (16:9–10). Again and again Acts highlights that the redefinition of God's people is happening at God's initiative.

God acts and calls people through a number of agents: angels (10:3–6), the Spirit (8:29), people (Peter, Stephen, Philip, and Paul are particularly prominent), and his word, which can be almost personified (over fifty times Acts uses "the word," frequently qualified by "of the Lord/God," esp. in 6:7; 8:14; 11:1; 12:24; 13:49; 19:10, 20).

In all of this activity God is a *saving God* (Green 19–22; Marshall, *Historian*), a wide-ranging category that includes physical healing (3:1–10 with 4:9; 14:9), reconciliation with God (2:21, 40, 47), forgiveness (5:31), and deliverance from a storm (27:20, 31). Throughout, God is the one who accomplishes these things, through Jesus (2:22; 10:38; 15:11; 16:31), who is the Savior (5:31; 13:23). Humans receive salvation by responding to the message in believing trust in Jesus (2:44; 3:16; 14:9; 16:31–32, 34) expressed in repentance and water baptism (2:38; 16:33; 22:16), resulting in becoming part of the believing community (2:39–42). Acts stresses the believers' unity (e.g., the use of *homothymadon*, "with one accord," in 1:14; 2:46; 4:24; 5:12; 15:25).

The believing community is presented warts and all, to the extent that believers can be a barrier, or at least resistant, to the new moves God is making. Thus, the Jerusalem believers criticize Peter for visiting Cornelius (11:2) and are persuaded otherwise only because they see that God is acting (11:18). The argument does not go away, for more Judean believers argue that circumcision and torah-observance are necessary for salvation

(15:1, 5). When this question is debated, there is repeated emphasis on what *God* is doing, to make clear that this is no human project (15:7–11, 12, 14–19).

So where does *Jesus* fit into this development? While he is not entirely absent from the narrative (e.g., 9:34), in Acts we generally hear *about* Jesus rather than encounter him acting personally. Jesus is the center of the apostolic preaching, especially his resurrection (2:24, 32; 3:15; 4:10; 5:30; 10:40–41; 13:30, 34, 37; 17:3, 31), which is stressed rather more than his death. Because of his resurrection and exaltation, Jesus is able to pour out the Spirit (2:32–33). Indeed, his resurrection shows that Jesus is truly Israel's Messiah and Lord (2:36), the fulfiller of Israel's hopes and God's promises (13:32–33), and it is on the basis of his resurrection that people are summoned to repentance and faith (2:38; 17:30–31).

The question of responsibility for the death of Jesus in Acts is strongly debated, particularly because of Sanders's claim that Luke holds the Jews responsible as a race. Though there are passages in which the apostles hold "you" responsible for Jesus' crucifixion, albeit in ignorance (e.g., 2:23, 36; 3:13–15, 17; 4:10), these passages are always found in and around Jerusalem locations. By contrast, when the evangelists speak to Jews from outside Jerusalem, it is "they" (the Jerusalemite Jews and their leaders) who are responsible for the death of Jesus (10:39; 13:27–29). Luke's view becomes clear in 4:27, where a combination of Herod, the Gentiles, and the Jewish people of the city are responsible for the death of Jesus. Thus Luke hints not only that God's salvation reaches to the whole world, but also that the whole world needs God to save them (on this issue, see Weatherly, esp. ch. 2).

In Acts, God is encountered personally most frequently by *the Holy Spirit*—when people turn to God, they receive the Spirit (2:38, a programmatic verse whose emphasis recurs in 9:17; 10:43–44; 11:15–17; 15:8; 19:1–7). Considerable debate exists over the nature of the Spirit's ministry in Acts, especially whether the Spirit exclusively brings empowerment for mission. Menzies argues that a soteriological ministry of the Spirit is a Pauline emphasis not found in Luke-Acts. Others assert that the Spirit also brings people into the experience of salvation and transforms them ethically (Dunn; Turner, *Power*—both agreeing with Menzies that the empowerment for witness theme is the major emphasis of Luke's pneumatology, but denying that it is exclusively so). That the Spirit's work likely includes more than witness is shown by, for example, the lack of any emphasis on witness among the Samaritan converts after they receive the Spirit (8:14–24)—indeed, Peter and John are the ones who preach in the other Samaritan villages (8:25).

A second important issue is whether the Spirit comes "once and for all" to believers at conversion or whether there is a subsequent "gateway" experience (frequently called "baptism in the Holy Spirit" by today's writers, although this is not a phrase found in the NT; on the wider issue, see the helpful compact discussion in Turner, *Baptism*). Pentecostal scholars appeal to accounts such as the delay in the Samaritan believers receiving the Spirit (8:14–17; Menzies 204–13), or the Ephesian "disciples" who had not heard of the Spirit (19:2; Menzies 218–25). However, others note the uniqueness of the Samaritan situation, where the gospel was reaching new territory (Turner, *Power*, 360–75), and the fact that Paul baptizes the Ephesian dozen in water in the name of Jesus (19:5), suggesting that previously they were not Christians, but disciples of John the Baptizer (19:3–4; Turner, *Power*, 388–97).

Acts in the Biblical Canon

Acts is properly to be read as the continuation of Luke's Gospel, and many seeds planted in the Gospel come to fruition in Acts. Thus, the hints of Gentile inclusion found in the infancy narratives (e.g., Luke 2:32) become a major theme in Acts. The new exodus motifs found in Luke, notably the use of Isa. 40–55 (e.g., Luke 3:4–6; see Pao, esp. ch. 2; Turner, *Power*, 244–50), are fully developed in the renewal and restoration of Israel in Acts (Pao, ch. 4), which now becomes a worldwide, ethnically inclusive community (note the echo of Isa. 49:6 in the key verses Acts 1:8; 13:47). The Lukan emphasis on the Spirit as the power of Jesus' ministry (Luke 1:35; 3:16, 21–22; 4:1 [twice], 14, 18; 10:21; 11:13) leads to Jesus promising the Spirit's power for the apostles' ministry (Luke 12:12; 24:49; Acts 1:5), and to the Spirit's coming to equip the believers for mission and ministry (Acts 2:1–4, 16–21, 38; etc.). To read Acts apart from Luke is to impoverish and badly skew one's reading of Acts (see Walton; Wenham and Walton, chs. 11, 13).

Reading Luke and Acts together, on the other hand, can explain some puzzles. Such an approach is suggestive for Luke's apparently diminished emphasis on the death of Jesus in Acts, for Luke has told this story clearly in his Gospel and, while writing Acts, can count it as read and known. The clear statement of Acts 20:28, seeing the blood of Jesus as "obtaining" his people, is the tip of a large iceberg of understanding of Jesus' crucifixion found in the Gospel, notably in Luke 23 (Wenham and Walton 235).

As Wall (26–32) highlights, the canonical location of Acts, sandwiched between the fourfold Gospel and the Epistles, also suggests a double relationship with the four Gospels on the one hand, and the Epistles, especially the Pauline Epistles, on the other. This location highlights the uniqueness of Acts within the canon, as telling the story of the earliest believers as a continuation of the story of Jesus, and as a preparation for reading the Epistles. Without Acts, the canon would provide a diminished understanding of both the divine power behind mission and the divine passion for mission, which together drove the growth of the earliest communities. Without Acts, we would lack models of how mission works out in different situations, for we would be left trying to reconstruct events from the even more fragmentary accounts in the Epistles. Without Acts, we would find it much harder to envisage a framework for the writing and events of the Pauline Epistles (although it must be said that it is hardly easy *with* Acts!). Equally, Acts provides insight into the varieties within earliest Christianity, such as in the Jerusalem meeting (15:6–29), which shows up tensions between believers who emphasize their Jewishness and those wanting to be open to Gentiles—tensions that can also be seen in the Pauline corpus (e.g., Galatians, Romans, Ephesians) and elsewhere (e.g., the Jewishness of James or Hebrews), but whose landscape would be harder to reconstruct without Acts.

Theological Significance of Acts

A major issue in interpreting Acts is the extent to which it is prescriptive, saying how the church is always meant to be, or descriptive, telling us how the church was at this particular period (Marshall, *Acts,* 101–5). One helpful tool in deciding case by case about this issue is to consider how far Luke presents clear patterns of events. For example, 2:38–42 presents a fivefold pattern of what it means to become a Christian, involving repentance from sin, water baptism, receiving forgiveness and the gift of the Spirit, and joining the renewed people of God. This pattern keeps reappearing in Acts, not always in the same sequence as in 2:38–42, but with the same elements present (e.g., 8:12–17; 10:44–48; 19:1–20). Using this "patterning" tool, we may identify three themes that address the theology and practice of today's churches.

First, Acts compels us to ask, and keep asking, what *God* is doing in our churches and our lives. At times the voice of God prevents believers from going the wrong way (e.g., 16:6–8), and at other times the divine call seems surprising (e.g., 8:26, taking Philip away from a growing new congregation in Samaria and to the desert). As we have seen, at times the church's instincts are misguided (e.g., 11:2; 15:1, 5).

The radical theocentricity of Acts highlights the constant temptation to anthropocentricity today, whether seen in advertising that panders to human self-centeredness or "tribalism" that will not act outside the parameters of our community. In practice, churches—and theologians—find it all too easy to believe that they need not pay attention to asking what God is doing, and therefore fall into the dangers of making God in their own image and limiting what they consider he can do to the parameters of their experience. Acts calls us to real and continuing openness to God and his agenda, and highlights the prayerfulness of the believing community, for that is how their dependence on God is expressed and experienced (e.g., 1:14, 24; 2:42; 3:1; 6:4; 9:40; 10:9; 12:5; 13:1–3; 14:23; 16:25; 20:36; 21:5; 28:8).

Second, Acts encourages an expectation that God will act and speak in order to bring people to himself. The emphasis on the expansion of the believing community "to the ends of the earth" (1:8) shows this theme on a large scale, and numerous individual incidents show God reaching out to people. Among Jews, most notably God touches the life of Saul, the persecutor of the church, and turns him round to become a passionate advocate of the faith that he attacked (9:1–22). Among Gentiles, God reaches beyond the bounds of the believing community by using angels (10:1–6) or guiding the missionaries into unexpected places (16:6–10)—and in the case of the journey to Philippi, they find themselves in prison when they follow this clear divine leading (16:19–24), a sign that to follow the divine voice and participate in the divine mission is far from an easy path. In this expansion God uses a variety of agents—most prominently the Spirit, as we noted above, but also angelic and human agents.

Western churches and theological thinkers today can easily have a low expectation that God actively seeks to draw people to himself, whereas such expectation can be stronger and fuller in parts of our world where the church is growing. Acts offers a challenge and encouragement that God truly is active in his world and has not abandoned it to its own devices in deistic fashion. Acts thus invites the construction of a *theo*-logy that sees God as its subject and not merely its passive object. Recent developments in pneumatological thought suggest that this emphasis is in the process of being recognized.

Third, the evangelistic speeches in Acts focus on the resurrection of Jesus, suggesting a corrective to today's evangelistic message and preaching. The speeches highlight the fact and implications of the resurrection of Jesus. A case that he has been raised from the dead is rarely offered. Most often, the evangelists are interested in communicating that it is God who has raised Jesus—the verbs used, *egeirō* and *anistēmi*, are found with God as their subject (e.g., 2:24; 17:31)—and that God's action in raising Jesus confirms Jesus' identity as Israel's Messiah and the world's Lord and judge (e.g., 2:36; 17:31). It is because of who Jesus is now known to be, postresurrection, that people are summoned to repent and turn to God (e.g., 2:38; 17:30).

This emphasis contrasts with the near-exclusive emphasis found in much of today's evangelistic preaching and christological thinking on the death of Jesus. While the cross is by no means unimportant to the evangelists of Acts, it is not the sole focus of their preaching and reflection in a way that 1 Cor. 1:23–24; 2:2 might suggest, if read in isolation from the rest of that letter and the NT. Resurrection from the dead is by no means easy to proclaim to skeptical, scientifically trained, Western ears, but today's Westerners, like their contemporaries in the east and south, are increasingly open to "spiritual" dimensions to reality, and Acts encourages today's evangelists to give greater attention to the resurrection of Jesus in their proclamation. It also invites christological reflection that sees the exaltation of Jesus, in his resurrection and ascension, as a key factor in understanding who he truly is, both then and now.

Bibliography

Allen, R. *Missionary Methods*. Robert Scott, 1912.

Conzelmann, H. *The Theology of St. Luke*. Faber & Faber, 1960.

Dibelius, M. *Studies in the Acts of the Apostles*. SCM, 1956.

Dunn, J. D. G. *Baptism in the Holy Spirit*. SCM/Westminster, 1970.

Green, J. "Acts of the Apostles." Pages 7–24 in *Dictionary of the Later New Testament and Its Developments*, ed. R. P. Martin and P. Davids. InterVarsity, 1997.

Haenchen, E. *The Acts of the Apostles*, trans. R. M. Wilson. Blackwell, 1971.

Jervell, J. *The Theology of the Acts of the Apostles*. Cambridge University Press, 1996.

Johnson, L. T. *The Literary Function of Possessions in Luke-Acts*. SBLDS 39. Scholars Press, 1977.

Marshall, I. H. *The Acts of the Apostles*. NTG. JSOT, 1992.

———. *Luke*. Paternoster, 1970.

Menzies, R. *Empowered for Witness*. JPTSup 6. Sheffield Academic Press, 1994.

O'Neill, J. C. *The Theology of Acts in Its Historical Setting*. SPCK, 1961.

Pao, D. *Acts and the Isaianic New Exodus*. Baker, 2002.

Peterson, D. "The Motif of Fulfilment and the Purpose of Luke-Acts." Pages 83–104 in *The Book of Acts in Its Ancient Literary Setting,* ed. B. Winter and A. Clarke. A1CS 1. Paternoster/Eerdmans, 1993.

Sanders, J. T. *The Jews in Luke-Acts.* SCM, 1987.

Squires, J. T. "The Plan of God in the Acts of the Apostles." Pages 19–39 in *Witness to the Gospel,* ed. I. H. Marshall and D. Peterson. Eerdmans, 1998.

Tannehill, R. *The Narrative Unity of Luke-Acts.* Vol. 2 of *Foundations and Facets.* Fortress, 1990.

Turner, M. *Baptism in the Holy Spirit.* Grove, 2000.

———. *Power from on High.* JPTSup 9. Sheffield Academic Press, 1996.

Wall, R. "The Acts of the Apostles." *NIB* 10:1–368.

Walton, S. "Where Does the Beginning of Acts End?" Pages 448–67 in *The Unity of Luke-Acts,* ed. J. Verheyden. BETL 142. Peeters, 1999.

Weatherly, J. *Jewish Responsibility for the Death of Jesus in Luke-Acts.* JSNTSup 106. Sheffield Academic Press, 1994.

Wenham, D., and S. Walton. *A Guide to the Gospels and Acts.* Vol. 1 of *Exploring the New Testament.* SPCK/InterVarsity, 2001.

6

Romans

CHRISTOPHER BRYAN

Genre

The book of Romans is a Greco-Roman letter. It contains elements characteristic of a family letter, notably, Paul's expressed desire to visit his addressees (1:1, 7, 8–10, 13) and his lengthy concluding salutations (16:3–16, 21–24); and it briefly takes the form of a letter of commendation when he speaks of Phoebe (16:1–2). But by far its greater part (1:16–15:13) consists of what the ancients would have called *logos protreptikos*—"a persuasive discourse." In philosophical tradition, such discourse was associated with the choice of a particular school, or with the choice of philosophy itself. Philosophers used protreptic to strengthen believers and convert outsiders. Ever since Aristotle's *Protrepticus* there had been a tradition of putting such discourses into letter form—as, for example, Lucian's *Nigrinus*. Philon of Larissa (ca. 160–80 BCE) identified two main elements in protreptic: dissuasion or refutation (*apelegmos*), and demonstration (*endeiktikos*). To those we should probably add a third: normally, such discourses involved personal appeal and exhortation (*parainesis*).

Occasion, Place, and Date of Writing

Paul wrote Romans on the eve of his final visit to Jerusalem, where he intended to deliver in person a collection that he had taken up from Gentile churches (15:25; cf. 1 Cor. 16:1). Though he evidently viewed the outcome of the projected visit with some uncertainty (15:30–31), the gift would, he hoped, show to the Jerusalem church the solidarity in Christ that existed between her "poor" and the Gentile believers of Achaia, Galatia, and Macedonia (15:26–27). That visit aside, and having preached Christ "from Jerusalem all the way round to Illyricum" (15:19), Paul evidently considered that his apostolate in the area of the eastern Mediterranean was complete. He now contemplated a mission to Spain, and he planned to go there by way of Rome, partly so that he might use the Roman church as a base (15:22–24, 28). (Note that in 15:24 Paul hopes "to be sent on [his] way [*propemphthēnai*]" by the Romans; Paul uses the word *propempein* elsewhere to speak of being sent on by a community with its support, as in 1 Cor. 16:6; 2 Cor. 1:16.)

Paul refers to Gaius as his host (16:23), so it is likely that Romans was composed in Corinth or Cenchreae (see 1 Cor. 1:14), perhaps during the winter of 56–57. This date would also fit with the positive view of Roman *imperium* in 13:1–4: at this period Nero was still under the influence of Burrus and Seneca, and he was generally regarded with high hopes.

Outline

In tracing the outline of Romans, it is easy to discern the three main elements of protreptic identified above.

Following the epistolary opening (1:1–15), the first part of the document (1:16–4:25) is a dissuasive, or refutation (*apelegmos*). These chapters seek, on the basis of Scripture, to dissuade Paul's hearers from a view of God's relationship with the world or with Israel that would see it as ever at any time or in any situation founded on anything except God's justice and grace. This is the point, not only of the long discussion of Abraham that concludes the section (3:27–4:25), but also of the entire denunciation of human sin (Jewish and Gentile) that runs from 1:18 to 3:20. This denunciation culminates at 3:21–26 with the affirmation of God's saving justice/righteousness "manifested apart from the law, although testified to by the Law and the Prophets" (3:21 AT). In other words, Paul claims that what he refers to as "my gospel" (2:16)—the proclamation of a God who, through the long-promised coming of the Messiah, has chosen to be gracious to all, Jew and Gentile alike—manifests the saving justice/righteousness of God promised through the prophets. Paul's gospel says nothing about that justice that was not implicit in the law given to Israel from the beginning.

This dissuasive involves Paul in making two other points. (1) The proclamation of God's universal graciousness does *not* strip Israel of her "special relationship" with God. The unshakable basis of that relationship is clear in Israel's possession of the Law (3:1–4). (This is important, for if God's graciousness *did* strip Israel of her privilege, then the universally gracious God would not be trustworthy, since God *promised* a special relationship to Israel.) (2) The God who is gracious to all is *not* on that account a God who is morally indifferent, so that in proclaiming such a God, Paul is *not* saying, in effect, "Let us do evil, that good may come" (3:5–8 NRSV).

The second part of the letter (5:1–11:36) is a positive demonstration (*endeiktikos*) of God's justice and grace at work in the life of faith—a life lived at "peace with God through our Lord Jesus Christ" (5:1). This demonstration involves defense, which means further reflection on the falsity of the two charges that Paul has already summarily denied. First, he considers the question of moral indifference (6:1–8:39). One who is "in Christ" no longer lives under the dominion of sin (6:14), has been "put to death to the law" (7:4 AT), and is freed from "condemnation" (8:1). Far from leading, however, to a life of moral indifference (6:1, 15), this leads to being "led by the Spirit of God" (8:14). Thereby we "put to death the deeds of the flesh" (8:13 AT) on the basis of a new relationship, as "heirs of God and joint heirs with Christ" (8:17 NRSV). Even suffering may be endured cheerfully (8:18; cf. 5:1–5), for Christians know that nothing can finally separate them from "the love of God in Christ Jesus our Lord" (8:39 NRSV). Second, Paul considers the question of God's special relationship to Israel (9:1–11:36). Paul argues that the fulfillment of the law in Christ (10:4), far from meaning that God has abandoned the promised special covenant relationship with Israel, means on the contrary that God is being faithful to *all* the promises, *including* the promises to Israel. Despite the disobedience of all—Jew *and* Gentile—it is God's will finally to "have mercy upon all" (11:32 RSV).

The third part of the letter (12:1–15:13) is taken up with appeal and exhortation (*parainesis*)—an exhortation springing directly out of the demonstration that preceded it. Those who know that they live only "by the mercies of God" (12:1 NRSV) certainly cannot lead lives of moral indifference. Far from conforming themselves "to this age," those who live "by the mercies of God" will look to be "transformed" by the "renewal" of their minds (12:2–3 AT). Within the life of the Christian community, this is going to mean mutual acceptance among those who feel called to obey the law in one way, and those who feel called to obey it in another (14:1–12). The basis of their actions will be plain—the example offered by Christ himself: "Welcome one another, therefore, as Christ welcomed you, for the glory of God" (15:7 RSV; cf. 12:1; 15:2–3).

The remainder of the letter is taken up with Paul's commendation of Phoebe, a deacon of the church at Cenchreae, his patron, and presumably the bearer of the letter (16:1–2), with final greetings and salutations (16:3–16, 21–24), and a note that was perhaps written in Paul's own hand (16:17–20).

Style

Ever since Rudolf Bultmann produced his dissertation in 1910 (*Der Stil der paulinischen Predigt und die kynisch-stoische Diatribe*), it has been common to associate Romans with diatribe. This is helpful, if "diatribe" is understood in accordance with ancient usage—which, unfortunately, has not always been the case. In connection with the kind of literature we are considering, the word "diatribe" (*diatribē*: "a way of passing the time," "an occupation") is properly used with reference either to the activity of teaching in a school or to texts describing that activity. Examples are Epictetus's *Discourses*—records of his lectures, noted down "so far as possible in his own words" by his student Arrian. By extension, "diatribe" is also applied to texts using rhetoric and pedagogy, which characterized education. As such, written diatribe has identifiable characteristics of both subject matter and style.

Regarding subject matter, diatribe is generally concerned with serious philosophical or moral issues. Clearly, Romans would be at home in such company. Regarding style, diatribe is marked by a whole battery of characteristics. Frequently there is discussion with an imaginary partner, whose role is to raise objections, offer false conclusions, and pose difficult questions. The teacher turns from his real audience to respond to such objections with direct, second-person discourse (9:19–20). False conclusions and suggestions may be set aside with a scornful *mē genoito!* "Of course not!" (3:4, 31; 6:2; 11:1). Suggestions and conclusions regarded as correct may be supported by citations from sources considered authoritative. In Epictetus, this means allusions to Homer, Plato, and others of the "canon" of Greek *paideia*; in Paul, naturally, it means appeals to Scripture. Some composers of diatribe like to personify abstractions, and so, at times, does Paul: "For Sin, seizing an opportunity in the commandment, deceived me and through it put me to death" (7:11 AT). Some use sarcasm, and so, at times, does Paul: "Will what is made say to its maker, 'Why have you made me so?' Or does not the potter have a right over the clay?" (9:20–21 AT). There are lists of virtues and vices (1:29–30).

This then is the style in which the Letter to the Romans is written: a style designed, above all, for leading those who heard it to the truth—often by correcting their assumptions or pretensions. It is a style not to be associated, as was at one time supposed, with public preaching on street corners to the masses, but with the lecture hall, the classroom, and the school—in other words, with education and instruction. It was a style, therefore, eminently suited to protreptic, which, as a genre, had the same associations.

Destination, Purpose, and Strategy

As his opening salutation shows (1:1–15), Paul is writing to a church that he does not know personally. On the other hand, if his closing salutations are to be taken seriously, he was acquainted with a good many individuals in it (16:3–16). There is no reason to suppose that he would not, through them, have come to know something of the situation at Rome, regarding both the believers' attitudes to each other, and their reactions to Paul or what they had heard of Paul's gospel. In addressing the Romans, then, Paul seems particularly to have been aware of two groups. First were some—mostly but not necessarily all of Jewish descent—who had accepted Jesus as Messiah but believed that Paul's admission of uncircumcised Gentiles to full fellowship simply on the basis of faith in Jesus was an abandonment of God's law. They saw in Paul's gospel of "grace for all" both an implicit denial of Israel's calling and a proclamation of moral indifference. Second were those—mostly but not necessarily all of Gentile origin—who resented the claims of the former group and felt, or claimed to feel, superior to those who were so hung up on questions of law and obedience. In Romans, Paul sought to address both groups, not with "a compendium of Christian doctrine" (as Philipp Melanchthon suggested), but with an account of how the gospel (which was also "my gospel" [2:16]) accorded with God's promises to restore creation (8:18–25) and redeem Israel (chs. 9–11), and how that should affect the attitude of believers to each other (12:1–15:13).

A strategic reason for Paul's undertaking to address the Roman congregations in this way is not difficult to see. He hoped for support from them for his projected mission to the West (15:23–24): clearly, the better they understood and accepted his apostolate, the sounder that support would be. Yet finally, it was more than a matter of strategy. Paul was convinced that an approach to the gospel that founded it on *anything* other than the justice and grace of God available for all who would put their trust in the Son of God amounted in fact to rejection of the gospel. "You who want to be justified by the Law," he wrote on another occasion, "have cut yourselves off from Christ; you have fallen away from grace" (Gal. 5:4 NRSV; cf. 1:6–9). Equally, Paul was convinced that those who did accept the gospel were committed by it to emulating the grace by which they were saved: "Welcome one another, therefore, just as Christ has welcomed you, for the glory of God" (Rom. 15:7 NRSV). In other words, not simply strategy, but the thing itself was at stake.

Genre is a tool of meaning. Protreptic was a form of address associated with the choice of a particular philosophical school, or with the choice of philosophy itself. Just why, then, did Paul choose to present his defense of the gospel in this form? Partly, he may have acted in the light of Jewish precedent. The Wisdom of Solomon, which appears to have influenced him in other respects (e.g., 1:24–32; cf. Wis. 14:22–27), certainly seems to have protreptic features. More decisive, however, was perhaps something in the nature of the gospel itself as the ancient world, including Paul, would have perceived it. The ancients generally seem to have understood what we call "religion" in terms of experience and ritual, whereas ultimate truth claims and demands for appropriate living were associated with philosophy. So Seneca:

> Who can doubt, my dear Lucilius, that life is the gift of the immortal gods, but that living well is the gift of philosophy? Hence the idea that our debt to philosophy is greater than our debt to the gods, in proportion as a good life is more of a benefit than mere life, would be regarded as correct, were not philosophy itself a boon which the gods have bestowed upon us. They have given the knowledge thereof to none, but the faculty of acquiring it they have given to all. . . . [Philosophy's] sole function is to discover the truth about things divine and things human. From her side awe of the divine (*religio*) never departs, nor duty, nor justice, nor any of the whole company of virtues which cling together in close united fellowship. (*Ep.* 90.3, altered)

Hence, joining a philosophical school involved many of the ideas, and even the emotions, that we associate with religious conversion. And so for the ancients, Christianity (like Judaism) was a confusing phenomenon. Insofar as it involved ritual and cult, it might naturally be described in

Latin as *superstitio*—the usual disparaging term for a foreign cult in the first century, as used by Pliny in his rescript to Hadrian about Christians in Bithynia (*Ep.* 10.96.10). On the other hand, insofar as Christianity presented itself as teaching doctrines describing what is ultimately true and requiring appropriate activity, it appeared to be a philosophical school. This, no doubt, was precisely the point. Paul's purpose in Romans was to persuade his hearers to a favorable view of his beliefs about God and God's promise—"my gospel." By using the protreptic form, he immediately declared to his contemporaries that he regarded what he was presenting *not* simply as an invitation to religious experience, but rather, and much more importantly, as also a witness to ultimate truth. It is "the power of God for salvation" (1:16 NRSV), in response to which no "rational worship" is possible other than total obedience, the presentation of one's whole being "as a living sacrifice" (12:1 AT; cf. NRSV margin).

In this connection, it is interesting finally to consider how Paul's pagan contemporaries might have reacted to Romans. No doubt they would have found it very Jewish, full of "questions about words and names and your own law" (Acts 18:15). If they were like Galen a century or so later, they might have said that while its "philosophy" could lead people to behavior "not inferior to that of genuine philosophers" (*Summary of Plato's Republic: Fragment*), yet it was full of "talk of undemonstrated laws" (*On the Pulse* 2.4). Nevertheless, in broad terms, they would not have been in any doubt about what Paul was trying to do. He was, in his own way, a "philosopher," seeking to persuade hearers to his particular "school."

Romans throughout Christian History

In August 386 a professor of rhetoric sat in his friend Alypius's garden in Milan and heard a child singing in a neighboring house, "Take up and read, take up and read!" Taking the scroll that lay at Alypius's side, he found himself reading Rom. 13:13b–14, "not in orgies and drunkenness, not in promiscuity and licentiousness, not in rivalry and jealousy. But put on the Lord Jesus Christ, and make no provision for the desires of the flesh" (AT). Augustine's reaction was immediate. "No further would I read, nor did I need to: at once, at the end of this sentence, a clear light flooded my heart, and all the darkness of doubt vanished away" (*Conf.* 8.29).

In November 1515, Martin Luther began lecturing to his students at Wittenberg (Germany) on the Letter to the Romans. He went on with his expositions until the following September; and as he did so, his own understanding changed.

> I greatly desired to understand Paul's Letter to the Romans, and nothing barred the way, save one expression, "the righteousness of God"—for I understood it to signify that righteousness whereby God is righteous and acts righteously in punishing the unrighteous. . . . Night and day I thought about this, until . . . I took hold of the truth, that the righteousness of God is that righteousness whereby, through grace and sheer mercy, he justifies us by faith. At which I felt myself to be born again, and to have passed through open doors into Paradise. The whole of Scripture took on a new significance, and whereas before "the righteousness of God" had filled me with hate, now it became for me indescribably sweet in greater love. This passage of Paul became for me a gateway to heaven. (WA 54:179–87)

In his journal John Wesley tells us how, in the evening of May 24, 1738, he "went very unwillingly to a society in Aldersgate Street [London], where one was reading Luther's Preface to the Epistle to the Romans. About a quarter before nine, while he was describing the change which God works in the heart through faith in Christ, I felt my heart strangely warmed. I felt I did trust in Christ, Christ alone, for my salvation; and an assurance was given me that he had taken my sins away, even mine, and saved me from the law of sin and death."

At the end of World War I, and in the chaotic years immediately following, Karl Barth, pastor in Safenwil (Switzerland), looked for a theology that might enable him to function amid the turmoil around him. "I sat under an apple tree and began to apply myself to Romans with all the resources that were available to me at the time. I had already learned in my confirmation instruction that this book was of crucial importance. I began to read it through as I had never read it before. . . . I read and read and wrote and wrote" ("Nachwort," 294). The result was *Der Römerbrief*, Barth's commentary on Romans. The first edition, published in 1919, fell (in Karl Adams's well-known words) "like a bombshell on the playground of the theologians."

These four vignettes may serve to illustrate the effect that Paul's Letter to the Romans has had, and continues to have, on Christian history. Other major interpreters throughout that history have included Chrysostom, Origen, Theodore of Mopsuestia, John Damascene, Oecumenius, Theophylact, Ambrosiaster, Hugh of St. Victor, Abelard, and Thomas Aquinas. To this day Romans continues to challenge the finest minds in Christendom.

Certainly, there are differences over details of interpretation. But in general, all who listen to Romans agree as to what it is overall: a proclamation of Christian freedom. Not surprisingly, then, it has again and again been a factor in the renewal of the church.

Theological Significance

Gratia sola: The Gift of Salvation

According to Paul, there is "no distinction; for all have sinned and come short of the glory of God, being justified [*dikaioumenoi*] by his grace as a gift, through the redemption [*apolytrōseōs*] that is in Christ Jesus: whom God set forth to be a propitiation [mercy seat; *hilastērion*], by his own blood, through faith (*dia pisteōs*)" (3:22b–25a AT). It is possible, though not certain, that Paul was here adapting a formula already familiar to the Roman church. In any case, the three metaphors that now fly past us like changing images on a cinema screen enable him to make his point with a force that has echoed through the centuries.

The first metaphor, "justified," is about law and judgment. "Justify" (Greek: *dikaioō*) means "to treat as just," or more simply, "to acquit." For Paul, "justification" (*dikaiōsis*) is God's declaration that we are not condemned, even though we are sinners; and through that declaration we are holy (set apart for God), for by it we are set in a positive relationship with the One who is holy. Hence, the believer is, in Luther's matchless phrase, *simul iustus et peccator*, "simultaneously justified and a sinner." This, as Karl Rahner finely said, is "God's justice, that in fact divinises us, [being] an unmerited gift of God's incalculable favor" (6)—and this is the justification that is brought about "through the redemption . . . in Christ Jesus" (3:24 NRSV).

"Redemption (*apolytrōsis*)" is a metaphor from the slave market, but has roots in Scripture. The cognate verbs *apolytroō* and *lytroō* (both meaning "obtain release on payment of a ransom") are used in the Septuagint (LXX) to speak of God's redemption of Israel from Egypt (e.g., Exod. 6:6; Deut. 7:8) and from Babylon (Isa. 51:11). "Redemption" therefore speaks of those who have been handed over, or fallen, into the power of something they cannot control—the dominant metaphor of Rom. 1:18–32, which has repeatedly spoken of humankind "handed over" into the power of sin.

Finally, "propitiation" (RSV: "expiation"; NRSV: "sacrifice of atonement") involves a metaphor from the cult. Greek *hilastērion* is a neuter noun formed from the (somewhat rare) adjective *hilastērios,* meaning "propitiatory" or "offered in propitiation." In the LXX this noun occurs regularly—and in the context of very important passages—in reference to the mercy seat in the temple (e.g., LXX: Exod. 31:7; 35:12). Since this seems to have become an accepted usage in Greek-speaking Judaism of the early Christian era (cf. Heb. 9:5; Philo, *Cher.* 25), there seems little reason to question that Paul, too, uses it in this way. If there was one thing in Judaism that was evidently forbidden to uncircumcised Gentiles, it was to come anywhere near the holy of holies, the place of the mercy seat, where once a year the high priest entered to make atonement by the sprinkling of blood (Lev. 16:14–16). There was therefore a peculiar poignancy in Paul's seeing Christ himself as a true mercy seat, "set forth" by God the Father for Jews and Gentiles to approach together—and that, not by the blood of animal victims, but "by his blood," the blood of the Messiah.

On what basis is Christ so "set forth"? It is "through faith" (*dia pisteōs*). Whose faith? God's faith? Christ's faith? Ours? Here is a question that continues to occupy the scholars. But the answer, as Barth saw, is surely "Yes," to all (42). Rooted in the faithfulness of God, the faithfulness of Jesus Christ invites our faithfulness in return: indeed, there is nothing else we can offer, no other basis on which we can stand with regard to God. Paul, as a good rhetorician, brings us full circle. In "his gospel," as he said from the beginning, "God's justice is revealed from faith for faith; as it is written, 'the just shall live by faith'" (1:17 AT).

We have, then, a hope of salvation, but it is solely on the basis of God's justice and mercy. Therefore, all human boasting is absurd—indeed, it is denial of the one God (3:27–30). Surely paganism—the deification of powers or forces within creation—undermines Hebrew monotheism from one side; but a claim to status before God that is based on something other than God's justice and God's mercy undermines it from the other side. It makes no difference whether the claim is (as among some whom Paul addressed at Rome) based on knowledge of God's law, or (as among some he addressed at Corinth) on knowledge of another kind, or on wisdom, or on gifts—*any* such claim undermines Hebrew monotheism. Any such claim asserts, by implication, that God is in some sense and in some measure *not* God of a part of the created order, or that there is something inherently wrong with a part of that order. In short, such a claim asserts a dualism (Rom. 3:27–31; 10:12; cf. 1 Cor. 8:4–6). Therefore, paganism and dualism alike must be confronted by the unyielding confession that none stand before God, save on the basis of God's justice and mercy (3:30).

On this basis Paul declares (among other things) that "all Israel will be saved" (11:26)—not thereby claiming that every single Jew will go to heaven, but certainly affirming his conviction that Israel as a whole, ethnic Israel, will find there is a place for her in the final salvation. Indeed, Paul went further, for he claimed finally, and on the same basis, that "God has consigned all . . . to disobedience, that he may have mercy upon all" (cf. 11:32). As to *how* that was to happen, Paul did not say. Like Dame Julian of Norwich centuries later, his confidence was simply in God's promise in Jesus Christ: "This is the great deed intended by our Lord God from the beginning, cherished and concealed in his blessed breast, known only to himself, through which deed he will make all things well" (*Revelations of Divine Love* 32).

Una ecclesia sancta: Unity in Christ

If none of us has any standing before God save on the basis of God's justice and mercy, what does that say about our relationships with each other, within the fellowship of faith? Paul's discourse to the Romans did not take only the form of a protreptic, but also that of a "family letter." Why? Because he regarded those whom he addressed not merely as individuals, but also as a household, God's household, and therefore unavoidably bound to each other, even if they disagreed with or disliked each other. For Paul, proclaiming and hearing the gospel led directly to forming communities "in Christ"—communities of the new age, which had begun with the Messiah's victory (Gal. 3:13–14). In short, the gospel led to the church (Rom. 12:1–5). Therefore, the important question for Paul about behavior was always not, "Does this square well with your conscience?" but, "Does this serve to build up your brothers and sisters in the community?" *Especially* is this the case if you happen to consider your brothers and sisters to be weaker than you are (14:1–15:13). And in any case, "Who are you to pass judgment on someone else's servant? Before his own master he stands or falls. And he will be upheld, for the Lord is able to make him stand" (14:4 RSV adapted).

The ancients, and presumably Paul among them, were as well aware as we are of the violence of the world (see 2 Cor. 11:24–25). Rome itself was a frightening and violent city. Yet Paul thought it possible for believers to create among themselves what François Bovon has called "zones of peace" (371)—caring for one another "with mutual affection" (12:10 NRSV). In Rom. 12:1–15:13 (and notably at 14:1–15:13) the apostle insists on continuing fellowship in the church among groups who evidently differed widely among themselves in a range of significant matters of faith and practice. This continues to challenge not only the behavior of Christians toward each other *within* congregations, communities, and denominations. It also challenges the feeble ecumenism that marks all major Christian denominations in their relationships toward each other at the beginning of the twenty-first century.

Vita venturi saeculi: Christian Hope

Protreptic is more than exhortation to a way of living. Protreptic bases its exhortation on a perception of how the world is and how it will be. "For you did not receive the spirit of slavery to fall back into fear, but you have received the Spirit of adoption, through whom we cry 'Abba! Father!' The same Spirit bears witness in support of our spirit that we are children of God, and if children, then also heirs, heirs of God and coheirs with Christ, given that we suffer with him, in order that we may be glorified with him" (8:15–17 AT). "For the creation waits with eager longing for the revealing of the children of God; for creation was made subject to futility, not of its own accord, but because of the one who subjected it, in hope—because the creation itself will be set free from the bondage of corruption and obtain the liberty of the glory of the children of God" (8:19–21 AT). Paul's hope, we should recognize, is not merely for the individual, or the church, or even humanity, but for "the creation." Only with the redemption and restoration of the whole creation will God's promises be fulfilled (Isa. 11:6–9).

To be "in Christ" is therefore by definition to "live in this hope" (Rom. 5:1–5; 8:24–25). Such hope (eschatology) is not simply an interesting idea, to be contemplated when we have leisure from more-pressing business (as one might indeed suppose from much of our contemporary preaching, even in the season of Advent). We do not have two lives, one transient and one (later on) that will be eternal. We have a single life, designed from eternity to be life in Christ Jesus. Because of that, it is worthwhile now to engage in the creative subversion that is Christian witness. Because of that, it is already "high time for you to awake from sleep. For now is our salvation nearer than when we first believed" (13:11 AT).

Bibliography

Barth, K. *The Epistle to the Romans,* trans. E. Hoskyns. Oxford University Press, 1933.

Bovon, F. "The Child and the Beast." *HTR* 92 (1999): 369–92.

Bryan, C. *A Preface to Romans.* Oxford University Press, 2000.

Byrne, B. *Romans.* SP 6. Liturgical Press, 1996.

Cranfield, C. E. B. *A Critical and Exegetical Commentary on the Epistle to the Romans.* 2 vols. ICC. T&T Clark, 1975–79.

Dunn, J. D. G. *Romans.* 2 vols. WBC 38A–B. Word, 1988.

Fitzmyer, J. *Romans.* AB 33. Doubleday, 1993.

Julian of Norwich. *Revelations of Divine Love.*

Käsemann, E. *Commentary on Romans,* trans. G. Bromiley. Eerdmans, 1980.

Moo, D. *The Epistle to the Romans.* NICNT. Eerdmans, 1996.

Rahner, K. *Theological Investigations.* 23 vols. Darton, Longman & Todd, 1961–92.

Seneca. *Ad Lucilium epistulae morales.* Vol. 2, *Letters 46–92,* trans. R. Gummere. LCL 76. Heinemann, 1920.

Wesley, J. *Journal from February 1, 1738–August 12, 1738.* Online: http://www.god rules.net/library/wesley/274wesley_a6.htm.

Wright, N. T. "The Letter to the Romans." *NIB* 10:393–770.

7

1 Corinthians

DAVID E. GARLAND

In the effective history of 1 Corinthians, the letter has been primarily mined for its contribution to debates about virginity (7:1–40), the mode of Christ's presence in the Lord's Supper (11:23–26), and the nature of the resurrection (15:1–58). Because Paul seems intent only on settling the practical problems that have arisen in the church, many in recent times think the letter lacks developed doctrine and contains only applied theology. Paul is assumed to be counteracting the Corinthians' spurious beliefs that have caused confusion about the importance of individual leaders, the nature of human sexuality, the nature of spiritual gifts, and the nature of resurrection—all of which have led to their behavioral excesses.

In the last century, these beliefs have been identified as antinomian Gnosticism. The letter became a favorite of later Gnostics in the tradition of Valentinus, who fastened onto Paul's statements about a spiritual body to buttress their view denying the resurrection of flesh and blood, but most are now skeptical of identifying the Corinthian opponents as Gnostics. Others attribute the problems to a Hellenistic Jewish religiosity, akin to Philo's, that focused on *sophia* and *gnōsis*. More recently, some claim that the problems are rooted in an "overrealized eschatology." The Corinthians presumably took literally Paul's statement "Behold, now is the day of salvation" (2 Cor. 6:2 KJV) and developed an overheated, spiritualistic illusion that they were already living in the kingdom come, as if the day of the Lord had come (1 Cor. 4:8; 2 Thess. 2:2). A theology of glory also caused them to downplay the cross.

Other recent studies find the problems in Corinth stemming more from the influence of their cultural setting than from specious theological beliefs. Paul's purpose is not to correct their theology but to get them to think theologically so that they would respond properly to their polytheistic, pluralistic culture. The cross and resurrection form the theological cornerstone of Paul's response. Karl Barth argues: "The discourse of the whole epistle proceeds from a single point and harks back to this point," the resurrection of the dead (113).

Shortly before his assassination, Julius Caesar reestablished Corinth as a Roman colony in 44 BCE. The Romans established colonies to foster the majesty of their culture, religion, and values. When Paul came to Corinth a century later to proclaim Christ's greater majesty, he found a city teeming with commerce as the vital link between Rome and its eastern provinces. This letter should be read against the background of a mercantile society imbued with Roman cultural values that fed a ruthless preoccupation with attaining public status, promoting one's own honor, and securing power. The scramble for scarce honor was as intense as the scramble for scarce wealth. Values of the dominant culture so antithetical to the message of the cross percolated into the church, destroying its fellowship and its Christian witness as some members vainly sought to balance secular mores with Christian norms. These secular values played havoc with Paul's attempt to build a community based on love, selflessness, and the equal worth of every member. Paul corrects their misconduct with carefully wrought ethical exhortations grounded in a correct theology.

Traditionally, the problems that Paul addresses in 1 Corinthians have been attributed to imagined theological disputes swirling around Peter, Apollos, Paul, and the elusive Christ party (1:12). These theological rivalries combined with the Corinthians' attraction to flashy displays of knowledge, wisdom, and spiritual gifts, and a gnostic worldview—all were assumed to be ripping apart the fellowship. A recent trend traces the problems in Corinth back to personality-centered politics and the members' social placement. The discordant factions within the community did not divide over fine points of theological interpretation but grew out of the rivalry of leading figures, who may have hosted different house churches.

The influence of secular ethics and the Corinthians' failure to grasp the full implications of the wisdom of the cross led to their competitive party spirit (1:10–4:21), their suing one another in pagan courts (6:1–11), their dangerous brushes with sexual immorality (5:1–13; 6:12–20), their dallying with idols (8:1–11:1), their humiliation of the have-nots at the Lord's Supper (11:17–34), and their vaunting of particular spiritual gifts (12:1–14:40). A Greek worldview caused them to believe in life after death without a resurrection of the dead (15:1–58). They failed to comprehend how an earthly body that is physical and perishable could be made suitable for a heavenly realm that is spiritual and imperishable.

Paul's letter has its genesis in his dismayed response to oral reports about what is going on in Corinth (1:11; 5:1; 11:18; cf. 16:17–18) and his answers to Corinthian queries in their letter to him (see 7:1). The problems emerge from the complexities of everyday life—a man living with his father's wife (5:1–13), lawsuits against fellow Christians (6:1–11), prostitution (6:12–20), celibacy and marriage (7:1–40), food sacrificed to idols (8:1–11:1), head dress in public worship (11:2–16), divisions at the Lord's Supper (11:17–34), the use of tongues in worship (12:1–14:40). Paul alternates between his reactions to oral reports and his answers to the Corinthian letter:

Oral reports (1:10–4:17 / 4:18–6:20)
Corinthian letter (7:1–40 / 8:1–11:1)
Oral reports (11:2–34)
Corinthian letter (12:1–14:40)
Oral reports (15:1–58)
Corinthian letter (16:1–12)

In each case, Paul draws out the theological implications of their behavior and the necessity of the norm of love and the wisdom of the cross for guiding all that they do, rather than issuing authoritarian directives. The theological core of this letter is his reiteration of the heart of his preaching—the feeble and stupid message of the crucified Christ, which nevertheless proves to have a power and wisdom no human eloquence possesses, since it is the power and wisdom of God himself.

Internal Dissension and the Wisdom of the Cross (1:10–4:21)

Paul first addresses the problem of the internal rivalries among the bigwigs in the church, who were scrambling for position in the community and dividing up Christ into lifeless fragments (1:10–4:17). The breakdown of community is caused by the infusion of "the spirit of the world" (2:12, synonymous with "the wisdom of the world" [1:20; 3:19] and "the wisdom of this age" [2:6]) into their attitudes, judgments, and behavior. Secular wisdom's baneful influence on church members, rather than some over-arching theological misconception, lies behind most of the problems that Paul addresses.

To bring an end to the Corinthians' political infighting and to uproot the worldly wisdom driving their behavior, Paul seeks to stimulate theological thoughtfulness that results in a cross-centered community adopting his own cruciform lifestyle (4:16). The death and resurrection of Jesus are the foundational events that determine Paul's vision of the Christian community, but Greco-Roman symbols and mythology competed with the cross to provide a framework for interpreting life. The Corinthians' quarreling reveals that they have uncritically absorbed the ideals and values of the pagan world around them. Paul seeks to replace a pagan paradigm, fascinated by displays of status and power, with God's paradigm, exhibited in the weakness of the cross. He does not sweep the crucifixion under the carpet as an unfortunate episode remedied by the glories of the resurrection but trusts the power of the cross to convict the audience of its truth. For those who claim honor on the basis of worldly wisdom, he offers the foolish wisdom of the cross that overturns human wisdom. For those who crave impressive displays of eloquence, he proclaims Christ's crucifixion in weakness, fear, and trembling, accompanied only by demonstrations of the Spirit's power.

The cross embodies the power of God to absorb all the blind rage of humanity and to avert its deadly consequences, but humanity, both Jew and Greek, fails to recognize that truth because it does not fit their categories and ways of thinking. Human wisdom is circumscribed by its partial knowledge, susceptible to self-deceit, and blinded by its own conceit and pride. Paul cites five passages from Scripture in 1:18–3:23 (1:19; 2:9, 16; 3:19, 20) to make the point that humans cannot grasp God's wisdom through their own effort. God has manifested his power and wisdom in sending his Son, allowing him to be crucified, proclaiming a seemingly weak and foolish message through apostles regarded by the world as weak and foolish, calling into being a church made up of those whom the world regards as nobodies, and uniting them to the crucified Christ, who becomes their righteousness, sanctification, and redemption. This wisdom can only be appropriated through the Spirit, whose most central work is not to be found in the visible things such as healings, glossolalia, and eloquent preaching but in leading believers to the crucified Christ (2:2) and calling believers into community. The Spirit, not an orator's eloquence, reveals the message's truth to the believer (2:4, 13).

For Paul, the message of the cross is the antidote to the human self-glorification poisoning the fellowship. Victory is won by giving up life, not taking it. Selfish domination of others is discredited. Shame is removed through divine identification with the shamed in Christ's shameful death. Paul further undermines the self-aggrandizement of the leading figures in the church by casting himself and Apollos as servants (3:4) and field hands (3:6–9), and he identifies apostles as figures of shame who are indistinguishable from the dregs of society (4:10–13). The image of building contractors (3:10–17) reminds them of their accountability in the final judgment. He expects submission to the cross to quash egoism and to lead all Christians to serve one another, and Christian leaders, in particular, to serve the community from below.

Ethics and Christ's Lordship of the Body (5:1–6:20)

The three issues that occupy Paul in 5:1–6:20 (incest, lawsuits, and visiting prostitutes) complement the previous discussion in chapters 1–4. In these opening chapters he insinuates that the church is riven by unnecessary strife, fed by unjustified spiritual pride. These cases expose their carnality (3:1) and serve to puncture the Corinthians' inflated arrogance. The immorality of church members has not only undermined any grounds for the church's boasting; it has wrecked the church's witness of God's transforming power to change lives. Christianity offers not only a completely new sexual ethos and a new ethos regarding material possessions; it also brings about a complete transformation of individuals through their washing, sanctification, and justification (6:11). God's grace does not simply whitewash sin. It is intended to transform sinners.

Paul's ethical exhortation is grounded in his view of the final judgment of all humanity and the resurrection of Christians. Each passage contains an eschatological affirmation: a hope that the incestuous man's spirit might be saved on the day of the Lord (5:5); an assertion that the saints will judge the world and the angels (6:2); and a reminder that the body will be raised (6:14). Paul seeks to shake them out of their blasé attitude toward sinful conduct and drive home the seriousness of their sin and their need for repentance. He argues that Christians should live in ways congruent with who they are—as those who belong to Christ and are destined to live with Christ (5:7–8; 6:11, 19–20). Christ's lordship lays claim on the Christian's body, which is destined for resurrection, so that those who belong to Christ are not free to do with their bodies whatever they please. Hiring a prostitute for sex essentially denies Christ's ultimate sovereignty by filching what belongs to Christ and handing it over to one who belongs to Satan.

Celibacy, Divorce, and Marriage and God's Calling (7:1–40)

In discussing questions about celibacy, divorce, and marriage in 7:1–40, Paul does not foist his own preference for celibacy on others but leaves room for believers to make their own decisions under Christ (see 7:6–7, 10, 12, 25, 28, 32, 35, 40). Some in Corinth must have regarded celibacy as a higher good, as evidenced by his opening quotation from their letter to Paul (7:1). While he believes celibacy is good, he knows that it is not good for everyone and certainly does not lift one to a higher spiritual plateau. His advice is grounded in his theological conviction that no condition presents an obstacle to living the Christian life, since a Christian is now defined by God's call (1:9) and nothing else. He develops this principle in 7:17–24, which seems from a casual reading to interrupt the discussion. These digressions (see also 9:1–10:22; 13:1–13) provide the theological underpinning guiding his counsel on the practical matters. Here Paul reminds them that the offer of salvation comes to believers without requiring them to alter their ethnic, social, or domestic status. What matters is keeping the commandments of God (7:19), in particular, avoiding fornication (7:2–5). Christians can keep the commandments of God whether circumcised or uncircumcised, slave or free, married or celibate. Any attempt to alter one's status in life for religious reasons gives more importance to that worldly status than it merits and controverts God's calling in Christ based on grace alone.

Again, Paul's advice is suffused with his eschatological perspective. The death and resurrection of Christ and the giving of the Spirit mean that the new age has invaded the present. Christians must evaluate their choices in life from the perspective of the end that has come so near (7:29–31). An end-time awareness should sharpen the focus of their decisions in the mundane matters of this world. Since the end is plainly in sight, Christians should see and judge more clearly what is and is not important and not allow the world's values and opinions (7:22–23) to cast them in the forge of its deadly furnace.

Idol Food and Christological Monotheism (8:1–11:1)

Paul's lengthy discussion of idol food (8:1–11:1) is grounded in his christological monotheism, which defines the people of God over against those
who worship many so-called gods and lords in their sundry guises. As a
cosmopolitan city, Corinth was a religious melting pot, with older and
newer religions flourishing side-by-side. Most persons could accommodate
all gods and goddesses into their religious behavior, and they could choose
from a great cafeteria line of religious practices. The Christian confession
of one God and one Lord, however, requires *exclusive* loyalty to God as
Father and to Christ as Lord (8:6). Paul rejects Christians participating
in any function that overtly smacks of idolatry because it poses a danger
to the Christian with a weak conscience, who might be sucked back into
idolatry's clutches (8:7–13). It also compromises the Christian witness to
one God, confirms the idolater in his idolatry, and will bring the Christian
under God's wrath (10:1–13). The Supper of the one Lord, which unites
participants to him, excludes eating idol offerings, which unite participants
to idols and their demons (10:14–22). Even a perfunctory or make-believe
show of fealty to an idol compromises the loyalty owed only to God and
Christ. Christianity breaks down the barriers that classify people by their
ethnic identity, social standing, or sexual gender; it also erects barriers that
create a distinctive Christian identity (cf. 10:32). Paul teaches that one's
presumed rights should be readily forfeited in the interest of saving others.
At stake is whether the church will keep religious syncretism at bay so that
it can remain holy to God, and whether the believer's allegiance to Christ
will override all other attractions and attachments.

Decorum in Public Worship and God's Creation (11:2–16)

Paul's advice on another mundane matter, wearing headdresses in public
worship, is grounded in his view of creation and how being "in the Lord"
alters how life is to be perceived (11:11). God's saving work through Christ
transcends society's gender hierarchy. Paul takes for granted that women
may pray and prophesy in the assembly as long as they have an appropriate
head covering. But Christians must avoid flouting what is culturally shameful (11:6; cf. 14:35). Wearing a head covering (11:13) is a sign of personal
rectitude for a woman, and its absence implies the opposite. Christians
should observe the proprieties of polite society in their public gatherings

to avoid bringing unnecessary dishonor to themselves and, concomitantly, to their Lord.

The Lord's Supper and Christ's Sacrifice (11:17–34)

In 11:17–34, Paul seeks to correct the Corinthian desecration of the Lord's Supper. The Lord's Supper should intensify group solidarity, but the Corinthians' supper has become a flash point highlighting their social inequality and alienation. No one ought to feel humiliated at the Lord's Supper, yet the Corinthians' manner of conducting the meal has left the have-nots feeling that they are beneath the notice of their fellow Christians (11:22). Paul appeals to the Last Supper tradition to correct their practice. The Corinthians act selfishly; Jesus acted unselfishly in giving his life for others. The Corinthians' actions will lead to their condemnation (11:29, 32); Jesus' action leads to the salvation of others. The combination of broken bread and cup conveys the nature of Jesus' ultimate sacrifice. Christ gave his body and sacrificed his blood in an expiatory death, which brings the offer of salvation to all persons, and each believer receives an equal share of the benefits of his sacrifice. That reality should be symbolized by what happens during the Lord's Supper. The Corinthians' observance of the Lord's Supper, in which one has more than enough and gets drunk, while another has too little and goes hungry, epitomizes the culture of selfishness and fails to proclaim the meaning of the Lord's death for all. Instead, they are to imitate Christ's example of self-giving, and everything they do in their meal should accord with his self-sacrifice for others. Consequently, Paul urges them to share what they have with each other (11:33).

Spiritual Gifts, Spiritual Persons, and Public Worship (12:1–14:40)

The lengthy discussion of spiritual gifts in 12:1–14:40 reveals that the Corinthians have limited the "spiritual gifts" to a handful of spectacular gifts and placed tongues above prophecy as a clear sign of supernatural power working in a spiritual person. In correcting their unwarranted spiritual pride and disorderly worship, Paul obliquely critiques their infatuation with speaking in tongues. He begins by asserting that all Christians are imbued with the Holy Spirit and are therefore spiritual by virtue of their confession "Jesus is Lord" (12:3), and he broadens the spectrum of grace gifts that manifest the Spirit (12:4–26). As throughout the letter, Paul develops the issue's theological implications, which they have overlooked. He makes clear that there are diversities of gifts, services, and activities, but only one Spirit who distributes them as he wills. Each gift is given to different persons for the common good. Consequently, each person is needed in the community. Inspired speech is only one among many ways the Spirit works in the body of Christ. No one should feel superior because he or she possesses a particular spiritual endowment. The Spirit decides who gets what gift and apportions them according to the need in the community, not according to the value of the recipient. All are gifted by God in some way and encouraged to contribute their gifts in ways that will build up the community. Spiritual gifts are not indicators of one's spiritual status.

The segmentation of the Corinthian congregation into cliques is the by-product of human depravity that spurs individuals to treat their differing spiritual experiences as a pretext for reinstating class divisions—now employing spiritual classifications—so as to elevate themselves over others. The seemingly unrelated digression in 13:1–13 praising love actually lays out the principle by which gifts should be exercised in the church. If any extol their own particular gift(s) as the highest and best, Paul demonstrates how devoid of value these gifts are without love. The question is not which gift is the most beneficial, stimulating, or spiritual. It is, instead, whether love is radiated in exercising their gifts. Though God and Christ are not mentioned, the cross of Christ as the manifestation of God's love for the world defines Paul's understanding. The principle of love embodied in the cross mandates that one should always seek honor for others, which stands in an absolute antithesis to the dominant value, which seeks honor only for oneself out of preening self-indulgence. Since almost every problem in the church is mentioned in 13:4–7, Paul implies that the source of their problems is their lack of love.

Paul holds up what contributes most to "building up" the church (14:3–5, 12, 17, 26) as the touchstone for ranking the relative value of gifts, particularly for public worship. The speech gifts that are intelligible to all, including outsiders, are the most fruitful and should be the most valued. Finally, he gives specific advice and commands on tongues and prophecy in worship (14:26–40), based on the theological conviction that the Spirit of ardor is also the Spirit of order.

The Resurrection of the Dead and God's Creative Power (15:1–58)

The climax of the letter is Paul's lengthy discussion of the resurrection in chapter 15. The Corinthians did not assume that the resurrection had already occurred (2 Tim. 2:18) but believed in an afterlife without the resurrection of the dead. Their error is not rooted in some deliberate doctrinal rebellion but in honest confusion, given their Greek worldview. They failed to comprehend how an earthly body that is physical and perishable can be made suitable for a heavenly realm that is spiritual and imperishable. Earthly bodies and heavenly existence are therefore deemed to be as different as chalk from cheese. The Corinthians assumed that at death the mortal body is shed like a snake's skin, and the immortal soul continues in a purely spiritual existence. Paul's argument for the bodily resurrection divides into two distinct sections. The first section, 15:1–34, makes the case for the reality of the resurrection. The second section, 15:35–58, explains how the resurrection is possible.

In the first unit recording the resurrection appearances of Christ (15:1–11), Paul is not trying to prove the resurrection of Jesus but arguing from it. Some of the Corinthians are saying that there is no resurrection of the dead (15:12), yet they accepted the unified apostolic proclamation that Christ has been raised. Their denial of the resurrection of the dead is theologically untenable (15:12–19). If there is no resurrection of the dead, Christ has not been raised. If Christ is not raised from the dead, then everything based on that belief collapses in a heap of broken dreams. Paul affirms that as Christ was resurrected from the dead, so also those who are in Christ and pattern their lives after him can hope to be resurrected by God. Jesus is the representative of others who also will be raised so that the end-time resurrection becomes the ineluctable sequel to Jesus' resurrection (15:20–28). This unit reveals why Paul so adamantly defends the resurrection of the dead. If there is none, then death will remain unconquered and still hold sway beyond the End as a power set over against God. This circumstance is theologically incongruous. Since God is all-powerful, death must in the end be vanquished.

Because the Corinthians could not comprehend how resurrection was possible, they assumed it was impossible. In 15:35–58, Paul does not explain how the resurrection happens but only makes the case that it can happen. He grants their assumption that a polarity exists between earth and heaven, and that earthly embodied existence is completely incompatible with heavenly spiritual existence. He makes clear that resurrection is not the resuscitation of the corpse. A body fit to inhabit this world must be changed before it is fit to inhabit the heavenly world. Nature illustrates that there are different kinds of bodies and that dramatic transformation can occur. As the bare seed that is sown is not the plant that miraculously sprouts from the ground, so the earthly body that is sown is not the spiritual body that is raised. As God chooses to give the seed a different body (15:37), so God will give humans, sown with a body animated by soul, a body animated by the Spirit in the resurrection (15:42–44a). As humans were dressed at birth in the clothing of the "man of dust," so Christians will put on the clothing of the "heavenly man" in the resurrection (15:47–49). What is mortal will be changed by the power of God so that those who are raised will be given a spiritual body that is consistent with its new celestial habitat. Divine agency must be accounted for in life and in death. Death is impotent before the power and mercy of God, who wills to forgive sins (15:3, 17) and to raise the dead.

Paul is concerned about the correlation of theology and morality throughout the letter. Bad theology can lead to bad behavior and vice versa. Belief in the resurrection impinges directly on how one is to live (6:12–14; 15:32–34, 58).

Bibliography

Asher, J. *Polarity and Change in 1 Corinthians 15*. HUT 42. Mohr, 2000.

Barclay, J. "Thessalonica and Corinth: Social Contrasts in Pauline Christianity." *JSNT* 47 (1992): 49–74.

Barth, K. *The Resurrection of the Dead*. Hodder & Stoughton, 1933.

Carson, D. A. *Showing the Spirit*. Baker, 1987.

Fee, G. *The First Epistle to the Corinthians*. NICNT. Eerdmans, 1987.

Furnish, V. P. *The Theology of the First Letter to the Corinthians*. NTT. Cambridge University Press, 1999.

Garland, D. *1 Corinthians*. BECNT. Baker, 2003.

Litfin, D. *St. Paul's Theology of Proclamation*. SNTSMS 83. Cambridge University Press, 1994.

Mitchell, M. *Paul and the Rhetoric of Reconciliation*. Westminster John Knox, 1992.

Rosner, B. *Paul, Scripture, and Ethics*. Biblical Studies Library. Baker, 1999.

Thiselton, A. *The First Epistle to the Corinthians*. NIGTC. Eerdmans, 2000.

Winter, B. *After Paul Left Corinth*. Eerdmans, 2001.

Wright, N. T. "Monotheism, Christology, and Ethics: 1 Corinthians 8." In *The Climax of the Covenant*. Fortress, 1992.

8

2 Corinthians

EDITH M. HUMPHREY

Second Corinthians is complex on several levels. Subtleties in language render it the student's nightmare and the exegete's playground. Because of debates regarding its integrity, it provides a convenient entrée into the ongoing conversation of Pauline scholars. Here, too, Paul deftly joins matters particular to the Corinthian church with larger theological questions. In all this we see the apostle at his most impassioned and his most astute, as he plays pastor, theologian, and even "fool." Throughout he uses a variety of literary and rhetorical strategies, grounding his concerns in the foundational principles of the faith.

History of Interpretation

Today's commentaries normally commence with the onset of the historical-critical method and the controversies sparked by the epistle in the last few centuries. Prior to this time, however, the letter served the church to a degree disproportionate to its size. It is, indeed, from 2 Cor. 3 that we derive the Christian categories of "old" and "new covenant." Augustine devoted an entire book of his *Literal Meaning of Genesis* (12.28, 34) to the intricacies of 2 Cor. 12:1–9. Chrysostom drew upon the letter in order to paint striking word-pictures of his favorite apostle (*Hom. 2 Cor.*). Gregory Palamas dwelt upon the epistle's theme of glory throughout his defense (*The Triads*) of the "hesychasts" who practiced "quietude" and so saw God's energies with natural eyes. Aquinas used 2 Corinthians to argue that, in their final beatific vision, the faithful will behold "the divine essence" (*ST* q. 12. art. 9. obj. 2) and in his discussion of reason and grace (*ST* q. 109. art. 1. obj. 3). Charles Wesley adapted 2 Cor. 3:18 to hymnody in his immortal lines "Changed from glory into glory / Till in heav'n we take our place."

By the late eighteenth century, the profound delight that the letter inspired in its readers was overtaken by more mundane concerns. J. S. Semler (1776) considered that 2 Corinthians must have been composed of at least two letters; A. Hausrath (1870) posited his "four chapters hypothesis" concerning chapters 10–13. The results of their source criticism were further complicated by Windisch (1924), who treated chapters 8 and 9 as two independent administrative letters. Current proponents of partition theories cite the apostle's name at 1:1 and 10:1, and a tonal change between chapters 9 and 10. They further point to ongoing correspondence between Paul and the Corinthians, seen in 1 Cor. 5:9; 2 Cor. 2:3–4, 9; and 7:8, 12. Some have believed that chapters 10–13 comprise the "tearful letter" of which Paul speaks. Most recently, the section 6:14–7:1 has been debated, with some dubbing it an Essene-like interpolation incompatible with Paul's theology, and others arguing for its authenticity (Webb). Such issues of integrity are interconnected with views of Paul's theology, career, and ministry. For convenient descriptions of the debates, see Gilchrist and Kreitzer (esp. 35–36).

Quite recently, some have prescinded from the source debate, turning to sociological, literary, and rhetorical concerns. An interest that links contemporary scholars with their forebears is the question of the identity of Paul's opponents—those "[*hyperlian*] super-apostles" who could, like Satan, "transform themselves" into agents of light (11:5, 14). Chrysostom, in the usual pragmatic manner of the Antiochene school, had identified these opponents as the much-debated "*skolops* [thorn]" in Paul's flesh (12:7; *Hom. 2 Cor.* 26.3–4). Through the years, critics have emerged with various pictures of this group—Judaizers (F. C. Baur [1833] and many others); proponents of Jesus as a miracle-working "divine man," or *Theios Anēr*; "enthusiasts" of various stripes, including early Gnostics (from Bultmann 1985 to F. Watson 1986). These questers have sought to make sense of the issues of apostolicity, gospel, and revelatory signs and wonders that run throughout the letter. (Again, for more players in this drama, see Kreitzer

71–82.) However, others wisely have urged caution in "mirror-reading" the epistle to locate opponents.

Then there is the study of Paul the visionary. Second Corinthians 12, despite its irony, inclines the reader to inquire in this vein. In antiquity, such concern led to the pseudepigraphical *Apocalypse of Paul*, and the use of 2 Corinthians in grounding the insights of spiritual theology. Today, Paul's "spirituality" is studied in an "academic" mode, with its major proponent from the Jewish community. Alan Segal views Paul as our best example of early rabbinic mysticism, followed by others who detect in 2 Corinthians *merkabah* mysticism (visions of the heavenly throne-chariot; cf. Ezek. 1). James D. Tabor likewise sees evidence that Paul privileged visionary experience.

The letter has also been grist for the mill of the literary and rhetorical critic. Richard Hays demonstrates Paul's subtle appeal to echo and allusion in such passages as 3:1–18. Others, beginning with Hans D. Betz, have turned their minds to the apostle's rhetoric, labeling chapters 10–13 a "Socratic apology" (Betz), a "philosopher's apology" (McCant), or a pastoral speech-act (Chevallier). F. Young and D. F. Ford argued that the entire letter follows the rhetorical template set down by classical rhetorical theoreticians, and so is unified. Paul's moves also have provided an entrée for sociological discussions of inner and external conflict and power-relations (Chow). Some have sought a deliberately integrative approach, such as Ben Witherington, or E. Humphrey, who demonstrates the intricacies of textual, cultural, and historical allusions in 2 Corinthians through an adaptation of V. Robbins's "textural" model.

Issues, Themes, and Messages

Principal themes of the letter include: true knowledge (a theme shared with 1 Corinthians), old and new covenants, suffering and patience, holiness in the authentic Christian life, vulnerable giving and receiving, the importance of the body and body of Christ, the loving resolution of conflict and reconciliation, the use and abuse of authority, and especially, revelation and transformation. Joining these disparate themes together is the person of Jesus himself. He gives knowledge of God, fulfills the old covenant and initiates the new, and is the patient Sufferer par excellence. He is himself the temple of the living God, "God's unspeakable gift" to humanity, and the one by whose body and in whom we become a body together. Through Christ, God reconciled the world to himself; in his life divine power was made perfect in weakness, and through him has come God's new creation. "For it is the God who said, 'Let light shine out of darkness,' who has shone in our hearts to give the light of the knowledge of the glory of God *in the face of Jesus Christ*" (2 Cor. 4:6 NRSV, italics added).

Despite the debates regarding unity, the letter is bound together by what could be called "apocalyptic discourse." With the apocalypses proper, 2 Corinthians presents a cosmic reality so that the life of the Christian community is understood in terms of God's disclosed actions in time, as well as in light of a weighty unseen world. However, Paul further reconfigures the world in terms of the decisive *apokalypsis* of God in the person of Jesus Christ. Hence, knowledge, austerity of life, sacrifice, charitable giving, authority, and even special revelation are not ends in themselves. All are of value because of Jesus, in whom the new creation has been established so that his body grows from glory to glory (3:18). From one perspective, the glory of Jesus is the only light in this letter, that before which every other light-source pales; from another perspective, it is because of his very light that all human endeavors, all struggles in the church, and all members of the new creation are utterly important. Paul calls the apostles "the glory of Christ" (8:23b NRSV), picturing the entire community growing into this likeness (3:18).

By this unflinching focus upon Jesus as the revelation of God, Paul sees human existence as both transitory and bound for glory. Currently we hold "treasures in clay vessels" (4:7 AT); our human and failing eyes have seen "the knowledge of the light of the glory of God in the face of Jesus" (4:6 AT). This visionary possession of Christ's body together is a gift that far surpasses the revelations of those great souls of old. Moses, Elijah, and Ezekiel glimpsed, in special visions, God's glory from afar, and so instructed God's people. But that hazy "appearance *of* the likeness *of* the glory *of* the LORD" (Ezek. 1:28b, italics added) has been eclipsed by the very light of God among us. Jesus, the seemingly "poor" (8:9), with veiled and vulnerable glory that the world thought to extinguish, blazed on the resurrection morning. As a result, the whole world has changed ("There is a new creation!" 5:17 NRSV) and has been granted a surprising fresh dignity. Because of Jesus, the new creation is being prepared.

Things are not as they seem, once it is acknowledged that the greatest apocalypse (Jesus himself) has been revealed. Mundane symbols such as clay jars and mirrors, as well as potentially sacred images such as fragrance and veils, are all taken up into Paul's dramatic vision. Here we are taught not to despise the work of God's hands, nor to overexalt it. Readers of the twenty-first century are reminded, in our time of crazy and undisciplined "spirituality," that if we are truly to live, our spiritual life must be cruciform and lived together in that particular Holy Spirit of God. Present faithful suffering displays the life of Jesus in mortal bodies (4:11) and prepares "an eternal weight of glory beyond all measure" (4:17 NRSV). So it is that the foundational story of Jesus the Messiah—his life, death, resurrection, and exaltation—casts its light upon the everyday and the terrible. So it is that the arduous and irksome life of God's people is assumed into the cosmic drama, taking on great significance. "I will welcome you, . . . and you shall be my sons and daughters, says the Lord Almighty" (6:17b–18 NRSV).

As he concludes a difficult correspondence, Paul summarizes, "For he was crucified in weakness, but lives by the power of God. For we are weak in him, but . . . we will live with him by the power of God" (2 Cor. 13:4 NRSV). In the apostle's own case, this weakness and power would mean a painful rectification of problems with and in Corinth. It would mean looking to see Christ's resurrection power working in difficult interchurch relationships. Our own needs may not be so very different, given the current crisis of authority in many congregations and communions. Be that as it may, we may give thanks for an epistle that is at once heavenly minded and earthly rooted, given to us "for building up and not for tearing down" (13:10 NRSV).

2 Corinthians and Canon

In its description of God's new covenant through Christ, 2 Corinthians exegetes the OT hope for a qualitatively new communion (Jer. 31:31–34; Ezek. 34; 37) between God and humanity, and among the faithful. The historical dynamic Paul offers is essential: we are not to disparage the Mosaic covenant, as though the ancient people of God had erred; we are nevertheless to fully honor the new covenant, made perfect in Jesus. There is both a continuity and a discontinuity, since God's glory has been revealed, first to Israel, and now fully in Christ. This is a historical understanding of the covenants that the church has not always heeded. In early centuries, some Christians missed this dimension of the gospel, forgetting that God "did something new" in Jesus whereby the law was fulfilled. Gnostics, Marcionites, and others in the subapostolic period mocked the ancient Hebrews for taking literally words that God had "intended" only to be taken metaphorically (e.g., Clement of Alexandria, *Paed.* 2.10). Today, the opposite error is in vogue: Christians ignore the finality of the Jesus apocalypse, positing two ways of salvation, one for Jew, one for Christian.

Paul will not leave us this option. In 2 Cor. 3–4, as in Rom. 10, he shows an undeniable continuity of the new covenant with the old, but the "veil" is only removed ("apocalypsed!") in Jesus. The Torah possessed a glory meant to be "set aside" (2 Cor. 3:13–14 NRSV) because it would come to completion in the One from whom the very light of God shines (on this, see Wright).

Paul relates this new story of Jesus and God's people by explicit reference to the OT, and also by allusion and echo, deeply inhabiting the old covenant story and demonstrating its new climax. Nor does he despise writings not strictly canonical, since he recalls (not uncritically) movements of Judaism (e.g., rabbinic mysticism) that we have long forgotten. Like the ancient poet Terence, Paul can say, "I consider nothing human to be alien to me"—but this he does with theological reason, for all is his, and he is in Christ, and Christ is God's. Close readings of 2 Corinthians dislodge unexpected allusions and memories of past writings, artifacts, and traditions. These discoveries enrich our own Christian world, so long as we maintain our focus upon the One in whom all things cohere.

2 Corinthians and Theology

The theological drive of 2 Corinthians is that of integration. Above all others, this letter reminds us that the pastoral, academic (scribal), and theological roles are best held together. Paul addresses the particular questions of his beloved church without losing sight of the larger picture. Here, if we will look, are answers to the "New Age" challenge, as Paul holds before us the One for whom new-agers thirst, but whom they do not recognize. Here are methods to resolve problems of authority and church structure—Paul embodies the vulnerable leader who uses his powerful role for the sake of his church. Here is a call to holiness that does not denigrate the body or the physical, but sees even the mundane as "sacramentals" disclosing the Holy One. Here is a written and luminous icon of the one who spoke worlds into being, and through whom has come and is coming and will come God's new creation. Paul does not here fully articulate the doctrine of the divinity of Christ, as he did in his reformulated Shema of 1 Cor. 8:5–6. In 2 Corinthians, that doctrine of Jesus as the LORD (through whom are all things) is assumed. Here Paul builds on that foundation, so as to nurture the common life made possible by "the Lord [who] is the Spirit" (2 Cor. 3:17). It is his lively hope that together we will be transformed into the image of that One who participates by right in the life of the Triune God. In the Spirit, Paul proclaims not himself, but Jesus Christ as Lord.

Bibliography

Baur, F. C. "Die Christuspartei in der korinthischen Gemeinde." Pages 1–76 of *Ausgewählte Werke,* ed. K. Scholder. 1963.

Betz, H. D. *Der Apostle Paulus und die sokratische Tradition.* Mohr/Siebeck, 1972.

Bultmann, R. *The Second Letter to the Corinthians,* trans. R. A. Harrisville. Fortress, 1985.

———. *Der zweite Brief an die Korinther,* ed. E. Dinkler. KEK 6. Vandenhoeck & Ruprecht, 1976.

Chevallier, M.-A. "L'argumentation de Paul dans II Corinthiens 10 à 13." *RHPR* 70 (1990): 3–15.

Chow, J. *Patronage and Power.* JSNTSup 75. JSOT, 1992.

Fitzmyer, J. "Glory Reflected on the Face of Christ (2 Cor 3:7–4:6) and a Palestinian Jewish Motif." *TS* 42 (1981): 630–44.

Gilchrist, J. "Paul and the Corinthians—The Sequence of Letters and Visit." *JSNT* 34 (1988): 47–69.

Hays, R. *Echoes of Scripture in the Letters of Paul.* Yale University Press, 1989.

Humphrey, E. "Apocalyptic Rhetoric and Intertextuality in 2 Corinthians." Pages 113–35 of *The Intertexture of Apocalyptic Discourse in the New Testament,* ed. D. Watson. SBLSymS 14. SBL, 2002.

Kreitzer, L. *2 Corinthians.* Sheffield Academic Press, 1996.

McCant, J. "Paul's Thorn of Rejected Apostleship." *NTS* 34 (1988): 550–72.

Robbins, V. *Exploring the Texture of Texts.* Trinity, 1996.

Segal, A. *Paul the Convert.* Yale University Press, 1990.

Tabor, J. *Things Unutterable.* University Press of America, 1986.

Watson, F. *Paul, Judaism, and the Gentiles.* Cambridge University Press, 1986.

Webb, W. *Returning Home.* JSNTSup 85. JSOT, 1993.

Witherington, B., III. *Conflict and Community in Corinth.* Eerdmans, 1995.

Wright, N. T. "Reflected Glory: 2 Corinthians 3." Pages 175–92 of *The Climax of the Covenant.* Fortress, 1991.

Young, F., and D. Ford. *Meaning and Truth in 2 Corinthians.* SPCK, 1987.

9

Galatians

JOHN K. RICHES

With an appropriateness that Paul could hardly have anticipated, Galatians is one of the most fruitful writings of the NT. Not only was it the foundational document of the Reformation; it was also widely influential throughout church history. Chrysostom, Jerome, and Augustine all composed commentaries on it within a few decades and a few hundred miles of each other at the turn of the fourth/fifth centuries, as Christianity began to expand under official recognition. Luther's commentary was itself enormously influential (even John Bunyan records his debt in *Grace Abounding*), in contrast to his commentary on Romans, published only in a provisional form in 1908 (critical ed. 1938). The letter is evidently written with deep passion and out of a great sense of care and anxiety for the Galatians, as they are tempted to follow those who argue that observance of the law is a necessary condition for membership in the people of God. It reveals the existence of deep controversy and conflict among the apostles over the issue of observance of the law. By contrast with the proponents of a law-observant Christianity, Paul insists that righteousness is to be found only by those who live by faith in Jesus Christ and who are led by the Spirit. Such people live in hope and out of the experience of the living Christ within them. This is the new life of freedom, which replaces the former life of bondage. Such a radical view of the newness of Christian existence (by contrast with all old ways, not only of the Gentiles but also of the Jews) raises some difficult questions about the relation of the OT to the NT, and of Paul to some of the other NT writers (Matthew and James) who place much greater emphasis on the law. At the same time it raises important questions about the nature of Christians' freedom and guidance by the Spirit. What weight are the churches to give appeals to the Spirit in the search for guidance and in times of controversy? Paul's assertion of the radical newness of believers' life in Christ also raises acute questions about the place of other forms of religious belief and practice within Christian understanding and practice, not least of members of the Jewish faith.

History of Interpretation

Guidance by the Spirit and Freedom from the Law in Galatians

In his argument with the Galatians, Paul clearly states that the role of the law in their lives (or the lives of the Jews?) was a temporary one. Before faith they were kept under the law, which acted as a custodian; once faith came they were all sons of God, "no longer under a custodian" (3:23–26 RSV). Clearly (not least in the light of the subsequent interpretation of this passage), Paul's use of this metaphor leaves a number of questions open: What precisely was the nature of this custodianship? Once Christian believers were no longer subject to the law as custodian, did that mean that their relationship to the law was then at an end? What was the nature of their new life in the Spirit, in which they had begun their Christian existence, such that the desire to return to practice of the law could be ironically described by Paul as a desire to perfect their new life "in the flesh" (3:3 AT)?

Marcion, one of the earliest commentators on Paul, saw the law as stemming from a different God than the God of Jesus Christ, and believed that the law of the just but cruel creator God had as its principal function the enslavement and punishment of human beings. The gospel brought by the Spirit liberated believers and allowed them to escape from the world of creation. This reading sets a mark for subsequent orthodox interpreters who seek to distance themselves from the teaching of Marcion. For Chrysostom, the law has two functions: the first as a bridle to curb the Jews; the second, more importantly, to teach the Jews the basic grammar of morality. The law is, as it were, a primary teacher who drills on the rudiments of the subject and is left behind when the pupil has learned all that he may and then moves on to be taught by a philosopher. It would be degrading for such a student to go back to his primary teacher, when he is already being taught by one much wiser and more learned. The role of the Spirit is also twofold: regenerating believers in baptism, thus liberating them from the desires of the flesh; also, instructing in the higher morality, so that believers may produce fruit. Augustine introduces a new motif into the understanding of the function of the law: it is there to humble those who seek justification by works, precisely because no one can perform all the works of the law. Thus, people are driven to seek the righteousness that comes by faith in Jesus Christ. The Spirit leads believers in the way of faith, but they constantly have to battle with the effects of original sin. Thomas Aquinas drew together the teaching of the fathers: the law was to restrain sins, to bring people to seek grace, to tame concupiscence, and also to serve as a figure of future grace. This last point allowed a more allegorical reading of the ceremonial aspects of the law.

Luther accepted that the law had a civil (political) use in promoting order and discipline in society; it also had a theological use: following Augustine, he described it as a hammer to break the proud and bring them to Christ. Through faith Christ enters the life of believers and through his Spirit guides and leads them, though they always have to battle with the power of sin in their lives. Until this point, few commentators attributed anything but a quite minor role to the law in the life of believers. At most, it is one source of ethical teaching, though a minor one compared with the teaching of the NT (Aquinas). For Calvin, this became more problematical. Faced with the Radical Reformers—who appealed to the inspiration of the Spirit to justify their pacifist and simple style of living—and inspired by a belief in the unity of the two covenants, Calvin appealed to the law as the true benchmark of Christian ethics. He thus proposes a third use of the law, which is the "principal use and more closely connected with its proper end. It has respect to believers in whose hearts the Spirit of God already flourishes and reigns. . . . That, by teaching, admonishing, rebuking, and correcting, it may fit and prepare us for every good work. . . . The law acts like a whip to the flesh, urging it on as men do a sluggish ass." But it also has a teaching function, even for believers in whose hearts "the Law is written and engraved." For them, "it is the best instrument for enabling them to learn with greater truth and certainty what that will of the Lord is which they aspire to follow, and to confirm them in this knowledge" (*Inst.* 2.7.12). Thus Calvin exalts the written law of the OT over the law written in the heart. This is taken up by later Puritan commentators such as

William Perkins, who see evidence of obedience to the law as a ground for assurance of the believer's election. Perkins gives some remarkable examples of what he sees to be the clear guidance of the written law, which includes not selling one's children into slavery. Among post-Enlightenment commentators, F. C. Baur saw the conflict between Peter and Paul at Antioch as representing the struggle between a law-based, particularist understanding of religion and the new law-free, universalist religion of Christianity, based on a new God-consciousness mediated through the Son. This new (idealist) understanding of Spirit was subsequently attacked by the history of religions school (Heitmüller), which located the understanding of Spirit in popular Hellenistic forms of effervescent religion, though Bousset argued that Paul's true religion of the Spirit transcended the popular cultic form of early Christianity. This characterization of Spirit-led belief as universalist, and Judaism with its own ethical traditions as particularist, easily led into various late-nineteenth-century portrayals of Judaism as legalistic and caught up in extreme forms of casuistry.

Justification by Faith and Not by Works

Commentators see Paul as contrasting two very different types of religious observance; one is based on works, driven by fear of the consequences of failing to obey the law; the other is based on faith in Christ's work in securing our forgiveness, which brings freedom to follow the Spirit (Chrysostom). There are questions, however, about the role of believers in the life of faith, how far they are restored/regenerated and able to act justly and lovingly, how far any such acts of righteousness are themselves the result of God's gracious action. Chrysostom believed both that our crucifixion with Christ in baptism leads to the killing of our passions and so to the end of sin, and also that there was a continuing need for ascetic discipline in the life of the Christian. Thus, he portrayed Paul as the ideal type of the Christian monk. Augustine believed that those who die to the law exchange a carnal for a spiritual understanding of the law. Moreover the law is no longer imposed, for now Christ lives in the believer, who thus acts out of love of justice. Nevertheless, although this might sound like a perfectionist understanding of Christian life, Augustine distinguishes between the present mode of Christ's dwelling in the believer and that which is to come. Now Christ lives in believers by faith only; in the life to come he will live in them by sight. In this life there is still a lack of clarity and certainty about relationship with Christ, which leads Augustine to become less confident in the bond.

For Aquinas, faith itself is a gift of grace and is informed by the gift of love (*fides caritate formata*); in this way God is understood as imparting the fullness of his gifts to believers. God assists our free will by his grace; Christians are released from the written law and instructed and directed by God himself; Christ directs the soul as the soul directs the body. Luther vehemently objected, saying this meant that faith not informed by love and therefore not issuing in works of love was viewed as nonsalvific; such teaching implied a doctrine of justification by works. The righteousness received through faith in Christ was a pure gift and not in any sense dependent on our activity. Christ entering the heart drives out Moses and brings grace and righteousness. With such a view, righteousness is not merely reckoned to the believer but, because it has its roots in the intimate union between Christ and the believer, issues in actual righteousness. In this sense, the believer is freed from the law. Nevertheless, while there is this union in the believers' hearts, they live out their callings in the world, where the law still obtains.

Calvin's reading of Gal. 2:15–21 first attacks the view of Jerome (and Origen) that it was only the ceremonial (as opposed to the moral) law that could not justify. While conceding that the original dispute was about ceremonial matters, he argues that Paul nevertheless moved from the particular to the general because he "was worried not so much about ceremonies being observed as that the confidence and glory of salvation should be transferred to works." He differs importantly from Luther, who takes "Through the law I died to the law" (v. 19) to mean renouncing it and being freed from it. For Calvin, it means rather that the law bears the curse within it, which slays us, not that we are liberated from its sphere. The new life of believers is engrafted into the death of Christ, from which they receive a secret energy. Believers are "animated by the secret power of Christ, so that Christ may be said to live and grow in [them]." The life of Christ in the believer depends on a "true and genuine communication with him" and has two possible senses for Calvin. First is the governance of the believer's actions by Christ's spirit. Second is participation in Christ's righteousness, so "that, since we cannot of ourselves be acceptable to him [French version], we are accepted in him by God. The first relates to regeneration, the second to the free imputation of righteousness." It is in the second sense that Calvin takes the present passage, though he indicates in the French version of his commentary that he would find it better if it could be taken in both senses. Thus both Luther and Calvin provide support for the dominant Reformed view that the righteousness of faith is an alien righteousness, imputed rather than imparted, a view linked with a negative view of the reality of the believer's sharing in Christ's righteousness. On the other hand, both these Reformers speak powerfully and movingly of the believer as united to Christ: "We so live in the world that we also live in heaven; not only because our Head is there, but because, in virtue of union, we have a life in common with him (John 14.1ff.)" (Calvin, *Galatians*, 42–43; *Commentaires*, 296–97).

Christian Anthropology—the Desires of the Flesh and the Desires of the Spirit: Gal. 5:16–18 and the Ethics of Desire

Paul states that the desires of the flesh and the Spirit are opposed to each other and engaged in struggle with each other in such a way as to bring a certain consequence: "You may not do what you want" (v. 17 AT). This statement is wonderfully ambiguous and has spawned a family of Christian anthropologies of very different temperaments. For dualists like Gnostics and Manichaeans, the flesh is seen as the creation of an alien principle, which holds the pure, incorruptible soul in bondage. The soul can, however, be released through saving knowledge of its plight. This knowledge of the fundamental opposition between flesh and spirit leads to renewal of the soul and a life of abstinence and asceticism, *not doing what one—wrongly—wants*. Such doctrines were vigorously opposed by the orthodox churches but nevertheless were influential and reflected in the adoption and idealization of ascetic lifestyles and the exaltation of virginity. Chrysostom saw flesh and spirit not as two opposed principles but as referring to different states of mind or judgment: those instructed by the Spirit knew clearly what the choices were that faced them and were *able to choose not to do what was wrong*. Again, this meant resisting the desires of the flesh and leading a life of (monastic) asceticism. Chrysostom portrayed Paul as the ideal type of the Christian monk, crucifying the flesh with its passions and desires (5:24). Aquinas follows the fathers in taking "flesh" and "spirit" to refer to different modes of the soul's willing. But rather than seeing fleshly desires as intrinsically wrong, he understands them as natural, wrong only insofar as they are taken to excess or allowed to distract the soul from the pursuit of spiritual, supernatural desires. For Aquinas, there is then a struggle within the Christian life to establish a proper balance between natural and spiritual desires, which means that we *cannot always do the good we want*. This tendency to see the Christian life as one of *continuing struggle in the will between the desires of the flesh and the Spirit* is given greater impetus by Luther, whose deep fears of judgment during his life as an Augustinian friar continued to disturb him later. He remained powerfully convinced of the continuing sinfulness of believers, and at the same time he also believed that those who were united to Christ were able to bear the fruit of the Spirit in their lives. This darker strain in Reformed theology was given yet greater impetus by Calvinist doctrines of total depravity, tendencies that were combated by Methodism and the holiness movements.

View of the Other in Galatians

Finally, we must consider the ways that readings of Galatians have influenced Christians' views of those outside the community of faith. With its sharp contrasts between those who follow the life of the flesh and those led by the Spirit—and between those who believe, are in Christ, and are sons and daughters of Abraham, Christ, and God and those who are not—Galatians can easily lead to a quite negative characterization of all those who are not Christian believers, indeed, to a very negative characterization of all forms of human difference (3:28). Such negative attitudes are clearly evinced in Chrysostom's *Discourses against the Jews* and in Luther's and subsequent Lutheran portrayals of Christianity as a legalistic religion of works and self-redemption. This is further developed in F. C. Baur's portrayal of Judaism as a particularistic, as opposed to a universal, form of religion (cf. Boyarin's reception and critique of Baur). But it is not only Jews who are thus categorized as alien and other: for Luther, all those who do not accept his doctrine of justification by faith are to be seen as pursuing some form of works-righteousness, whether Jews, Turks, schoolmen, philosophers, or monks. The list presumably is extendable.

Place within the Canon

The radical nature of Galatians' theology of the Spirit and its doctrine of the temporary nature of the law raise a number of questions. In the first place, it is argued that Paul's own views of the law change between Galatians and Romans (describing the law as "holy and just and good" in 7:12 NRSV). This does not necessarily entail any contradiction between Galatians and Romans, though there is certainly a difference of tone and emphasis. There are much greater difficulties in plotting the relations between Galatians and works like Matthew and James, which emphasize performing works of the law and doing all that Jesus commanded. Certainly, Luther felt that it was not possible to reconcile Paul and James, which he famously dismissed as an "epistle of straw," just as commentators have continued to see Matthew's emphasis on judgment by works as inimical to Paul's teaching on justification by faith. However, there are similar tensions within Paul's own writings, which should prompt the theological interpreter to question a too-simplistic resolution. Yet Marcion raised more radical questions about the relation of Paul's works (pruned to suit Marcion) to the rest of the canon and in particular to the OT, which for him was testimony to a different, creator God, opposed to the merciful and gentle God of Jesus Christ. Even though orthodox Christian interpreters have fiercely resisted such views, they continue to find powerful supporters. Harnack was one such, and this support for Marcion was coupled with a deeply negative view of Judaism. He saw it as a labyrinthine religion of legalism—transcended by Jesus' teaching of the fatherhood of God and a higher righteousness in the form of an ethic of intention. Even among those who have held that the law plays an integral part in the history of salvation, there is, as recognized, a radical dispute about the nature of its continuing role in the life of the believer.

Galatians presents us with one of the sharpest statements of the giftedness of Christian existence, its dependence not on human effort but on gratitude and faith in God's grace in Christ, a life lived in union with Christ. That life neither springs from nor is subsequently conditional upon human observance of the law of the OT, though it will indeed bear the fruit of the Spirit. Such a vision of the Christian life as a wholly new mode of existence, free from the "bondage" of the old life of the flesh, has never been easy to sustain or indeed to reconcile with the continuing evidence of disharmony, conflict, and other "works of the flesh" in the life of Christian communities. At one extreme are those who have emphasized the perfectionist strand in Paul's thought, asserting the possibility of a new life wholly freed from the flesh, where the soul is free to follow the guidance or instruction of the Spirit. At another extreme are those who have regarded such perfection as something to be achieved only in a future state, since the present life is still dominated by the power of the flesh to create disorder in Christian lives. Hence, the law remains necessary both as a whip to scourge the flesh and as a clear guide for Christian conduct. In this life the human will remains weak; hope, in the face of imminent judgment, resides in the imputation of Christ's righteousness to the believer: "Just as I am, without one plea" (C. Elliott). While perfectionist readings may run up against the hard facts of Christian communal existence, the more negative views seem largely deaf to the promises that Paul makes to Christians in this life and to his despair that those who have once tasted such a life should be willing to turn their backs on it. Readings like those of Aquinas, and to a degree Augustine and Luther, are more alert to the tensions within Christian existence between Spirit-led freedom and the "desires of the flesh," and thus seem more faithful to the text and offer creative ways of appropriating it. In particular, they offer encouragement to Christians to take more seriously their own moral experience as they are led by the Spirit, and to have the courage to explore new ways of living that are governed not by the letter of the law but by the fruit they bear.

Bibliography

Baur, F. C. *Paul*. Williams & Norgate, 1876.

Bousset, W. *Kyrios Christos*. Abingdon, 1970.

Boyarin, D. *A Radical Jew*. University of California Press, 1994.

Bunyan, J. *Grace Abounding to the Chief of Sinners*. Clarendon, 1962.

Calvin, J. *Commentaires de M. Jean Calvin sur toutes les epîstres de l'Apôtre Sainct Paul*. S. Honorati, 1563.

———. *The Epistles of Paul the Apostle to the Galatians, Ephesians, Philippians, and Colossians*. Eerdmans, 1965.

———. *Institutes of the Christian Religion*, ed. J. McNeill, trans. F. L. Battles. 2 vols. Westminster, 1960.

Chrysostom, J. "Commentary on Galatians." Vol. 13 of *NPNF*[1].

Harnack, A. von. *Marcion*. Wissenschaftliche Buchgesellschaft, 1996.

Heitmüller, W. *Taufe und Abendmahl bei Paulus*. Vandenhoeck & Ruprecht, 1903.

Luther, M. *A Commentary on St. Paul's Epistle to the Galatians*. J. Clarke, 1953.

Perkins, W. *A Commentary on Galatians*. Pilgrim, 1989.

Plumer, E., trans. *Augustine's Commentary on Galatians*. Oxford Early Christian Studies. Oxford University Press, 2003.

Thomas Aquinas. *Commentary on St. Paul's Epistle to the Galatians*. Magi Books, 1966.

10

Ephesians

MAX TURNER

No NT writing more joyfully celebrates God's grace in the gospel than does Ephesians, nor does any contain so rich and concentrated a vein of theological gold. This short letter's profound and extensive influence on the church's thought, liturgy, and piety ranks with that of the much longer Psalms, John, and Romans (on the letter's history of influence, see Schnackenburg 311–45). It was Calvin's favorite letter, and Coleridge was later to pronounce it "the divinest composition of man." In more recent times Ephesians has come to be thought pseudepigraphical, and consequently marginalized in Pauline studies. In the meantime, contemporary focus on both *ecumenical* theology and on *canonical* readings of the biblical writings has helped to maintain something of the letter's former prominence.

History of Interpretation

Ephesians has been a central text throughout the history of the church, the subject of many commentaries from Origen, Chrysostom, and Jerome onward, and continually thereafter ransacked for its spiritual and theological treasures. With the Reformation, and the modernist quest that followed it, the letter came increasingly to be read as a unified discourse with its own distinct message. This tendency was radically sharpened by increasing doubts in the nineteenth and twentieth centuries concerning its authenticity and its Ephesian destination.

Increasingly interpreters propose that "Ephesians" was written by an admiring disciple of Paul, late in the first century—one who wrote in a different style from the apostle. This author was far more heavily dependent on Colossians than Paul ever was on his own writings (about a third of the wordings of Colossians, and many of its main themes, appear in Ephesians) and was offering what he saw as the essential legacy of the apostle's theology for a new time and circumstances. It is argued that the (pseudonymous) writer no longer actively hopes for an imminent return of Christ and, indeed, has replaced the whole shape of Paul's largely *future* hope with a realized eschatology, in which believers are *already* raised from death and exalted with Christ into the heavenly places (2:1–10; 1:3–4; allegedly contra 1 Cor. 4:8; 15:1–54; and Rom. 6:1–11; *but* see Col. 2:11–13). It is held that the writer has left Paul's theology of the cross for a theology of glory instead, and that he has given ecclesiology a radical new direction and extravagant prominence as the "universal church" (whereas, it is often asserted, Paul himself uses *ekklēsia* only of *local* congregations; but per contra, see Gal. 1:13; 1 Cor. 10:32; 12:28; 15:9; Phil. 3:6). It is also said that he has moved toward a supersessionist view of Israel and the law, in which the church replaces Israel as the people of God (2:14–18; contra Rom. 9–11; for an accessible account of all these alleged shifts, see, e.g., Lincoln and Wedderburn, ch. 8).

Other interpreters, however, consider Ephesians authentic and see most of the claimed shifts as either exaggerated or already present in its "companion" letter, Colossians (cf. Col. 4:7–8//Eph. 6:21–22), and/or generated by the letter's more general, doxological, visionary, and exhortatory purposes (so, e.g., Arnold, Moritz, and the major commentaries by Barth, O'Brien, and Hoehner).

The Style of Theologizing in Ephesians

Unlike other Pauline letters, Ephesians does not directly tackle some particular local or immediately strategic concerns. Yet it was probably intended primarily to be read *alongside* Colossians in the Lycus valley churches (possibly as the "letter from [nearby] Laodicea," Col. 4:16), and as a partial prophylactic against the danger there of syncretistic veneration of angelic powers (see Arnold). Instead, Ephesians is dominated by (1) blessing of

God for the cosmic reconciliation he has begun in Christ (1:3–14 [esp. 1:9–10]; 3:20–21); (2) prayer that the readers might spiritually comprehend this gospel and be fully grasped by it (1:15–2:10; 3:1, 14–21); and (3) an integrally corresponding ethical exhortation to live out that good news *together* in a unity that exemplifies it to the cosmos (4:1–6:17).

The writer deliberately builds important stages in the letter around material already regarded as core "creedal" tradition in the Pauline churches, including a significant vein of OT texts largely read christologically (cf. Pss. 8 and 110 in 1:20–23; Isa. 52 and 57 in 2:14–18; Ps. 68 in 4:8–10; Isa. 26 and 60 in 5:14; Gen. 2:24 in 5:30–32; and Isa. 11, 52, and 59 in 6:10–17: see Moritz, passim; Best, *Essays*, ch. 3). And this short letter is so densely packed with the apostle's major themes that it has been hailed as the "crown" and "quintessence" of Paulinism. But the style of address is not Paul's usual "argument" or expository discourse as much as it is thankful, prayer-filled celebration and exhortation, written with the zeal, idealism, and burning enthusiasm of the visionary. The writer almost certainly feels that he himself powerfully experiences the very "Spirit of wisdom and revelation" which he prays for his readers (1:17), and that the eyes of his own heart have thereby been opened to comprehend the rich glory of the gospel (1:18–2:8; 3:2–10). He senses that by this Spirit he is already deeply united with the ascended Lord (1:3; 2:5–6). By the same Spirit (3:16) he has already begun to know the depths of Christ's love and to be filled with the eschatological fullness of God (3:18–19). And it is as one full of this Spirit (5:18) that he pours out his doxological and edificatory address.

The form and style of address—together with the concrete content of Paul's prayer for his readers in 1:17–2:10 and 3:1, 14–19—underscore that the apostle regards authentic theological understanding (the sort that enlivens and transforms) as *fully possible only* in the *community* (not in mere "individuality") that *experiences the charismatic self-revealing and transforming presence of God's Spirit.*

The Substantive Content, Shape, and Contribution of the Letter's Theology

For the sake of brevity, in what follows I distribute, under separate headings (like so many separated bones, muscles, and other organs), parts that Ephesians holds together in interconnected, full-bodily motion.

Theology

Written from a Jewish-Christian perspective, from the very outset (1:3–14) Ephesians patently blesses *Israel's* God. He is the almighty author of creation and the promised new creation (1:4; cf. 2:15; 3:11 [cf. 4:6]; 4:24), working out his sovereign pretemporal will to the eschatological praise of his glorious grace (1:6, 11–14). That grace focuses on fulfillment in Christ of the promises made to Israel of corporate "sonship" (now, yes, but primarily eschatological: 1:5–6, as in Rom. 8:23); new-exodus "redemption" from slavery/sin (1:7); "sealing" (with the Spirit: 1:13); and final "inheritance," in which God takes full possession of his people (1:14; cf. 1:18). At that point he will bring all things into the open cosmic unity and harmony of reconciliation with himself, which has already begun in the church in and through Christ (1:9–10; cf. 1:22–23; 3:19).

In Pelagian and especially in Reformation and later debates, attention fell on the opening eulogy's emphasis on *God as the sovereign source of election and predestination* (1:3–5, 9–11), and on what it means to affirm that this is accomplished "in Christ." Unresolved is the question whether behind the evident *corporate* nature of the election (the "we"/"us" stands for the *congregation* of God's people in Christ) there is also an implied election/predestination of *individuals* into the church: the latter is exegetically improbable (but not theologically thereby excluded).

But (as with other NT writings) God's identity is *supremely* revealed as "the God and Father *of our Lord Jesus*" (1:3 NRSV, italics added; cf. 1:17)—not so much on the basis of the number of times such expressions are used, as on the letter's profoundly christocentric (proto-binitarian) shape.

Christology

In most ways Ephesians recapitulates the teaching of Paul's other letters, including emphasis on Jesus as (1) the Christ; (2) the unique Lord (exalted to God's right hand, and thence as "head of all things," sharing his cosmic rule: see esp. 1:20–23; cf. 4:6); and (3) the Son of God. As elsewhere, he is also an Adamic figure who is the beginning (1:4), the paradigm (4:20–24; 5:1–2, 25–32), and the end of God's purposes with humankind (1:10; 4:13, 15–16). As in other Paulines, the Lord is invoked as the *co-source*, with the Father, of "grace and peace" (1:2; cf. 6:23), but uniquely also of "love and faith/faithfulness" (6:23–24). Paul usually refers to God as providing the "grace" of his apostolate and other ministries, through the Spirit, and Ephesians maintains the same (e.g., 3:2, 7), but much more explicitly than at (e.g.) 1 Cor. 12:5, describes the ascended Christ as the (co-)*giver* of the varied ministry gifts (4:10–12). Similarly, in Ephesians the risen Christ, like God, uniquely "fill[s] all things" (4:10), especially the church (1:22–23). Grasping the infinite love of Christ means to be filled with all the fullness of God (3:17). All this amounts to a deep-level "binitarian" Christology. It is matched by Paul's first explicit exhortation that Spirit-filled congregational worship should regularly involve singing and making melody *to* the Lord Jesus as well as giving thanks to the Father *through* (or "in the name of") the Lord Jesus (5:18–20). To mark Jesus as the expected recipient of full and regular worship, alongside the Father, was thus to include him within the identity of the One God/Lord of Israel (cf. 4:5–6; 1 Cor. 8:5–6; and the Shema [Deut. 6:4], on which they depend). That in turn was self-consciously to move into some form of *binitarian* monotheism (see Hurtado), and to provide the basis for pronounced liturgical developments.

Two more distinctive christological emphases may be mentioned: (1) Eph. 4:8–10 speaks of a descent and ascent of Christ. In conjunction with 1 Pet. 3:18–19, this has been taken (from the fathers onward) as a descent from the cross to hades (e.g., to harrow the imprisoned spirits), followed by resurrection-ascension. But this is exegetically implausible (in both letters!) and breaks the contextually required symmetry of the ascent-descent pattern, which might be ascent to heaven followed by corresponding re-descent (in the gift of the Spirit: so Lincoln; Harris). More probably it is the incarnational descent from heaven to earth, and then to the humiliation of the cross (= "the very lowest parts" AT), followed by corresponding ascent in resurrection-exaltation (see Schnackenburg; O'Brien; Hoehner). (2) The confession of Jesus as "head" of the ecclesial body is said to shift from the image of the local church as a whole body (including head, ears, eyes, etc., in 1 Cor. 12) to a universal church seen as an otherwise headless torso-and-limbs. But more probably as head to the church, Christ is portrayed as a lordly husband to his bride in a "one-body" union (5:22–31).

Pneumatology

The teaching on the Spirit in Ephesians is far more extensive than in its companion letter, Colossians, but also much closer to that of Paul's other letters (contra Adai; see Hui). The Spirit is the self-manifesting, transforming, and empowering presence of God—*and* of Christ—most probably the personal executive power by which both the Father and the Son indwell and "fill" the church (cf. 2:18, 22; 3:16–19), and direct (3:5; 4:30; 6:18), shape (1:17–19; 4:3), inspire (5:18), and empower it (1:17–19;

6:17; cf. 4:10–16). As such, the Spirit is essentially proto-trinitarian in character (Turner, "Trinitarian").

Salvation/Reconciliation/Cosmic Unity

At the theological heart of Ephesians glows the multifaceted jewel of the ineffable "mystery" revealed in the gospel (cf. 1:9–10; 3:3–4, 6–9; 5:32; 6:19; cf. Caragounis). This, while planned in eternity, was "set forth" paradigmatically in the Christ event (1:9 ESV, NRSV) as God's eschatological intention to (re-)unite "all things" in cosmic harmony with himself in Christ (1:10; cf. Col. 1:18–20). Many fathers from Irenaeus onward took the key verb *anakephalaiōsasthai* to mean "recapitulate" (i.e., to restore in the new head, Christ, all that was lost in the old, Adam). Others preferred to see a simpler allusion to 1:23, and took the verb to mean "to bring under (the) one head, Christ" (cf. NJB). The majority, however, recognize the verb means "to sum up/gather up" as under one *kephalaion* (= heading). The background assumption (as at Col. 1:18–20) is that creation has been plunged by sin into a chaos of alienations. Correspondingly, the hoped-for "summing up" takes the specific form of the reuniting of all things (or "reconciling" thereof: so Col. 1:20) in cosmic peace and harmony. *This is the vision that fundamentally stamps all else in the letter* (see Turner, "Mission"). It is a vision the author believes has been decisively inaugurated through Christ's redemptive (1:7), and especially in his *reconciling*, death (2:14–18). In a horizontal dimension the cross tears down (in principle) the wall of alienation dividing the two ancient divisions of humankind (Jew and Gentile), previously generated by the law, and allows the former two to be re-created as one *new* humanity in Christ (2:14–15). But in a vertical dimension the cross also reconciles both these groups *to God* (2:16–17), creating a church that thereby already exemplifies (to the world and to the *heavenly hosts*: cf. 3:10!) the beginnings of the cosmic reunification and messianic peace (2:18) in 1:9–10. That salvation has at least fully dawned in the transforming faith-union that joins Jew and Gentile with the exalted Lord (2:6, 8), even though it has yet to be consummated.

Eschatology

Contrary to the assertion of some interpreters, the author does *not* believe the vision of 1:9–10 is already fully accomplished. He looks out onto a still largely benighted unbelieving "old" humanity, alienated from God, from the church, and from each other; dead in sin; and under the malign influence of the evil one (cf. 2:1–5; 4:17–20; 5:11–14). Even for the church itself, the days are evil (5:15; 6:13) and beset by encircling hosts of opposing powers (6:10–17; 4:27). Its day of redemption and inheritance (1:11–14, 18; 4:30) still essentially lies in the temporal future, which readers will naturally identify (from Col. 3:4, or from the Pauline tradition more generally) with the parousia. Ephesians does, however, take up the Pauline apocalyptic belief that the eschatological blessings already exist in the heavenly places, and that believers already share in these by virtue of their union with Christ. Ephesians gives distinct emphasis to this (esp. 1:3–14) and in 2:6 can even assert that believers are raised up and enthroned with Christ there (themes closely paralleled in Col. 2:12–13; 3:1–4). But this does *not* mean a shift to an overrealized eschatology, as is so often asserted. It is partly the regular bold assurance of eschatological benediction. More specifically, though, it is joyful affirmation of faith's close, partly reciprocal, indwelling between the believer and the heavenly Lord. Just as experience of the Spirit as "down payment" (1:14) of our inheritance is a foretaste of the eschatological fullness of Christ (1:23; 3:18–19; 4:10), so by the same Spirit we are now present *to* Christ, and so "with him," and share in his exaltation. And this sharing "with" him in the heavenlies is no triumphalism: it does not lift the believer out of earthly existence, with all its individual, household, and community responsibilities to live the cruciform life of openness, meekness, love, and service (see below).

People of God/Church/New Humanity/Ministry

In no Pauline letter is the church so remarkably prominent (see Schnackenburg 293–310, 321–31; Best, *Critical and Exegetical Commentary* 622–41). Ephesians develops many ecclesiological themes present in other Pauline letters, especially Colossians. Thus, the church is the holy "people of God" (= the saints), fulfilling the destiny of Israel. It is the body over which Christ is the head (Eph. 1:22//Col.1:18; 2:10; Eph. 4:15//Col. 2:19). It is God's *ekklēsia* (assembly), probably meaning the multiple and distinct earthly representation of the one heavenly and eschatological assembly (against the view that it is simply the universal earthly church, see O'Brien), the temple he indwells (Eph. 2:20–22; cf. 1 Cor. 3:16–17; 2 Cor. 6:16–18). But Ephesians brings distinctive emphases to bear. The temple is being built on the foundation of the fundamental apostolic/prophetic revelation of its essentially concorporate nature (fusing Jew and Gentile; 2:20–22; 3:5–6).

The church is also portrayed as a single developing body, one growing harmoniously from childhood toward Christlike (eschatological?) maturity, the "complete man." In this growth it is shaped, and held together, by the ministries that the Lord gives (4:10–16). Or to vary the metaphor again (sharply so in gender!), it is a body that is Christ's *bride*, and he is head over it as a husband to his wife (5:22–32; cf. 2 Cor. 11:2, but there the bride is a single congregation, and Paul its "best man"). The church is also the one new-creation humanity (2:15; 4:20–24), which, while not effacing the Jew/Gentile distinction (readers can still be addressed as "You Gentiles," 2:11; 3:1), embraces both in a unity that transcends such distinction (and any other racial division). It has a fundamentally "Israel" bias and shape and fulfills its hopes and destiny (2:11–18, esp. 12–13), but takes its singular most-defining identity from the ultimate *reconciling* self-giving of the (Jewish) Christ (4:20–21, 32; 5:1–2). In a context of Jewish mysticism, where the veneration of the heavenly beings was a potentially divisive threat (see Colossians), the soteriology, eschatology, and ecclesiology of the letter could hardly be more sharply relevant.

Ethics

Not surprisingly, the *one main and urgent task* of the church (as the writer composes his three chapters of ethical exhortation) is to maintain, and *visibly live out*, the cosmic unity/harmony begun in Christ (4:1–3). This means much more than merely ensuring that Gentile converts are treated on fully equal terms with Jewish believers (2:11–20; 3:5–6): it also means that *all* must renounce the old-creation patterns of alienated and alienating behavior (4:17–31; 5:3–15). Instead, they must adopt the cruciform virtues that recognize the authentic self, in God's likeness (*not* the smothered self of totalitarian regimes!), as belonging to and for the other. Thus they embrace ways of being/living that build the community's varied relationships and thereby give them previously unimaginable and joyful depth (esp. 4:25, 29; 4:32–5:2; 5:15–20, but throughout: cf. Turner, "Mission," 148–60). No better paradigm can Paul provide than that of authentic marriage, which models the Christ-church relationship (5:22–32), and none has been more influential. But we would miss the apostle's point entirely if we took it just to be his later, more-considered teaching on marriage than that in 1 Cor. 7: he intends this portrayal of marriage to illumine *all* Christian relationships.

Powers and Spiritual Warfare

No Pauline letter—other than the sister letter, Colossians—gives such attention to principalities and powers. Arnold has argued that this is evoked by Ephesian fears of demonic magical powers associated with the

Artemis cult. Perhaps more probable is that Paul fears the influence of Jewish-Christian teaching (primarily in the Lycus valley) about mystical heavenly ascent, and concomitant undue reverence for angelic beings. In terms of the history of interpretation, pride of place has certainly been given to Eph. 6:10–20. But while this passage has regularly been taken as a kind of specialist appendix on how to deal with the evil powers, it is much more convincingly understood as a fitting summary and conclusion to the themes of the whole letter (Lincoln).

Ephesians and the Canon

With relatively few exceptions, those who consider Ephesians pseudonymous still warmly commend its message. Its place in the canon restores a reading of it as complementary to Paul's letters and, indeed, even the "crown of Paulinism," rather than as any kind of substantial reassessment of it. As recognized above, it also dramatically highlights the universal, heavenly, and eschatological nature of the church as a community of cosmic reunification.

Ephesians and Theology

There is hardly a sentence of Ephesians that has not been deeply influential on Christian theology. But it is the letter's ecclesiology of cosmic reunification that has deservedly given it a place of singular import in contemporary theological discussion. Ephesians 2 has sparked important discussion of racial hostility (Rader). Ephesians 4:1–3, 7–16 has profoundly inspired various kinds of ecumenical theology of church and ministry. Many of these constitute a challenge to an evangelical tendency to point to Christ *rather than* to the church (which Ephesians would surely have seen as a false antithesis and even possibly as a betrayal of the church's calling). But the letter also emerges in theology as a challenge to contemporary individualism, and as a call for a radically new and engaging understanding of the "self" and authentic personhood (see, e.g., Ford).

Bibliography

Arnold, C. *Ephesians*. Cambridge University Press, 1989.
Barth, M. *Ephesians*. 2 vols. AB 34–34A. Doubleday, 1974.

Best, E. *A Critical and Exegetical Commentary on Ephesians.* T&T Clark, 1998.

———. *Essays on Ephesians.* T&T Clark, 1997.

Caragounis, C. C. *The Ephesian "Mysterion."* Gleerup, 1977.

Ford, D. *Self and Salvation.* Cambridge University Press, 1999.

Harris, W. H., III. *The Descent of Christ.* Brill, 1996.

Hoehner, H. *Ephesians.* Baker, 2002.

Hui, A. W. D. "The Concept of the Holy Spirit in Ephesians." *TynBul* 44 (1993): 379–82.

Hurtado, L. *Lord Jesus Christ.* Eerdmans, 2003.

Lincoln, A. *Ephesians.* WBC 42. Word, 1990.

Lincoln, A., and A. J. M. Wedderburn. *The Theology of the Later Pauline Letters.* Cambridge University Press, 1993.

Moritz, T. *A Profound Mystery.* Brill, 1996.

O'Brien, P. T. "The Church as a Heavenly and Eschatological Entity." Pages 88–119 in *The Church in the Bible and the World,* ed. D. A. Carson. Baker, 1987.

Rader, W. *The Church and Racial Hostility.* Mohr, 1978.

Schnackenburg, R. *The Epistle to the Ephesians.* T&T Clark, 1991.

Turner, M. "Mission and Meaning in Terms of 'Unity' in Ephesians." Pages 138–66 in *Mission and Meaning,* ed. A. Billington, T. Lane, and M. Turner. Paternoster, 1995.

———. "'Trinitarian' Pneumatology in the New Testament?—Towards an Explanation of the Worship of Jesus." *Asbury Theological Journal* 58 (2003): 167–86.

11

Philippians

N. T. Wright

Paul's letter to the Christians in Philippi is a small gem. Though it covers a good many well-known theological topics, including particularly Christology, soteriology, and eschatology, its chief and largely unremarked value for theological interpretation is the way in which it hammers out a Christian view of what it means to live within a pagan society. "Let your public behavior be worthy of the gospel of the Messiah" (1:27 AT). This refers not simply to Christian ethics, but also to how Christians behave in the public arena. Most modern readers of Paul have not considered the extraordinary challenge facing the young church, of how to negotiate a totally new way of living. What would it mean to give allegiance, in a city like Philippi, to Jesus as the world's true Lord (2:11)?

The letter is written from prison, to thank the Philippian church for their financial support. Those held in ancient prisons were not provided for by the authorities, and so were utterly dependent on family and friends. In Paul's case, traveling from place to place, this meant that he had to rely on the churches he had founded, and Philippi had come to his help (1:5; 2:25–30; 4:10–19). Many suppose the prison to be in Rome; a good case can be made for Ephesus, though not much turns on this. (Ephesus had its own Praetorian guard; 1:13.) Paul, it seemed, was aware that the charges against him could result in his death (1:18–26), though in prayer he had glimpsed that he still had work to do and so reckoned that he would be released.

The word he uses to describe the "partnership" into which he and the Philippians have entered, the business partnership in which they will support him when he needs their help (1:5, 7), is *koinōnia*, often translated "fellowship." As with some of Paul's other key terms, this word has often been allowed, in the history of interpretation, to slide into referring simply to the way in which Christians feel toward and with one another; but for Paul it was severely practical. It meant a sharing in common life that resulted directly in mutual support; and also it meant that Paul and his supporters belonged to one another with a family identity. What happens to one, happens to all. The fact that in 1:7 it is not clear whether Paul means that he holds them in his heart, or that they hold him in theirs, tells its own story, as does the whole opening paragraph (1:3–11). Initial theological reflection on Philippians ought to focus on the nature of *koinōnia* and the strange fact that so many modern churches manage to ignore it.

So what does it mean for the Philippians that Paul is in prison? Most likely, some kind of threat: if that is what the authorities are doing to our apostle, what will happen to us? This threat was already well known in Philippi, judging from the hints in various parts of the letter (e.g., 1:28–30). Living as Christians in the pagan environment of northern Greece (on the main road from Rome to the East, with a well-established Roman colony supplying some of the leading citizens) must have posed all kinds of problems. Christians would not join in the regular pagan festivals, including those in honor of the emperor. They would not offer sacrifices at pagan shrines, or take part in the other street-level pagan practices. Some of them might already have suffered in business from their newfound faith, as clients became suspicious or scornful and went elsewhere. Others may have run into actual verbal or physical abuse. Does this mean they have made a dreadful mistake? No, replies Paul; but from here on, you need to think through how to live appropriately within the world that has suddenly become strange to you and in turn is likely to regard you as a stranger.

That is what he is praying for the church in Philippi (1:9–11). First, he prays that they will love one another more and more (like *koinōnia*, the word *agapē* refers first and foremost to something you do, not something you feel). Second, he prays that they will do so "with knowledge and all discernment, so that they may be able to make right judgments about things that differ, so that they may be blameless and innocent for the day of the Messiah" (AT). Since Paul more or less repeats and expands this in

2:12–16, it ought to be clear that we are here in touch with one of the key aims of the letter. He is not, again, simply talking about "how to live as good Christians"; he is talking about how to work out what it means to live as a follower of Jesus Christ in a world where there are many things that are good and many things that are not. They are neither to reject everything in the surrounding world nor to embrace everything. They need to develop a keen sense of discrimination. If this set of questions fails to register as a topic in theological interpretation, it is a sign that the Scripture-reading church has forgotten part of its basic calling. It is much easier to decide either to go along with everything in the world or to reject everything in the world than to work out a mature, wise, and discriminating path of loyalty to Jesus as Lord amid the pressures and problems of life and society.

Paul brings them up to date with what has been happening to himself (1:12–26), and in doing so introduces one of the main themes of the letter: the union between the Messiah and his people. Paul is in prison because of his loyalty to the Messiah, and his life is so bound up with that of Jesus that his sole hope is for whatever happens to him to bring glory to his Lord. It is not entirely clear to whom he is referring when he speaks of some "announcing the Messiah because of envy and rivalry" in 1:15, 17 (AT). They may be rival Christian missionaries, but a good case can be made instead for seeing them as pagans who, affronted that Paul is declaring a crucified Jew to be the Lord of the world, are telling others that this is what he is saying. That, for Paul, would constitute "announcing the Messiah"; for him, "proclaiming Christ" (1:15) does not mean trying to persuade people to accept Jesus, but simply making the announcement, like a herald: Jesus, the Messiah, is Lord! As long as people are saying that, Paul declares, he will be content (1:18).

The main appeal of the letter is stated in 1:27–30. The Philippians must figure out how to live within their surrounding social and cultural world in a manner worthy of the announcement of the Messiah's good news. Central to this will be the unity of Christians, a favorite theme in Paul; opposition and persecution might threaten to split the church, but they must stand firm. Paul then develops this appeal in 2:1–4, which heaps up what to us appear almost impossible demands: think the same thing, have the same love, share the same soul, always seek one another's advantage and not your own. This is the radically different lifestyle that must characterize the Christian community and enable it to stand out, and stand firm, within the watching, curious, and potentially hostile world.

All of this is then undergirded and given specific focus and direction by the spectacular poem of 2:6–11. This is the point at which much of the history of the interpretation of Philippians has been concentrated, and especially on 2:6–7. These verses appear to give an account of the way in which Jesus can be identified with and as the preexistent divine being who became incarnate by "emptying himself" (2:7). Some nineteenth- and twentieth-century Lutheran and Anglican theologians have spoken of "kenotic Christology" (from the Greek *ekenōsen*, "emptied" [2:7 NRSV]) and have used this passage as a key to explore what aspect of Jesus' divinity was abandoned or put on hold when he became a human being. This inquiry goes back to the patristic period, but no special theories were worked out then. However, this is not Paul's concern. For him, as for John, the point is not that we know in advance who "God" is and can then, as it were, fit Jesus into that definition, but that only when looking at Jesus himself do we discover who the true God really is. The second half of the poem (2:9–11) insists, with its opening "therefore" (*dio*, 2:9), that the honor given to Jesus in his exaltation is the result of what has been accomplished in incarnation and crucifixion: he has done what only God can do. For theological as well as grammatical reasons, the key phrase in verse 6 should be translated, "He did not regard his equality with God as something to exploit." Jesus was always equal with God, and, so far from compromising his divinity, expressed that equality in incarnation and crucifixion. This passage stands at the heart of the theological reinterpretation of Jewish traditions in early Christianity. To Jesus is now given the glory that Israel's one and only God declares he will not share with another (Isa. 45:23; 48:11; Phil. 2:10–11).

All this wonderful Christology is placed in the service of Paul's deeply subversive critique of Caesar and his world. The implicit contrast throughout the poem, as in Mark 10:42–45, is between the way in which earthly rulers normally rule and the way in which Jesus expressed his divinity and arrived at his world sovereignty. And this leads back to the appeal of 2:13–14. Over against many interpretative traditions worrying about Paul telling people to "work out your salvation," as though this might compromise justification by faith, Paul means precisely: Therefore, figure out, calculate, and reckon it up, what your kind of "salvation" will mean in practice. Caesar offered one kind of "salvation": live under my rule and I will look after you—a kind of global protection racket. The salvation Jesus offered was of quite a different type, and it is up to communities of Christians to work out how to live within it. More particularly, they must bear in mind their calling to live as lights in the dark world.

The second chapter ends with an extensive recommendation for Timothy, and a warm passage about Epaphroditus, the Philippians' messenger to Paul. Both are held up as examples of the selfless service that Paul commends throughout.

The second half of the letter has sometimes been thought to be a separate composition, and certainly the link in 3:1 feels a bit jerky. But 3:2–21 has so many close thematic and linguistic connections to the earlier chapters, and to 2:6–11 in particular, that it looks as though Paul is consciously building on what he has just said. His appeal in chapter 3 is for the Philippians to be "imitating" him (3:17 NRSV), but this is initially strange. In 3:2–11 he describes in detail how he has abandoned his pride of ancestry and "righteousness under the law" (3:6 NRSV) so that he might find his identity and life as a member of the Messiah's people. He himself follows the pattern of renunciation and resurrection foreshadowed in 2:6–11. This passage integrates closely with the more-developed statements of "justification by faith," rather than by "the works of the law," as in Romans and Galatians. It strengthens the argument for seeing justification not simply as a truth about how sinners get saved but also as a truth about how Jews and Gentiles come together in a single family. The Philippians have no such ancestry or background in the Jewish law. But they do have pride of civic status, as one of the premier Roman cities and colonies in northern Greece. Maybe Paul is saying—this, too, is something with which theological interpretation of Philippians needs to reckon—that they must be prepared to regard their social and civic privileges in the same way that he has regarded his. They need to look at the world in which they live, not in its own terms, but from the perspective of the gospel. According to the gospel, the Lord Jesus, the royal Messiah, will come from heaven with all power vested in him, and will transform both the present situation of the little beleaguered church, surrounded by the wicked and idolatrous world (3:18–19), and the frail, mortal bodies of individual Christians. Paul here applies 2:9–11 to the particular situation of the church in a pagan environment. This is what it means to give allegiance to Jesus, not Caesar, as the world's true Lord.

This is what it means to "stand firm in the Lord" (4:1 NRSV). We should recognize, as a matter of urgently needed theological revision, that when Paul says "our citizenship is in heaven" in 3:20 (NRSV), he does not mean, "Therefore that is where we shall go when we die." That is not how the logic of citizenship worked. Roman citizens living in Philippi would not expect to return to Rome upon retirement, but to be agents of Roman civilization in Philippi and the surrounding countryside.

The central appeal of chapter 4 is, once more, to live within the wider world, not in a state of nervous anxiety at what may happen, but in total trust in the Lord himself (4:4–7) and in readiness to pray about every concern. This leads to the remarkable double command of 4:8–9. On the one hand, they are to think about anything at all that has the stamp of truth, holiness, justice, and so on. Paul is well aware, and wants them to be so aware, that the world is full of beauty and truth, and that they must celebrate it and not pretend that it is all confined to the church. On the other hand, when they think about how to behave, they must once more, as in 3:17, reflect on Paul's own modeling of Christian living in the world. Here is a point of theological interpretation that the twenty-first century church needs more than ever. Christian leaders have an awesome responsibility to model the life that the gospel produces. Others will follow their lead, for better and for worse.

The letter closes, as we saw, with further detailed thanks for the gift the Philippians have sent to Paul, and with reflections on the way in which God works strangely but powerfully to meet the needs of those who live and proclaim the gospel. Philippians, after all, is a severely practical letter, even though the Christology of 2:6–11 and the soteriology of 3:2–11 are among Paul's finest pieces of condensed theology. But that, too, is part of the point. Theological interpretation of Scripture needs constantly to remind itself that we know what true theology is, just as we know who the true God is, by looking at what it means to take the form of a servant.

Bibliography

Bockmuehl, M. *The Epistle to the Philippians.* BNTC. Black/Hendrikson, 1998.

Fee, G. *Paul's Letter to the Philippians.* NICNT. Eerdmans, 1995.

Oakes, P. *Philippians.* SNTSMS 110. Cambridge University Press, 2001.

O'Brien, P. *The Epistle to the Philippians.* NIGTC. Eerdmans, 1991.

Wright, N. T. *The Climax of the Covenant.* Fortress, 1992.

———. *What St. Paul Really Said.* Eerdmans, 1997.

12

Colossians

Sylvia C. Keesmaat

History of Interpretation

Throughout the history of Christian thought, Colossians has played a central role, particularly in relation to Christology and soteriology. The church fathers focused primarily on the hymn in Col. 1:15–20, where Paul's description of the Son as the image of the invisible God and the firstborn of all creation (1:15) provided the basis for the doctrine of the preexistence of Christ. This in turn gave rise to the doctrine of the two natures of Christ: "The pre-existent one is also the incarnate one and who yet at the same time bears the whole divine being in himself" (Schweizer 253; Gorday 12–14). Such an emphasis provided the impetus for seeing the work of God in the OT as continuous with the work of Jesus. Calvin later argued that 1:15–20 is not about the two natures but rather describes Jesus as the one who has made God visible to believers. The emphasis shifts, therefore, from Jesus' relation to God to his relation to believers and the result of such a relationship in their lives.

The second major contribution of Colossians in the history of interpretation was to discussions of soteriology, primarily whether salvation includes all of the natural world, the whole of the cosmos, and even all people (Gorday 15–21). More recently, Sittler has carried this theme forward in arguing that 1:15–20 shows that redemption embraces both history and nature and therefore has political, and especially ecological, implications. The radical nature of this redemption for all dimensions of life has continued to shape the soteriological thrust of discussion of Colossians into the present.

Ethically, Colossians initially provided the basis for condemnations of ascetic practice. For much of the history of interpretation, readers paid relatively little attention to the household codes of Col. 3:18–4:1, using them primarily to counteract the abuse of Christian freedom and equality. More recently, however, this passage has played a central role in ethical discussions concerning the role of women and the institution of slavery. Such discussions generally interpret Colossians as endorsing a restrictive social ethic that justifies both slavery and the subordination of women (D'Angelo; Martin). Such interpretations have provided one of the bases for the position that Colossians is post-Pauline. In such a context Colossians is seen to be evidence of a tendency toward a more hierarchical ethic in the development of the early church. While such views on the post-Pauline character of Colossians are widespread, they are by no means unchallenged (Wright, *Colossians*; Cannon).

The Message of Colossians and Its Relation to the Canon

Paul's letter to the Colossians is rooted in the story of Israel and in the story of Jesus. These two stories function as a challenge to the dominant story facing the Colossian Christians: the story of Rome. Such a challenge is evident from the outset of the letter, where Paul describes the gospel as bearing fruit and growing in the whole world (1:6), and later describes the Colossians themselves as bearing fruit and growing in the knowledge of God (1:10).

For the inhabitants of Colossae, the language of gospel (*euangelion*) carried strong imperial overtones. A central claim of Rome was that the empire achieved and guaranteed universal peace, the Pax Romana. The imperial gospel, moreover, assured the Colossians that fruitfulness and fertility was all around them. It was a claim that incessantly called everyone to acknowledge Rome as the source of abundance. Partaking in such abundance in the midst of scarce resources required fidelity to the empire and its structures, oppressive or not.

This was no new claim. Throughout its history, Israel constantly grappled with an empire's claims to be the source of abundance, security, and fertility.

But there was also a countertestimony within Israel's story, a witness to an alternative social vision that challenged the claims of empire. The fruitfulness of Yahweh, and the fruit that Israel was called to bear, was central to that countertestimony. Fertility and fruitfulness in the land on the one hand, and peace and security on the other, are rooted in a rejection of the militaristic consumerism of empire and the social and economic practices that support it. The language of such blessing is the language of fruitfulness (Lev. 26:3–6; Isa. 5:1–7; Ezek. 34:25–31; Mic. 4:1–5; Zech. 8:1–16).

These themes come to their climax in Jesus. The community that Jesus envisions is not only judged by its fruit but is itself a manifestation of the fruitfulness of Yahweh. At key points in the narrative—some of them foundational, some of them climactic—we meet the metaphors and language of fruitfulness (Matt. 13:23//Mark 4:20; Luke 8:15; Matt. 7:16–20; Luke 6:43–45).

By using the language of fruitfulness, with all of its overtones from the story of Israel and the preaching of Jesus, Paul in Colossians is proclaiming a different gospel, which bears fruit fundamentally different from the fruit of the empire.

Before Paul discusses that way of life, he describes the cosmic scope of this gospel and the nature of the reconciliation it brings. In 1:15–20 Paul alludes to Adam as the image of God; however, he does so in his description of Jesus, the second Adam. He also alludes to the creation of wisdom in Prov. 8:22, the firstborn of creation. There is a faint echo of Gen. 9:8–17, where God reaffirms the covenant with all living things, and the phrase "all living things" or "all flesh" is repeated nine times in the Greek. In Col. 1:15–20, the repetition of "all things" or "everything" occurs seven times. By confessing that in Jesus God reconciles all of creation to himself, Paul is reaffirming God's most foundational covenantal promise to be faithful to all of creation.

The identification of Jesus with God, and the linking of God's covenant promise to creation with the reconciliation of all things in Jesus through the cross, is a clear challenge to the empire. Not only does the language of image evoke Adam, it also evokes Caesar, whose images were ubiquitous throughout the ancient Roman world both in statues and on coins. The claim that Jesus is above all thrones, dominions, rulers, or powers challenges the throne, dominion, rule, and power of Rome. And while the Pax Romana is achieved and maintained through the public crucifixion of those who challenge Rome's rule, Jesus' blood shed on such a cross radically subverts imperial rule and establishes a more profound peace.

Here Paul is asserting the primacy of the story of Jesus over against the story of Rome. This alternative story line, with its proclamation of a different peace, is rooted deeply within the story of Israel. That story, however, is redefined in Jesus, in whom its central character finds expression.

In Col. 2 Paul reinforces this by describing a worldview that is attempting to capture the imagination of the Colossian Christians. Paul's description of this worldview echoes the scriptural prophetic polemic against idolatry (Walsh 8–9). Perhaps the best way to draw out the parallels is in the form of a chart.

The Colossian Philosophy	Idolatry
1. The philosophy is captivating (Col. 2:8).	1. Idolatry makes repentance and knowledge of God impossible (Hos. 5:4).
2. The philosophy is empty deceit (2:8), and a shadow without substance (2:17).	2. Idolatry is worthless, vanity, nothingness (Pss. 97:7; 115:4–7; 135:15–18; Isa. 44:9; 57:13; Jer. 2:5).
3. The philosophy is a human tradition (2:8), a human way of thinking (2:18), that imposes human commands and teaching (2:20).	3. Idols are constructed by human hands (Ps. 115:4; Isa. 2:8; 41:6–7; 44:11; Jer. 10:1–10; Hos. 8:4, 6; 13:2; Hab. 2:18).
4. The philosophy is puffed up without cause (2:18) and deceives people by employing so-called plausible arguments (2:4, 8).	4. Idolatry results in a deluded mind and a fundamental lack of knowledge (Isa. 44:18–20; Hos. 4:6); an idol is a teacher of lies (Hab. 2:18).
5. The philosophy is of no value in checking the flesh (2:23).	5. Idolatry is impotent, without value, and does not profit (Pss. 115:4–7; 135:15–18; Isa. 45:20; 46:1–2; Jer. 2:11; Hos. 7:16; Hab. 2:19).
6. The philosophy disqualifies, insists on self-abasement (2:18), and promotes severe treatment of the body (2:23).	6. Idolatry is a matter of exchanging glory for shame (Ps. 106:20; Jer. 2:11; Hos. 4:7; 7:16; 13:1–3; Rom. 1:23).

In these verses Paul's language evokes the prophetic critique of idolatry, and in so doing his critique of the empire finds a context in larger biblical tradition. For instance, "the proclamation that Christ triumphs over the rulers and authorities on the cross (2:15) is clearly rooted in the prophetic confession that Yahweh is Lord and shares glory with no idols (Isa 42:8; 48:11)" (Walsh 9). These overtones are heightened when put in parallel with Col. 1:15–20. The prophetic critique of idolatry is rooted in the confession that Yahweh, not the idols, is Creator of heaven and earth (Pss. 115:16; 135:5–7; Isa. 40:12–26; 44:9–28; 45:12, 18; Jer. 10:11–16; 51:15–19). So also Paul's critique of the philosophy is rooted in the assertion that Jesus is the one through whom and for whom all things were created (Col. 1:15–17).

As the results of such an echo, Paul alludes to empire and asserts that Jesus is the true image, not Caesar. Jesus is over all thrones, dominions, rulers, and powers. He is the head in whom all things hold together, not Caesar. And Jesus is the one in whom the Deity dwells. All of these assertions are rooted in the larger biblical narrative of Yahweh as the one who offers a salvation that defeats the captivity, deceitfulness, vanity, shame, and impotence of idols and the empires that image them.

Here we return to competing stories. If a life directed by idolatry constitutes forgetfulness of Yahweh's covenant in Israel's Scripture (Deut. 4:15–31; 6:10–15; 8:11–20), the succumbing to imperial idolatry means that the Colossian Christians have forgotten that they indwell the story of Jesus. "In Christ" they have died (2:20; 3:3), were buried (2:12), and were raised from the dead (2:12; 3:1). They set their minds on the ascended one (3:2–3) and anticipate his coming (3:4). Christ's death, burial, resurrection, ascension, and return form the narrative heart of the counterimperial ethic Paul elucidates in 3:1–17.

This alternative story and ethic culminate, however, in Paul's description of the "household code" in 3:18–4:1. Here Paul's argument is made or broken. It doesn't matter if Paul uses language that subverts the empire and its violent and oppressive practices, if in the end he affirms a patriarchal household structure that reinscribes economic control and violence. I have argued elsewhere that rather than reinscribing the hierarchy of the household in these verses, Paul is subverting them (Walsh and Keesmaat, ch. 11). Paul's instructions to the household have three surprising and subversive aspects. Many scholars have recognized the first aspect: Paul directly addresses not only the head of the household—husband, father, and master—but also women, children, and slaves. This has the effect of giving the dignity of participation to those who would have seldom been addressed as having status in the relationship.

Second, and often lost in English translation, is Paul's play on the language of Lord, or Master (*kyrios*). This is most striking in the section to slaves, where the rhetorical effect of the constant movement from the "masters according to the flesh" to "the Master" undermines the ultimate legitimacy of these earthly masters.

Third, when Paul tells slaves that they will receive an inheritance (3:24), he is evoking the language of slaves receiving an inheritance in the year of Jubilee (Lev. 25). For those with ears to hear, Paul's language suggests that in the story of Jesus, slaves are to be set free, for they too are to receive an inheritance. As a result, in these verses Paul challenges the most fundamental hierarchy in which power was centralized in the Roman Empire.

These verses are thus shown to be a working out of Paul's words in 3:12 and following. There a self-sacrificing love, manifesting itself in compassion, kindness, humility, meekness, and patience, comes to its culmination in an ethic of forgiveness, love, and the rule of peace. This is not the peace of the empire (the Pax Romana), but the peace of a different ruler, Christ (3:13–15). In light of these verses, and in light of v. 11, where Paul proclaims that "there is no longer Greek and Jew, circumcised and uncircumcised, barbarian, Scythian, slave and free" (NRSV), a subversive word to slaves that proclaims their liberation makes perfect sense.

For the Colossian Christians, Paul's allusions to Israel's Scriptures provide an alternative story line that fundamentally challenges the claims of the story of the empire.

The Theology of Colossians

The challenge that Colossians provides to its imperial context is overwhelmingly rooted in a strong theology of creation. Paul describes himself as the servant of a gospel that "has been proclaimed to every creature under heaven" (1:23). This assertion comes after the hymn of 1:15–20, with its echoes of creational monotheism (Wright, "Poetry") and its repeated affirmation that *all things* in heaven and on earth were created in Christ, through Christ, and for Christ. It is because all things were created good in Christ that all things are now reconciled in Christ.

At the heart of the philosophy was its insistence on self-abasement, asceticism, and severe treatment of the body (2:17, 20–23). As we saw above, Paul describes these practices as idolatrous and emphasizes Jesus as the one who has triumphed over all other thrones and rulers and powers. Thus he asserts that God in Jesus is the true Creator of the heaven and earth, over against the idolatrous forces that seek to enslave the Colossian Christians (2:8). Jesus is the one who is now the Creator of all, and in the face of all that would seek to deny the goodness of his creation, Paul is asserting that as Creator he has not only vanquished all other creation-denying rulers (2:15), but has also renewed the creation.

In addition, not only is Jesus the true image of the Creator God, but those who have clothed themselves with the new self are "being renewed in knowledge according to the image of [the] creator" (3:10). The Colossian Christians themselves bear the image of that Creator and hence witness to the world the forgiveness, love, and reconciling peace that Jesus has achieved through the blood of the cross (1:20; 3:13–15). At the end of this letter, Paul's subversion of the household codes reveals how far-reaching this creational reconciliation goes. The household structure he is describing was the basic economic, social, and political unit of first-century culture. Hence, Paul is daring to assert that those who image the Creator will act differently in social, economic, and political spheres. From what we know of the church in the first century, this was indeed the case.

In a culture such as ours, where the idolatry of the market necessarily results in disregard for almost every creature under heaven, Colossians provides a word of hope. Just as in the first century Paul proclaimed that Jesus, not Caesar, was the one who had reconciled the whole of the world, so Paul proclaims to us that Jesus, not globalization, reconciles the whole of the world. Just as Paul proclaimed to the Colossians that the forces that deny the goodness of this creation are idolatrous, so he proclaims to us today that those economic and political practices that destroy the creation and those in it are idolatrous. And just as Paul proclaimed that the lordship of Christ challenged the imperial structures for familial, social, and economic life, so Paul proclaims to us today that the lordship of Christ challenges our societal structures that shape familial, social, and economic life in service of empire and its oppression.

Paul ends Colossians by asking the believers to remember his chains (4:18). We do well to remember them, for they indicate where such a subversive theology could lead, not only in Paul's time, but also in ours.

Bibliography

Cannon, G. *The Use of Traditional Materials in Colossians*. Mercer University Press, 1983.

D'Angelo, M. "Colossians." In *A Feminist Commentary*. Vol. 2 of *Searching the Scriptures*, ed. E. S. Fiorenza. Crossroad, 1994.

Dunn, J. D. G. *The Epistles to the Colossians and to Philemon*. NIGTC. Eerdmans, 1996.

Gorday, P. *Colossians, 1–2 Thessalonians, 1–2 Timothy, Titus, Philemon*. ACCSNT 9. InterVarsity, 2000.

Lincoln, A. *The Letter to the Colossians*. NIB 9. Abingdon, 2000.

Lincoln, A., and A. J. M. Wedderburn. *The Theology of the Later Pauline Letters*. Cambridge University Press, 1993.

MacDonald, M. *Colossians and Philemon*. SP 17. Liturgical Press, 2000.

Martin, R. *Colossians and Philemon*. NCB. Eerdmans, 1981.

Schweizer, E. *The Letter to the Colossians*, trans. A. Chester. Fortress, 1981.

Sittler, J. "Call to Unity." *Ecumenical Review* 14 (1961–62): 177–87.

Walsh, B. "Late/Post Modernity and Idolatry: A Contextual Reading of Colossians 2:8–3:4." *Ex Aud* 15 (1999): 1–17.

Walsh, B., and S. Keesmaat. *Colossians Remixed*. InterVarsity, 2004.

Wilson, W. *The Hope of Glory*. Brill, 1997.

Wright, N. T. *The Epistles of Paul to the Colossians and Philemon*. TNTC. Eerdmans, 1986.

———. "Poetry and Theology in Colossians 1.15–20." Pages 99–119 in *The Climax of the Covenant*. T&T Clark, 1991.

13

1 Thessalonians

Charles A. Wanamaker

First Thessalonians holds a unique place among the writings of the NT in the view of many contemporary scholars because it is widely believed that 1 Thessalonians is not only Paul's first extant letter, but also the earliest extant writing of Christianity. If this is correct then 1 Thessalonians gives us our earliest window on the theology of nascent Christianity. Strikingly, this theology is communicated in the form of a letter and through the medium of apocalyptic discourse. Both of these points are significant. Beker (*Paul*; and "Recasting") argues that Paul's letters are characterized by contingency and coherence. The contingency results from the unique situation addressed by each letter; the coherence derives from Paul's interpretation of the Christ event through the master symbolism of Jewish apocalyptic thought. A proper interpretation of 1 Thessalonians requires that both of these points be kept in mind.

History of Interpretation

The earliest extant commentaries on 1 Thessalonians come from the Antiochene school of theology in the fourth and fifth centuries. The school approached Scripture as a historical document and as a result sought the meaning intended by the inspired author. This posed a problem for them since in 4:15 Paul seems to place himself among the living at the time of the parousia, but if this is what he intended, history proved him wrong. As a result the tendency was simply to deny that Paul referred to himself in order to avoid the apostle being wrong. Some contemporary commentators follow the same approach.

During the Middle Ages commentators often merely reproduced the church fathers or resorted to allegorical exegesis. With the Protestant Reformation allegorical interpretation was replaced by grammatical and literal interpretations. The legacy of the early Reformers meant that scholars became interested in historical questions with respect to the Bible. In the case of 1 Thessalonians Hugo Grotius in the early seventeenth century raised questions regarding the order in which Paul wrote the Thessalonian letters, arguing for a reversed sequence to the canonical order. The issue that he first posed, the relation between the Thessalonians letters, has remained a significant part of Thessalonians studies to this day. Grotius's arguments for the priority of 2 Thessalonians have been developed significantly during the last two centuries. But others have claimed that 2 Thessalonians is a post-Pauline forgery.

In the nineteenth century Baur questioned the Pauline authorship of 1 Thessalonians, but his view failed to carry conviction. More recently some (e.g., Richard, *Thessalonians*) have claimed that it is a compilation of two or more letters based on form-critical considerations regarding the multiple thanksgivings. Several scholars (e.g., Pearson) have claimed that 2:14–16 is a Deutero-Pauline interpolation because of its anti-Jewish character. A recent debate has also emerged over whether 2:1–12 is an apostolic apology against opponents criticizing Paul (Weima), or whether the apostle was employing a self-description derived from the ideal philosopher (Malherbe, *Paul*). As with other Pauline letters, interpreters have been interested in the question of whether Paul was making use of various Jewish and Christian traditional materials in composing his letter. In the last twenty years rhetorical analysis has been employed extensively in the interpretation of 1 Thessalonians in order to understand Paul's persuasive strategy (e.g., Jewett), and Malherbe (*Paul*) has attempted to show that the pastoral nature of Paul's letter was indebted to the tradition of moral philosophers of antiquity.

Hearing the Message of 1 Thessalonians

The message of 1 Thessalonians originally addressed a community of recent converts from paganism (1:9–10). Following their acceptance of

Paul's gospel, they experienced serious opposition from their fellow citizens (1:6; 2:14; 3:3). In spite of persecution and the premature departure of Paul (2:17), they remained faithful to Christ and loyal to Paul (3:6). In this situation the essential message of the letter served the twin pastoral functions of encouraging and exhorting the Thessalonians. Paul presented his message through a carefully constructed introduction (1:2–10) that introduces the main themes of the letter, an extended narrative of his relationship with the Thessalonians (2:1–3:10), and an exhortative section (4:1–5:22), which includes an eschatological clarification regarding the resurrection (4:13–18).

Much of 1 Thess. 1–3 reads like a narrative devoted to recounting aspects of Paul's and the Thessalonians' experience. Beneath the surface, however, Paul seeks to encourage his readers by reminding them of how they impressed other Christians by their response to persecution (1:4–10), and by showing them that through suffering they became imitators of himself and the Lord (1:6), as well as the Judean Christians (2:14–16). He also indicates that he has a special affection for them (2:7b–12, 19–20; 3:1–10). In 2:1–12 Paul's account of his ministry among the Thessalonians functions to reconfirm the Thessalonians in the pattern of Christian behavior that they had seen him demonstrate in his ministry.

In the main exhortative section Paul introduces a discussion about how the readers should live as Christians. His first topic concerns sexual ethics appropriate for those called to holiness (4:3–8), while in 4:9–12 he directs them to love one another as God has taught them to do and to behave appropriately toward those outside the community of faith. Paul then offers an important theological clarification regarding participation in the parousia of Christ (4:13–18), followed by an exhortation to ethical and religious vigilance as they wait for the coming of their Lord, through whom they are to obtain salvation (5:1–11). Before concluding the letter, Paul offers a series of short exhortations on how to live the Christian life (5:12–22).

1 Thessalonians and the Canon

Among the letters of Paul, 1 Thessalonians does not appear to be a very significant theological writing because it primarily served a pastoral function and as such contains little doctrinal material on topics like sin and the law, justification by faith, and the cross and resurrection of Christ. Nevertheless, 1 Thess. 4–5 does have theological importance within the context of the canon of Scripture. First, these chapters contain a great deal of ethical exhortation and community instruction that contribute to our understanding of what Christian identity is and how Christians should live lives of holiness in order to please God. Second, 4:13–17 contains an important discussion of the parousia, or return of Christ. In a number of respects 4:13–17 shows conceptual connections with the eschatologically charged passages of Mark 13, Matt. 24, and Luke 17. The fact is that Paul identifies what he is saying in 4:15–17 as "the word of the Lord" (NRSV). The close verbal similarities between these verses and Matt. 24:29–31 and 40–41, in particular, suggest that this passage may be a reference to the Jesus tradition regarding the coming of the Son of Man from heaven. The coming of the day of the Lord "like a thief in the night" (5:2) may also derive from the apocalyptic tradition of the coming of the Son of Man found in Matt. 24:23–27.

Although the OT is nowhere directly cited, there are allusions to it, particularly in the apocalyptic eschatological sections. For example, the expression "the day of the Lord" in 5:2 was taken over from the OT "day of Yahweh" (e.g., Amos 5:18–20; Joel 1:15; 2:31–32). Similarly, the metaphor of judgment coming like "sudden labor pains" in 5:3 is well attested in judgment passages in the OT (e.g., Isa. 13:6–8; Jer. 6:22–30), as is the light and darkness metaphor in 5:4–5 (e.g., Job 22:9–11; Ps. 82:5; Isa. 2:5; 9:2). Thus, Paul either directly or through Jewish apocalyptic traditions makes important use of the OT.

1 Thessalonians and Theology

At the center of the theological thought of 1 Thessalonians stands the belief that God elects (1:4) and then calls (2:12; 5:24) believers through the message of the gospel (1:5; 2:13), and that he appoints them to future salvation through Jesus Christ, who died for them so that they might live with him at his victorious coming from heaven (5:9–10). The future salvation to which they are called means that, unlike those who do not believe, they will not be subject to divine wrath on the day of judgment (1:9–10). From this central theological point flow several other key considerations.

First, faith represents the necessary response to the message of the gospel for those who would be saved (1:5–10). But it is more than this. It designates the trust, commitment, and loyalty that form the core elements in the Christian's relationship with God and Jesus Christ. The Thessalonians demonstrated their faith in God by remaining loyal in the face of persecution by their fellow citizens. Such faith, maintained under adverse circumstances, can provide encouragement to others (3:7). But more importantly, God reciprocates with faithfulness toward those whom he has called. Therefore, those who trust in God may rely upon God to keep them safe and without blame until the parousia of the Lord Jesus Christ (5:23–24).

Second, God wills that believers should be holy or sanctified (4:3). Malherbe (*Thessalonians*, 343) identifies this theological theme, along with the election and call of believers, as the two main themes of the letter. Fundamental to the concept of sanctification is the idea of separation from what is impure (4:7). This separation involves both divine action and human effort. God's call through the gospel of Christ involves believers' sanctification by God (4:7). Nevertheless, God will only complete the process of sanctification at the parousia of Jesus Christ (3:13; 5:23). At the same time sanctification requires moral endeavor on the part of believers. In 4:3 sanctification, separation from all forms of immorality, constitutes the ethical response of believers as they seek to please God (4:1). It also serves to distinguish them from their pagan neighbors (4:5). To reject this requirement of the faith is to reject divine authority itself (4:7–8). Positively, sanctification is closely associated with the love that Christians are called to show toward fellow members of the community, as well as to outsiders (3:12–13). Just as much as maintaining ethical purity separates Christians from those who are not believers, so doing deeds of love toward one's brothers and sisters in the faith also distinguishes and therefore separates Christians from outsiders (4:9–10; 1:3; Yarbrough 86–87).

Third, the theme of hope suffuses the letter. In introducing the main topics to be covered, Paul twice alludes to his readers' eschatological hope (1:3, 9–10). The main body of the letter, 2:1–5:22, is bracketed by 1:9–10 and 5:23, in which Paul stresses the eschatological hope of the Thessalonians. In 3:13 Paul invokes the theme of eschatological hope in the transition to the main exhortative section of the letter. Elsewhere in the letter Paul refers to eschatological hope in 2:12, 19; 4:13–18; 5:1–4, 9–10. With so many references, particularly at crucial points in the structure of the letter, it is clear that the eschatological hope of apocalyptic thought plays a fundamental role in the letter. Like moral purity and love for the family of God, Christian hope also serves to separate the followers of Christ from outsiders (4:13). First Thessalonians 4:15–17 offers a word from the Lord Jesus himself regarding the coparticipation in the parousia by both living and deceased Christians and the promise of eternal life in his presence. Knowledge of this hope means that death has lost its power for the believer in Christ, unlike those who lack this hope. The hoped-for salvation of Christians stands in complete contrast to the destiny of those without faith, who will be subject to divine wrath at the coming of the Lord. Theologically, hope for eternal life requires vigilance and ethical preparedness on the part of Christ's followers (5:1–11).

Finally, and often unnoticed, 1 Thessalonians provides resources for a theology of ministry. Paul sets out the character of his own ministry in 2:1–12. The goal of his ministry was to declare the gospel in order to please God, not other humans (2:2–4), and to build up his converts in the faith (2:11–12). The passage also underscores the ethical qualities of his ministry as well as the exemplary character of his commitment to the Thessalonians (2:3–8, 10–11). All of this is every bit as relevant today as in Paul's time, as is his instruction to the community to love and respect those who minister to them (5:12–13).

From this brief discussion of the themes in 1 Thessalonians, we may conclude that the theological value of 1 Thessalonians for Christians today is perhaps much greater than has often been recognized. It speaks to how Christians should live in the world while waiting with hope for the parousia of Christ.

Bibliography

Beker, J. C. *Paul the Apostle*. 1980. Reprint, T&T Clark, 1989.

———. "Recasting Pauline Theology: The Coherence-Contingency Scheme as Interpretive Model." Pages 15–24 in *Thessalonians, Philippians, Galatians, Philemon*, ed. J. Bassler. Vol. 1 of *Pauline Theology*. Fortress, 1991.

Chapa, J. "Is First Thessalonians a Letter of Consolation?" *NTS* 40 (1994): 150–60.

Collins, R., ed. *The Thessalonian Correspondence*. BETL. Leuven University Press, 1990.

Donfried, K. *Paul, Thessalonica, and Early Christianity*. Eerdmans, 2002.

———. "The Theology of 1 Thessalonians." Pages 1–79 in *The Theology of the Shorter Pauline Letters*, ed. K. Donfried and I. H. Marshall. Cambridge University Press, 1993.

Jewett, R. *The Thessalonian Correspondence*. FF. Fortress, 1986.

Lyons, G. *Pauline Autobiography*. SBLDS. Scholars Press, 1985.

Malherbe, A. *The Letters to the Thessalonians*. AB 32B. Doubleday, 2000.

———. *Paul and the Thessalonians*. Fortress, 1987.

Marshall, I. H. *1 and 2 Thessalonians*. NCB. Eerdmans, 1983.

Meeks, W. "Social Function of Apocalyptic Language in Pauline Christianity." Pages 687–705 in *Apocalypticism in the Mediterranean World and the Near East*, ed. D. Hellholm. Mohr, 1983.

Pearson, B. "1 Thessalonians 2:13–16: A Deutero-Pauline Interpolation." *HTR* 64 (1971): 79–94.

Plevnik, J. *Paul and the Parousia*. Hendrickson, 1997.

Richard, E. J. "Early Pauline Thought: An Analysis of 1 Thessalonians." Pages 39–51 in *Thessalonians, Philippians, Galatians, Philemon,* ed. J. M. Bassler. Vol. 1 of *Pauline Theology*. Fortress, 1991.

———. *First and Second Thessalonians*. SP 11. Liturgical, 1995.

Wanamaker, C. "Apocalyptic Discourse, Paraenesis and Identity Maintenance in 1 Thessalonians." *Neot* 36 (2002): 131–45.

———. *The Epistles to the Thessalonians*. NIGTC. Eerdmans, 1990.

Weima, J. "The Function of 1 Thessalonians 2:1–12 and the Use of Rhetorical Criticism: A Response to Otto Merk." Pages 114–31 in *The Thessalonians Debate,* ed. K. Donfried and J. Beutler. Eerdmans, 2000.

Wiles, G. *Paul's Intercessory Prayers*. SNTSMS 24. Cambridge University Press, 1974.

Yarbrough, O. *Not like the Gentiles*. SBLDS 80. Scholars Press, 1985.

14

2 Thessalonians

CHARLES A. WANAMAKER

In the modern period the interpretation of 2 Thessalonians has proved far more controversial than 1 Thessalonians because of three related uncertainties. First, the letter's relationship to 1 Thessalonians has been the subject of considerable debate. Second and closely related to the first, scholars have frequently contested the Pauline authorship of the letter. Third, because of the first two uncertainties and the limited information in the text, the precise situation addressed by the letter has proved elusive. Naturally, the position taken on these issues has a significant bearing on the general interpretation of the letter and more specifically on its theological interpretation (Bassler, "Peace").

History of Interpretation

The general history of commentating on 2 Thessalonians closely parallels the history for 1 Thessalonians. The elusive nature of the apocalyptic discourse in 2 Thess. 2:1–12 has made it a fertile ground for exegetical speculation from the patristic period onward. Because most interpreters up until the modern period understood the passage to be prophetic, they linked their explanations of 2:1–12 to historical circumstances of their own period. The "man of lawlessness" (2:3–4) was early identified with the antichrist of the Johannine letters. Tertullian thought that the figure would arise on the ruins of the Roman state. He, like Chrysostom, believed the restraining force mentioned in 2:6–7 to be the Roman Empire, though Chrysostom mentions that some thought the restrainer was the Holy Spirit. The reference to the temple of God (2:4) was often taken literally, and some interpreters therefore believed that the temple in Jerusalem would have to be rebuilt for the prophecy to be fulfilled. Others understood the temple metaphorically as a reference to the church.

For the Reformers, 2:1–12 proved an invaluable scriptural weapon in their attack on the papacy. Calvin, for example, regularly referred to the pope as the antichrist, citing 2:3–4. He claimed that the papacy had arrogated to itself the honor and glory due to God alone, fulfilling the prophecy in 2:4. Some Protestants even claimed that the seat taken by the antichrist in the temple was the seat of the apostle Peter, usurped by the pope.

In the seventeenth century Hugo Grotius set the course for the modern study of 2 Thessalonians when arguing that 3:17, with its reference to Paul's own signature, only made sense if written at the end of Paul's first letter to the Thessalonians, not his second letter. His study raised the wider issue of the relationship of 1 and 2 Thessalonians.

Around 1800 J. Schmidt maintained that 2 Thess. 2:1–12 was an interpolation into an otherwise authentic letter. He based his conclusion on two points. First, he claimed that a contradiction existed between the sequence of events prior to the parousia of Christ in 2:1–12 and the suddenness of the parousia in 1 Thess. 4:13–5:11, and second that the antichrist fantasy in 2:1–12 was un-Pauline in character. The supposed tension between the eschatology of 1 and 2 Thessalonians has been a recurring feature in subsequent claims rejecting Pauline authorship of 2 Thessalonians.

In 1839 F. Kern rejected the authenticity of 2 Thessalonians. He maintained that 2 Thessalonians showed signs of literary dependence on 1 Thessalonians, and that 3:17 was part of the attempt by a forger to secure acceptance of his work in the name of Paul. At the turn of the twentieth century Wrede further developed Kern's literary approach. His work largely set the parameters of the debate for those rejecting Pauline authorship until the work of Trilling in 1972. Trilling consolidated and further developed the argument against Pauline authorship to the extent that, it is fair to say, a majority of critical scholars now reject the Pauline origins of 2 Thessalonians. Trilling's case, however, is far less compelling under scrutiny than is often appreciated (see Wanamaker, *Epistles*, 17–28; Malherbe, *Letters*, 364–70).

Hearing the Message of 2 Thessalonians

The starting point for hearing the message of 2 Thessalonians, like all of Paul's letters, begins with the recognition that the message of the letter is contingent upon the circumstances that Paul believed himself to be addressing. The message that we hear when listening to 2 Thessalonians depends heavily on the assumptions we make regarding the three uncertainties mentioned in the first paragraph. In this article I assume the following: (1) Paul wrote 2 Thessalonians. (2) He did so prior to writing 1 Thessalonians. (3) He did so at a time when he believed that the Thessalonian Christians were experiencing persecution on account of their new faith in God and Jesus Christ (see Wanamaker, *Epistles*, 17–28, 37–45).

The letter deals with three main issues. First, in 1:4–12 we find the theme of retributive justice, in which an eschatological reversal is promised. The current persecutors of the community are threatened with divine vengeance on the judgment day, while the persecuted are promised relief from their affliction. The promise of retributive vengeance to bring comfort and encouragement is unusual in Paul. Since he addressed it to a community that was powerless in the face of persecution and believed that God was just, it is at least understandable. Second, in 2:1–2 Paul exhorts the readers not to believe that the day of the Lord has already come. Presumably their experience of persecution may have led some to believe that the woes associated with the parousia of the Lord had come (Aus, "Relevance," 260–65). Paul presents evidence in 2:3–12 that the day of the Lord cannot have come yet by outlining an apocalyptic, eschatological scenario leading up to the day of the Lord. As part of this, Paul includes an etiology for the lawlessness or evil that has led to the persecution of the Thessalonians (2:7–12). The apocalyptic scenario in 2:3–12 is unparalleled in Paul or anywhere else in the NT for that matter (Malherbe, *Letters*, 427).

Finally, in 3:6–15 Paul both instructs and exhorts regarding the problem of idleness among some members of the community who were not making any effort to provide for themselves. Russell has shown that the problem may have had its origins in the poor entering into client relations with better-off members of the community, thereby putting their Christian patrons under financial pressure. Paul begins by instructing the readers not to have fellowship with believers who are refusing to work for a living

(3:6, 10–11). Such behavior, he indicates, runs contrary to the example that he set when preaching in Thessalonica (3:7–9). He then both commands and exhorts those who are living in idleness to mend their ways by working for a living and living quietly (3:12). In closing, he exhorts the hearers of the letter to break fellowship with any who do not obey what he has instructed, but also to continue admonishing such people to reform themselves (3:14–15).

Apart from the main points, Paul seeks to encourage and comfort his readers in their difficult circumstances through thanksgivings in 1:3–4 and 2:13–14, as well as through his wish-prayer in 2:16–17 and his prayer-request and promise of assurance in 3:1–5.

2 Thessalonians and the Canon

In the modern era 2 Thessalonians has not been considered a very significant writing. Its limited and highly contextual message, colored by apocalypticism, has marginalized it within the canon.

Not surprisingly, 2 Thessalonians is most closely related in vocabulary, content, and function to 1 Thessalonians. Several of its features, however, are connected to other canonical writings. The theme of the avenging retribution of God, which plays an important role in the book of Revelation (Collins), derives from the OT. Aus ("Relevance"), for example, has demonstrated a close relation between 2 Thess. 1 and Isa. 66, where the theme of divine vengeance occurs. Paul himself employs this theme in Rom. 12:17–21, although the context is quite different from 2 Thessalonians, and Rev. 6:9–17 and 19:2 utilize the theme of retributive vengeance specifically in relation to the persecution and martyrdom of the people of God. Although no OT passage is directly quoted, Bruce (149–53) has identified a number of OT passages parallel in thought or wording to various phrases and ideas found in 1:5–10. The judgment scene in 1:9–10 has some affinities with the coming of the Son of Man in the Gospel tradition (Wenham 347–49), and with the separation and destruction of the unrighteous in Matt. 25:31–46.

The eschatological gathering of Christians mentioned in 2:1 is redolent of a number of OT passages (e.g., Isa. 43:4–7), but the apocalyptic scenario of 2:3–12 is unparalleled in the canon. Nevertheless, several of the individual features of the scenario are connected to the OT. For example, the lawless one who defiles the temple of God should be read against Dan. 11:31, 36. His arrogation of divine status is perhaps modeled on Ezek.

28:1–10 and Isa. 14:4–20. The idea that God sends a deluding influence (2:11) is well known from the OT (e.g., 2 Sam. 24:1), and occurs in the NT (Rom. 1:24–32).

2 Thessalonians and Theology

The highly contextual and pastoral character of the letter means that Paul's theological thought is narrowly focused on addressing specific issues for his readers, issues that do not resonate very well with many Christians today. This naturally has limited the theological value of 2 Thessalonians for the contemporary church.

In relation to 1:4–12 and 2:8–12, Donfried points to a theology of divine justice, typical of Jewish and Christian apocalyptic thought, but this is a component of what Aus and Bassler ("Enigmatic Sign") have called a theology of suffering. In their account, the theology of suffering emerged in Judaism during the second and first centuries BCE. This theology believed in God's retributive justice and understood the present suffering of the righteous as the means by which they satisfied the just demands of God for their own sins in order to be made worthy of future salvation. Malherbe (*Thessalonians*, 408) suggests that Paul selectively employs this tradition. In 1:4–5 (part of the sentence running from 1:3–11 in the Greek) the suffering of the Thessalonians is not described as satisfying God's justice for their own sins; instead, it makes them worthy of the divine kingdom. In doing so it demonstrates God's justice toward them. A second component of this suffering theology maintains that God will send affliction to punish the godless, who currently afflict the righteous, leading to a just reversal of current unjust circumstances. In 1:6–10 Paul makes this very point. The combination of future blessing for the suffering righteous and punishment for evildoers because they afflict the righteous has often provided encouragement to the oppressed people of God, but Collins rightly warns of the potential dehumanizing effects of the desire for vengeance.

The scenario in 2:3–12, which demonstrates that the day of the Lord has not come (2:1–2), takes us to the heart of Paul's own apocalyptically oriented eschatology. The obscure thought of the mythic-symbolic language occurring in the passage is theologically difficult for contemporary Christians to deal with at face value. For example, the temple of God (2:4) has not existed for nearly two millennia. If the mystery of lawlessness (anarchy) was already at work in Paul's day (2:7), and Paul expected the return of Christ during his lifetime (1 Thess. 4:17), what are we to make of the last 1,900 years of human history? One possibility is to look at what led to Paul's apocalyptic eschatology. The answer seems to be a sense of powerlessness and alienation caused by pervasive evil within the social, economic, political, and religious structures of the day. This same sense is not unknown to contemporary Christians in many parts of the world, as is the refusal of people to accept the truth of the gospel and instead to engage in evil without constraint (2:10–12). In the face of this, 2:3–12; 2:13–17; and 3:1–5 provide a reminder that God is ultimately in control of human destiny. Those who perpetrate evil will suffer God's recompense of condemnation; those who receive the gospel will share in the glory of the Lord Jesus Christ at his coming. Christian hope assures us that God's justice will ultimately triumph over all forms of evil, and that God's elect who already have "eternal comfort and good hope" in the present (2:16 NRSV) will be empowered for Christian living (2:17).

Bibliography

See also bibliography for chapter 13, "1 Thessalonians."

Aus, R. "God's Plan and God's Power: Isaiah 66 and the Restraining Factors of 2 Thess 2:6–7." *JBL* 96 (1977): 537–53.

———. "The Relevance of Isaiah 66:7 to Revelation 12 and 2 Thessalonians 1." *ZNW* 67 (1976): 252–68.

Bassler, J. "The Enigmatic Sign: 2 Thessalonians 1:5." *CBQ* 46 (1984): 496–510.

———. "Peace in All Ways: Theology in the Thessalonian Letters: A Response to R. Jewett, E. Krentz, and E. Richard." Pages 71–85 in *Thessalonians, Philippians, Galatians, Philemon*, ed. J. Bassler. Vol. 1 of *Pauline Theology*. Fortress, 1991.

Bruce, F. F. *1 and 2 Thessalonians*. WBC 45. Word, 1982.

Collins, A. Y. "Persecution and Vengeance in the Book of Revelation." Pages 729–49 in *Apocalypticism in the Mediterranean World and the Near East*, ed. D. Hellholm. Mohr/Siebeck, 1983.

Donfried, K. "The Theology of 2 Thessalonians." Pages 88–113 in *The Theology of the Shorter Pauline Letters*, ed. K. Donfried and I. H. Marshall. Cambridge University Press, 1993.

Giblin, C. *The Threat to Faith*. AnBib 31. Pontifical Biblical Institute, 1967.

Jewett, R. "A Matrix of Grace: The Theology of 2 Thessalonians as a Pauline Letter." Pages 71–85 in *Thessalonians, Philippians, Galatians, Philemon*, ed. J. Bassler. Vol. 1 of *Pauline Theology*. Fortress, 1991.

Krentz, E. "Through a Lens: Theology and Fidelity in 2 Thessalonians." Pages 71–85 in *Thessalonians, Philippians, Galatians, Philemon*, ed. J. Bassler. Vol. 1 of *Pauline Theology*. Fortress, 1991.

Rigaux, B. *Saint Paul les épitres aux Thessaloniciens.* ÉBib. Gabalda, 1956.

Russell, R. "The Idle in 2 Thess 3.6–12: An Eschatological or a Social Problem?" *NTS* 34 (1988): 105–19.

Trilling, W. *Untersuchungen zum zweiten Thessalonischerbrief.* St. Benno, 1972.

Wenham, D. "Paul and the Synoptic Apocalypse." Pages 345–75 in vol. 2 of *Gospel Perspectives,* ed. R. T. France and D. Wenham. JSOT, 1981.

15

1 Timothy

I. HOWARD MARSHALL

With 2 Timothy and Titus, 1 Timothy is one of the three "Pastoral Epistles" addressed by Paul to his co-workers rather than to congregations. It deals with the task of Timothy as overseer of the congregation(s) in Ephesus and is largely concerned with the danger of opposition and heresy in the church, the need for measures to ensure the proper maintenance of congregational life (including care for widows and the conduct of elders), the development of reliable leadership (overseers and deacons), the responsibilities and personal life of Timothy as local pastor, and the curbing of disturbing influences (unacceptable teaching by both male teachers and women). It is not primarily concerned with articulating theology, but nevertheless has considerable theological importance.

History of Interpretation

The origin of the letter is disputed. Until modern times it was accepted as a letter of Paul, probably written toward the end of his life around the same time as 2 Timothy and Titus, with which it has close links in style and content. Recognition of its unusual style and the impression that it reflects a post-Pauline situation led to the hypothesis that it is a pseudonymous composition, possibly from the early second century. In it a partisan of Paul endeavors to call the church back to a Pauline position, although in so doing he presents a theology that has developed beyond Paul in an early catholic direction. Thus, it is counted as emphasizing the static reproduction of tradition; the creation of a fixed church order, with leadership by appointed officers replacing the less-structured, informal charismatic ministry of an earlier period; and the development of a way of life that conforms more to the patterns of secular society and wards off criticism and persecution.

Alongside this majority position that the document is substantially later and reflects interests around the turn of the first century, strong support is still being expressed for composition by Paul himself (perhaps with an active amanuensis). A related option is for the use of Pauline materials (oral or written) by a close associate in the immediate post-Pauline period via a letter intended to maintain Paul's influence without any attempt to deceive readers. Since in my view there is no compelling evidence for a late date, 1 Timothy should be read as a document that belongs to the period around the close of Paul's life, whether from his lifetime or soon afterward.

Hearing the Message of 1 Timothy

First Timothy reflects an understanding of the gospel that centers on God as Savior, who wants all people to be saved and to know the truth (2:4). The purpose of God makes universal provision for salvation even though it is clear that salvation becomes a reality only in the case of believers (4:10). The presupposition is that all people are sinners and therefore need to be delivered from sin and its consequences. Christ Jesus came into the world to save sinners; he is depicted as the mediator between God and humankind, the implication being that sinners stand under divine judgment (1:15; 2:5). The statement that Jesus gave himself as a ransom for all (2:6, echoing Mark 10:45) constitutes the gospel to which people respond in faith. Paul himself is an example of such belief; he was shown mercy and forgiven because he had sinned ignorantly in unbelief (1:12–13). The clear implication is that to continue knowingly in sin and unrepentance leads to judgment. It is not stated whether people who have sinned ignorantly can be forgiven without hearing the gospel or coming to faith.

The letter is opposed to the kind of idle speculations that lead to heterodox views. Nevertheless, it contains an important statement enshrining the remarkable revelation by God that constitutes the truth at the heart of the faith. This is the cryptic description of Christ: "He was revealed in flesh, vindicated in spirit, seen by angels, proclaimed among Gentiles, believed in throughout the world, taken up in glory" (3:16 NRSV). This statement affirms the reality of Christ's incarnation (and so probably implies his preexistence) and then of God's affirmation of him, presumably in response to his humiliation and death, "in spirit" (which probably refers to the sphere in which it happened, in contrast to his earthly life "in flesh"). The vindication continues in that he was seen (acknowledged) by angels in heaven. Back on earth he was the object of preaching far and wide, and this led to people believing in him everywhere (possibly in contrast to the comparative lack of belief among the Jews). Finally, he was taken up to be with God in glory; although this clause comes after the mention of the worldwide mission, it can only refer to the ascension. The whole statement emphasizes the vindication of Christ in both heaven and earth, and implicit in it is the church's task of participating in that vindication by preaching Christ to the Gentiles, among whom there will be a positive response to him.

God's purpose for the church as "the pillar and bulwark of the truth" (3:15 NRSV) leads to the calling of specific people to be heralds, charged with making it known. This is the role of Paul himself, who emphasizes his mission especially to the Gentiles (2:7; cf. 2 Tim. 1:11). He also encourages the right people to take on responsibility in the congregations. Normative requirements for overseers (or bishops) and deacons (including "women," who are probably female deacons rather than the wives of deacons) are laid down (3:1–13). These are a mixture of freedom from anything that would give them a bad reputation in and outside the church, competence in leadership skills, and a firm hold on the faith (3:9 of deacons, and implicitly also expected of overseers). Later in the letter (5:17–25) instructions are given regarding proper recognition of the "elders" in the congregation and appropriate disciplinary measures if any fall into sin. It is to be presumed that the elders are identical with the overseers, or perhaps the term embraces both overseers and deacons.

The task of the church is to be faithful to the Christian message. Misguided teachers have been sidetracked into strange speculations based on Jewish myths and have developed commandments based on the Jewish law that they are promulgating as the conduct required of Christians. Paul regards all this as nonsense, with which it is difficult to have any useful debate (1:7); although pursuit of it is spiritually fatal (1:19), the victims are not beyond the hope of repentance and restoration (cf. 2 Tim. 2:23–26).

In place of fruitless controversy he advocates the place of prayer in the congregation, both for peaceful conditions in which evangelism is possible, and for people of all kinds to be saved (2:1–10). In this connection Paul warns against the danger of the men in the congregation behaving inappropriately by quarreling, probably as a result of the false teaching. He then warns against the women dressing extravagantly and possibly also seductively. As a kind of appendix to this (2:11–15), he further requires that a woman should not teach or have authority over a man but should be "silent" (or quiet).

1 Timothy and the Canon

First Timothy is part of a canon that includes the earlier letters of Paul. If the letter is genuinely by Paul, it forms part of the total evidence for his theology, and it can be argued that his other letters should be read in the light of it. Such a reading of both 1 Timothy and the other letters would need to bear in mind any special circumstances attaching to their individual composition. If, for example, 1 Timothy were the work of Paul in old age and there had been a decisive shift in his manner of thinking and theological position, then this would have a bearing on the exercise. However, there is no evidence whatever that Paul's age (still less an aging process) is a factor to be considered. If the letter is substantially distanced from Paul, then it can be interpreted on its own. The question that then arises is whether it differs from, or even contradicts, Paul. I see no signs that it is attempting to provide a normative reinterpretation of Paul for a much later situation. Rather, it provides appropriate teaching for a specific situation that stands in the tradition of the earlier Pauline letters. It does lack much of the kind of theologizing that is characteristic of the earlier letters, and like Luke-Acts it might be thought to show less depth of theological thinking. But it does an appropriate job in its own setting.

1 Timothy and Theology

1. For a letter that is of necessity much concerned with false teaching and congregational order, 1 Timothy contains a warm theology of salvation that preserves the mystery of the gospel and emphasizes the primacy of grace. Like 2 Timothy and Titus, it inculcates an attitude to Christian living that stresses the need for obedience to a conscience operating in close conjunction with faith and on the basis of sound teaching. This lifestyle produces

an orderly and self-controlled life that wins respect from non-Christians, commends the gospel, and gives us important insights into the character and duties of Christian leaders. The author holds to an essentially missionary theology in which apostles are church planters, but the responsibility of the church planter includes the continuing care of the church and its preservation from error. It can be safely assumed that, had it not been for the demands of this necessary task, the need for active evangelism would have been closer to the forefront of his concerns.

2. First Timothy significantly develops the concept of the church as the household of God. Whereas the metaphor of the body, as expressed in Rom. 12 and 1 Cor. 12, has little to say about leadership and structure in the congregation (though 1 Cor. 12:28 should not be overlooked), the household metaphor does recognize the need for direction in the church. It was perhaps inevitable that such structuring would resemble the pattern in the society of the time, but the letter does not imply that this particular form is appropriate for all time. A solution to the problems of congregational organization today will be found by holding together the concepts of the body and the household in a fruitful and creative tension, not by assuming that either is necessarily superior to the other and following either model exclusively.

3. The instruction to women to learn in silence remains controversial. Some congregations today accept women into "ministry," specifically the ordained pastoral ministry, with the authority that accompanies it. There are debates over whether a woman can function as a priest in denominations where the ordained ministry is understood as a form of priesthood confined to males. Apart from that, there is strong resistance to women taking an active part in preaching and ordained ministry in some congregations where high regard is paid to what is regarded as the "plain teaching" of Scripture.

In the first-century situation with its generally patriarchal society, where women played little part in public affairs, teaching by women could be regarded as an unacceptable breach of behavior patterns, whether among Jews or also among some Gentiles. Accordingly, the restriction can be interpreted as a culturally shaped prohibition that is no longer binding in a different setting.

The difficulty is in the appeal to Scripture that is used to back up the prohibition. It has a twofold argument that Adam was created prior to Eve (and therefore is superior), and that it is Eve who was deceived by the serpent (with the implication that women are still more likely to be deceived than men). This seems to be a doctrinal rather than a cultural consideration and is decisive for those who believe that the authority of a passage of Scripture must be accepted even when it seems to run against the grain of NT teaching generally (e.g., Gal. 3:28).

Other factors must be brought into consideration. (1) If it were not for the presence of this passage (together with 1 Cor. 14:33–36, though its significance is not agreed upon), probably nobody today would hold that women should be prohibited from teaching. (2) In an ancient society, where illiteracy and lack of education were common, it was especially the women who would suffer from these disadvantages. (3) The evidence of 1 Tim. 5:13 and 2 Tim. 3:6–7 suggests that women were especially susceptible to the prevalent false teaching in these specific congregations. (4) The argument that women are for all time more likely to be deceived than men because Eve was deceived is groundless. In any case, there is no way of knowing whether, if the serpent had spoken to Adam rather than to Eve, he would not have fallen just as readily as she had. (5) The argument that priority in creation places men in such a position of su-periority over women (or a husband over a wife) that a woman should not teach is untenable. (6) Eunice and Lois are commended for teaching the faith to the boy Timothy; evidently, therefore, it is not the teaching that is at fault, but rather the implication that the teaching woman is exercising authority over a man. (7) The very rare verb "have authority over" (Gk. *authenteō*) most probably expresses an unacceptable form of dominance. (8) Some women may have been arguing that they needed to teach in order to be saved, whereas the writer insists that this is not so, and reminds them that bearing children (which may also have been an issue; see 4:3) was a proper fulfillment of their Christian calling.

One possible interpretation is that, even if a woman should not have authority over a man, the exercise of teaching or the holding of ministe-rial office in the church should not be regarded as infringing this principle in contemporary society. Another possibility is that there may have been women teaching that women were superior to men on the basis of a faulty interpretation of Genesis, and the author is concerned simply to refute this and to stop the women giving false teaching. Hence, nothing more may be involved than a correction of a false interpretation of Genesis in a specific situation.

Certainty in interpretation of this difficult passage is difficult to achieve, but there is at least sufficient doubt concerning the validity of the patri-archal interpretation as a ruling for practice today to make it very unwise to impose it upon the church.

4. There is no uncertainty, however, over the full-scale treatment of the dangers of wealth, both the desiring of it and the misuse of it (6:3–19; cf. 2:9–10; 5:6). The author is quite clear that these are real dangers, against which Christians must be extremely vigilant, and he is very serious about the right use of income and possessions and the dangers of greed and envy. In a world where many Christians cannot avoid earning relatively high incomes, where there are many opportunities for lavish expenditure, and where equally many people are living in various degrees of poverty—the lesson of 1 Timothy is uncomfortably relevant and challenging.

Bibliography

See also bibliography for chapter 17, "Titus."

Campbell, R. *The Elders*. Studies of the New Testament and Its World. T&T Clark, 1994.

Donelson, L. *Pseudepigraphy and Ethical Argument in the Pastoral Epistles*. HUT 22. Mohr/Siebeck, 1986.

Kidd, R. *Wealth and Beneficence in the Pastoral Epistles*. SBLDS 122. Scholars Press, 1990.

Köstenberger, A., et al., eds. *Women in the Church*. Baker, 1995.

Oberlinner, L. *Die Pastoralbriefe*. HTKNT 9/2. Herder, 1994.

Quinn, J., and W. Wacker. *The First and Second Letters to Timothy*. ECC. Eerdmans, 2000.

Roloff, J. *Der erste Brief an Timotheus*. EKKNT. Benziger/Neukirchener Verlag, 1988.

Webb, W. *Slaves, Women and Homosexuals*. InterVarsity, 2001.

16

2 Timothy

I. HOWARD MARSHALL

With 1 Timothy and Titus, 2 Timothy is classified as a "Pastoral Epistle"; it is addressed to an individual engaged in mission and oversight, dealing with his personal lifestyle as a pastor and his relationships with the congregations under his supervision. Unlike the other two letters, it has no formal material on congregational structures and leadership. It reflects Paul facing up to the impending end of his life and deals primarily with the future mission of his younger colleague Timothy without supervision. It considers the nature of apostleship, the incipient dangers from within the church, and the need to respond to them, plus the external threats of persecution and even martyrdom.

History of Interpretation

From earliest times 2 Timothy was accepted as the last surviving letter of Paul, written from imprisonment in Rome, whether that described in Acts 28 or a subsequent imprisonment after a presumed further period of missionary activity (Eusebius, *Hist. eccl.* 2.22). Critical scholarship in the nineteenth century called into question the authenticity of all the so-called Pastoral Epistles on grounds of style and apparent reflection of a later period of composition. Some regard 2 Timothy as entirely fictitious. Others hold that it includes substantial fragments of Pauline material. Scholars who hold that it is fully Pauline generally hold to the traditional dating; some place it earlier (from prison in Ephesus or Caesarea), but the necessary reinterpretation of 1:17 is unconvincing. This is the Pastoral Epistle that has the strongest claims to be genuine or at least to be a reworking of Pauline material, including a letter from prison to Timothy. The closeness in style and content to 1 Timothy and Titus strongly suggests the final composition was from a hand other than Paul's (whether an amanuensis in his lifetime or a later compiler).

On the traditional understanding, 2 Timothy is an authentic or near-authentic expression of the mind of Paul as he faces the end of his active career and is concerned for the continuation of his mission, possibly through Timothy as his successor. If it is a later fiction, it is thought to be patterned on Jewish testament literature, in which a godly person is represented as facing impending death and conveying memorable last instructions and encouragement to his family or successor. This context distinguishes 2 Timothy to some extent from 1 Timothy and Titus, which convey instructions ("mandates") from an active apostle to his colleagues in mission.

Hearing the Message of 2 Timothy

The message is summed up nicely as "do the work of an evangelist" (4:5). Timothy is a member of Paul's mission team, which carried out evangelism, involving both the planting of congregations and their nurture. The letter is largely concerned with Timothy himself; the self-references by Paul function by way of example and stimulus, although in chapter 4 they are also concerned with his own situation and requirements.

Even in a letter to a close colleague and friend, Paul writes self-consciously as an apostle with a calling related to the "life that is in Christ Jesus" (1:1). Apostleship is the key to Paul's self-understanding, the position of a missionary authorized by the risen Lord to preach and teach (1:11), but also called to the possibility of suffering for the sake of the gospel like any other believer (3:12). He therefore leads a life that should be exemplary for other missionaries, both in the things that happened to him but also in the way that he lived (3:10–11).

Timothy was apparently tempted to lack of courage and thus to maintaining a low profile. Paul still refers to him as his child, which may imply that he was comparatively young (2:1). He had a pious upbringing by his mother and grandmother; his father (Acts 16:1) is not mentioned. As a young believer, Paul took him along as a junior colleague. At some point Paul prayed and laid hands upon him for his work as a fellow missionary, so that he might have the appropriate gifts of the Spirit, in this case "a spirit of power and of love and of self-discipline" that needed to be kept burning brightly (1:6–7 NRSV).

Paul's opening exhortation (1:3–18) is backed up by an appeal first of all to the power of God and to Timothy's colleagueship with Paul. Through participating with Paul in a ministry carrying the risk of suffering, Timothy shares in the power of God. The thought is developed through using a traditional formulation of the gospel that is quite similar to the teaching in Titus, with its correlation of what God did before ages began and what he has now revealed through the epiphany of Christ. Here the stress, however, is more on the "life and immortality" brought by the gospel (1:10), probably to provide an incentive in the face of threats of death against the missionaries (cf. 2:11–12). Paul comments on the suffering that he endures as a missionary but declares his trust in God, who delivers him from being "ashamed," from the feeling of shame that results from failure. His concern is not for his own resurrection but for the safe preservation of the gospel, no matter what happens to himself. God will guard to the last day what Paul has entrusted to him: the gospel (rather than Paul's own self; but the interpretation of 1:12 is disputed).

Against this background, Paul appeals to Timothy to hold fast to the faith, in the sense of proclaiming and transmitting it faithfully, and especially of standing up to corrupting influences within the church. At the same time, he can be told to "be strong in the grace that is in Christ Jesus" (2:1). There is an irreducible tension between the appeals to human faithfulness and the promises of divine empowerment.

Timothy is called to total commitment to his pastoral work (2:1–26). His tough assignment demands self-denial, self-discipline, and self-commitment. There is a broad appeal to the example of Jesus, who was "raised from the dead" (2:8), an expression doubtlessly implying that first he submitted to death, but God was faithful in raising him. There is a further appeal to the pattern of Paul in his suffering and commitment, so that God's people may attain to salvation without falling away; here is the reminder that, although the messengers may be imprisoned, the word of God cannot be fettered. And there is the sure knowledge that those who are prepared to suffer with Christ will share in his resurrection and reign. This trustworthy statement also warns against the consequences of falling away and again insists that even if some of God's people are faithless, he will continue faithfully to uphold them, since that is his very nature (2:11–13). Further reassurance is provided by the fact that, despite the activity of false teachers, the church has a firm foundation laid by God himself. Here again the tension recurs. God knows his people and (it is implied) watches over them; at the same time it is their responsibility to turn aside from wickedness. Even if people do turn aside, nevertheless, the opportunity for repentance and escape from the shackles imposed by the devil remains, and the faithful pastor will continue to persuade them to repent.

In the remaining instruction (3:1–4:5), the context for Timothy's work is the further spread of godlessness and error in the church but with the assurance that it will not triumph. Once again, he is reminded of how Paul's mission was not free from opposition and persecution, but the Lord rescued him. The stress now is on the danger of error, into which even Timothy might fall. The antidote lies in holding firmly and faithfully to the original Christian teaching received from people whom he knows to be reliable. It is rooted in the sacred writings, the Scriptures.

The conclusion of the letter (4:6–22) offers a further picture of Paul as the representative missionary, who is assured of his reward from the Lord. Deliverance in this situation is not only protection from the attacks of enemies, but also preservation of Paul in the faith so that he will reach God's heavenly kingdom.

2 Timothy and the Canon

This letter makes a distinctive contribution to the canon in various ways.

1. Even more than 1 Timothy, it is concerned with the personal life of the Christian and especially of the congregational leader. It may seem strange that a letter to a close colleague should be couched in this rather formal style and give advice with which Timothy would have been already familiar. However, Ignatius writes to Polycarp as a fellow Christian leader in a similar manner. And although the letter is addressed to Timothy himself, in its canonical form the letter is to be read by a wider audience, doubtlessly including both church leaders and members (cf. "you" [plural!], 4:22).

2. It gives a fuller picture of Paul himself, his own situation, and his self-consciousness. To some scholars it reads like an ideal picture of a missionary who is beginning to be a legend, an exaggerated portrait from a later date. Paul, it is said, has here become almost part of the gospel, a paradigm of conversion and perseverance. Certainly, the picture can be

read exemplarily, just as Paul presents himself implicitly as an example in Philippians, but it may also well be authentic.

3. The importance of preserving the gospel unchanged and sharing Paul's message with a wider circle of teachers is appropriate at this later stage in the growth of the church. Although the admonition (2:2) has been interpreted solely in terms of passing on the message to the next generation of leaders, there is also a concern for widening the influence by equipping local congregations with leaders so that they are not dependent upon a teacher like Timothy himself.

4. The place of the Holy Spirit in equipping congregational leaders is stressed. With the growth of a leadership of people appointed to serve, perhaps with little previous Christian experience and no training, it was vital to emphasize the provision of divine enabling for leaders. Yet, although the leaders are doubtlessly especially in mind, the gift of the Spirit is common to all believers.

2 Timothy and Theology

1. A major contribution of this letter is its statement of the inspiration and usefulness of Scripture. It contains the only biblical use of the term *theopneustos*, "breathed by God," which is applied to "all" or "every [passage of] Scripture." There is no mention of the Holy Spirit in this connection (contrast 2 Pet. 1:21). Nor do we have the suggestion that God "played" on the human writers like a musician playing on an instrument. The point is rather that Scripture teaches the Christian understanding of salvation and provides whatever the believer needs for instruction in Christian living. The corollary of the inspiration of "all Scripture" is that any passage may have value for the Christian. Its origin in God implies its authority, truthfulness, and usefulness. The extension of applying the text to apply to the NT is fully justified, and there is at least the possibility that some early Christian writings were being regarded as Scripture by this date.

2. The Christian life is understood to be empowered and guaranteed by God and yet dependent on the faith and commitment of the believer. The author places these two facts side by side without saying anything to suggest that the believer is automatically brought safely through every danger and temptation to a heavenly reward, or that everything depends on the believer's personal commitment and effort. Alongside the falling away of some Christians like Demas, there is the assured conviction of

Paul himself. Perseverance to the end is expressed in terms of trust in God's faithfulness.

Bibliography

See also bibliography for chapter 17, "Titus."

Oberlinner, L. *Die Pastoralbriefe*. HTKNT 11/2. Herder, 1995.

Prior, M. *Paul the Letter-Writer and the Second Letter to Timothy*. JSNTSup 23. JSOT, 1989.

Quinn, J., and W. Wacker. *The First and Second Letters to Timothy*. ECC. Eerdmans, 2000.

Stott, J. *Guard the Gospel*. InterVarsity, 1973.

17

Titus

I. Howard Marshall

With 1 Timothy and 2 Timothy, Titus is one of three letters ostensibly addressed to missionary colleagues of Paul and collectively known since the eighteenth century as the "Pastoral Epistles." Although its brevity and similarity in content to 1 Timothy have encouraged its neglect, it has its own distinctive and valuable contribution to make to the theology of the NT.

History of Interpretation

Until the nineteenth century Titus was understood as a letter of Paul, written during the final period of his life to his junior companion, Titus, in charge of the congregations in Crete (1:5). They were less developed than those in Ephesus (as reflected in 1 Timothy). Negatively, the letter is concerned with the danger caused by "rebellious people" teaching material eccentrically based on Jewish mythology and commandments; they are criticized for their greed, deceit, and general immoral behavior (1:10–16). Positively, the letter advocates the appointment of local congregational leaders of good character and sound faith (1:5–9) and the inculcation of a respectable way of life characterized by self-control, submission to authority, abstention from time-wasting controversy, and devotion to good works

175

(2:1–15; 3:1–11). This exhortation is backed up by two reminders of the way in which God acted graciously in Christ to achieve the redemption of believers and to save them personally from their previous sinful way of life (2:11–14; 3:3–7). The letter is a mature statement of Pauline theology and ecclesiology that encourages an orderly way of life but is redeemed from dullness by its inspirational teaching on the nature of salvation.

This traditional understanding has been challenged by a different view, based on the increasingly severe objections raised against Pauline authorship (especially by Holtzmann). Titus, along with its companion letters, was held to be a pseudonymous composition of a considerably later date (perhaps even from the early second century). Its general purpose was to rehabilitate Paul during a period of declining influence by presenting the kind of teaching that he would have given if still alive and encouraging people to be loyal to his brand of Christianity. However, the teaching actually presented is significantly different from that of Paul, it was alleged. Detachment from the hypothesis of Pauline authorship allowed modern critical scholars to emphasize the differences and see the three letters in their own light rather than to conform them to the pattern of the earlier Paul. At the same time there is the danger of seeing the letters as different facets of a common agenda, although some scholars are now recognizing that each must be appreciated for its own worth. Two things characterize the new outlook.

1. Later books of the NT were regarded as "early catholic" in their outlook. They represented and promoted the type of ecclesiology found in second-century Christianity, with an emphasis on fixed traditions handed down from the past. The theology has become static. Pauline creativity has disappeared. The church is the dispenser of salvation and is developing a fixed, hierarchical church structure, in which "office" has replaced the less-formal charismatic congregational ministry (e.g., prophecy) of an earlier period. The Holy Spirit's activity is increasingly confined to the ordained leaders.

2. Dibelius characterized the way of life in the Pastoral Epistles as "bourgeois," by which he meant that the church was adopting the patterns of Hellenistic-Roman society, living according to its ideals and becoming so innocuous as to avoid persecution. The ethic is characterized by sobriety, self-control, and good works. Orderliness and submission to authority are paramount. Slaves, in particular, are to be obedient and submissive. There is little that is specifically Christian.

Such an evaluation of Titus is essentially negative and pejorative. Superficially, it may seem to be plausible. For example, the actual amount of theological teaching in the letter is small in comparison with the ethical and ecclesiastical material. Nevertheless, there has been a justified reaction against it.

On the one hand, there is a continuing and vigorous defense of Pauline authorship (whether directly or through an amanuensis) by scholars who cannot be accused of a blind traditionalism (Fee; Johnson; Knight; Mounce; Spicq). They have demonstrated the essential harmony of the letter with Paul's earlier writings.

On the other hand, there has been recognition of the creative, theological character of the letter by scholars who find it hard to recognize the literary style and manner of thinking as those of Paul himself (so variously Marshall; Oberlinner; Quinn). One approach attempts to do justice to the Paulinism of the letter by seeing it as a nondeceptive presentation of what Paul would have said to the church in the period fairly soon after his death. It is conveyed by a follower who makes use of the kind of things that Paul actually did say to his colleagues. This view and that which attributes the letter to Paul himself, assisted by an amanuensis, are not far apart.

The result has been a recognition of a much more vigorous theology in Titus than earlier scholars detected, whether through their seeing Titus in the shadow of the major Pauline letters or through assessing it as typical of early catholicism. At the same time there has developed recognition of the contribution that literary and social-scientific approaches can make to a fuller appreciation of the letter.

Hearing the Message of Titus

In the lengthy opening salutation (1:1–4), the self-description of Paul as an apostle becomes a mini-statement of the gospel, setting out the correlation between the eternal plan of God the Savior and its realization in the proclamation of the gospel. The apostle is concerned to promote knowledge of the truth and faith in God's people as leading to a life characterized by godliness and hope. The Father's character and purpose are summed up in his title of "Savior," and his purpose for humankind is salvation. Jesus Christ stands alongside him as "Savior" (1:4).

The "proclamation" is an integral part of the accomplishment of God's plan of salvation; the saving act is the revelation of God's grace (2:11), which includes both the coming of Christ and the apostolic mission. Special importance attaches to the work of the apostles and those who share in their work by continuing it where the apostles are absent, whether geographically or no longer active.

The growth of error leads to great emphasis on "sound doctrine" (2:1). Knowledge figures prominently alongside faith as a characteristic of God's people, and there is a greater tendency than in earlier literature to see faith not only as a relationship of personal trust and commitment to God, but also as acceptance of the true teaching enshrined in Christian tradition.

The first doctrinal passage (2:11–14) complements the salutation. The word "grace," which could have been dismissed as a formal element in a stereotyped greeting (1:4), is now forefronted as the key quality of God. The whole of what God has done and is doing to save people is "grace," and in a remarkable statement it is "grace" that has been revealed rather than God's Son (contrast Gal. 1:15–16). A further clarification appears in 3:4 (NRSV), where "the goodness and loving kindness" of God appears; the language of human benefaction is used to explain in simple terms the beneficence of God. The term "appeared," related to the noun "epiphany," picks up on language used to express the saving intervention of divine beings in the world. The same terms are used both for the future coming of the Savior to wind up God's saving action in the world and for the historical action in the incarnation of Jesus and the associated events.

The saving action is also described in traditional language as redemption (2:14), quite deliberately echoing Ps. 130:8 and Mark 10:45. God acts to rescue people from a sinful life (rather than simply from the penal consequences of sin) to live a life of goodness worthy of himself.

Such a life looks forward to the end of the present age in which we live in a sinful world, and eagerly longs for the manifestation of the glory of Christ. But here there is a surprise: the awaited one is "our great God and Savior, Jesus Christ." This explicit application of the term "God" to Jesus Christ has been challenged by some who would render the phrase "of the great God and our Savior Jesus Christ," but the evidence strongly favors the former interpretation. Although anticipated earlier (Rom. 9:5), this statement is the climax in the growing recognition that Jesus Christ is alongside the Father in the complex identity of God.

The second doctrinal passage (3:4–7) shifts the emphasis to the way in which God has acted savingly in the lives of believers. The Pauline stress on "not by works" is affirmed; this is probably in response to Jewish stress on the commandments as the means of salvation, and it reiterates that salvation is entirely dependent upon God's action. A picture is painted of people living such sinful lives that they do not in fact have any goodness that might count in their favor; they are justified by divine grace. They are entirely dependent on divine mercy, and mercy is exercised in a radical change, like being born again, brought about by the agency of the Holy Spirit. The Spirit is said to be poured out on them, echoing the language of Pentecost, but acts inwardly to renew them. Thus, as in Romans, justification and regeneration by the Spirit are brought together as the two essential aspects of God's saving work. Out of this fundamental saving action of God, the obligation to a new way of life emerges. The practical teaching that Titus is to give is to be "consistent with sound doctrine" (2:1 NRSV).

Titus and the Canon

1. The doctrinal teaching in Titus, though expressed in new ways, is in fundamental agreement with that of the earlier Pauline letters in its teaching about the gracious saving action of God, justification by grace and not by works, and regeneration by the Spirit. The unity of the saving revelation in Christ and in the proclamation of the gospel is likewise already present (2 Cor. 5:18–21). The Christology, implicit and explicit, ranks God the Father and Jesus Christ together as the sources of salvation and draws the logical conclusion that the term "God" is equally applicable to both. Nevertheless, the term "Son" is not used.

2. Ethical teaching is addressed to the different groups in the congregation (rather than in the family): older men and women, younger women and men, and slaves. The instruction to slaves is particularly significant in that, while inculcating the need for submission to their masters, it nevertheless insists that the lowest class in society can be "an ornament to the doctrine of God our Savior" (2:10 NRSV).

3. There are the first detailed instructions regarding the choosing of local congregational leaders. Here only elders are mentioned, functioning as overseers or "bishops" (1:5, 7), with no mention of deacons (contrast 1 Tim. 3). The importance of their being able to teach positively and also to refute error is highlighted. However, the appointment of local leaders is nothing new (cf. Phil. 1:1). There is the risk here that addressing leaders like Titus and concentrating on the work of local church leaders could promote an early "catholic" type of ecclesiology; within the canon the teaching in the Pastoral Epistles must be balanced by the more "charismatic" ecclesiology found elsewhere.

Titus and Theology

Like its companions, the letter to Titus is brief and written in a specific situation. Therefore, care must be taken in appropriating its theological message for today, and it must be seen as part of Scripture as a whole. Nevertheless, it sets an important precedent in two ways.

1. Titus is an important example of recontextualizing the gospel within the NT and its first-century context. The author holds fast to the apostolic doctrine and institutes measures in the church to maintain it in pure form against the inroads of opposition and incipient heresy. Teaching based on the gospel is crucial. So too is the careful appointment of congregational leaders who are of sterling Christian character, possess the gifts of leadership, and are able to teach. It is probable that a plurality of leaders in each local situation is in mind rather than one for each Christian group.

2. While the author holds fast to the Pauline teaching, it is expressed in new ways, using a fresh vocabulary that will speak meaningfully and so communicate successfully in the Hellenistic world. Christian communication today not only takes over the language of Titus (as well as that of the NT generally) but also follows its example in searching out relevant ways of expressing the gospel and the imperatives of Christian living in the contemporary world.

Bibliography

See also bibliography for chapter 15, "1 Timothy," and chapter 16, "2 Timothy."

Dibelius, M., and H. Conzelmann. *The Pastoral Epistles*. Hermeneia. Fortress, 1972.

Fee, G. *1 and 2 Timothy, Titus*. NIBCNT. Hendrickson, 1988.

Harding, M. *What Are They Saying about the Pastoral Epistles?* Paulist, 2001.

Holtzmann, H. *Die Pastoralbriefe, kritisch und exegetisch behandelt*. Engelmann, 1880.

Johnson, L. T. *Letters to Paul's Delegates*. NTC. Trinity, 1996.

Knight, G., III. *Commentary on the Pastoral Epistles*. NIGTC. Eerdmans/Paternoster, 1992.

Lau, A. *Manifest in Flesh*. WUNT 2.86. Mohr/Siebeck, 1996.

Marshall, I. H. (with P. Towner). *A Critical and Exegetical Commentary on the Pastoral Epistles*. ICC. T&T Clark, 1999.

Mounce, W. *The Pastoral Epistles*. WBC. Word, 2001.

Oberlinner, L. *Die Pastoralbriefe*. HTKNT 22/2. Herder, 1996.

Quinn, J. *The Letter to Titus*. AB 35. Doubleday, 1990.

Spicq, C. *Les Épîtres Pastorales*. ÉBib. J. Gabalda, 1948, 1969.

Stott, J. *The Message of 1 Timothy and Titus*. InterVarsity, 1996.

Towner, P. *The Goal of Our Instruction*. JSNTSup 34. Sheffield Academic Press, 1989.

Young, F. *The Theology of the Pastoral Letters*. NTT. Cambridge University Press, 1994.

18

Philemon

Daniel R. Streett

Because of its brevity and relative lack of extended theological reflection, Paul's letter to Philemon has often been overlooked or ignored by those interested in constructing a theology of Paul or the NT. It has not fared much better in the churches or in the devotional life of most Christians. At various times, however, when the political and societal setting was right, this short epistle, with its controversial subject matter, has become a storm center of debate. Some interpreters find in Philemon a liberating message of redemption, while others detect a capitulation to the status quo and a failure to realize the radical implications of the gospel.

Returning a Redeemed Slave

Likely written during Paul's Roman imprisonment, Philemon is a letter of intercession to accompany the return of a slave, Onesimus, to his master, Philemon, in Colossae. In the body of the letter, Paul uses various techniques of persuasion to win Philemon's compliance, including a subtle appeal to his authority as an old man and an apostle, his role in Philemon's salvation, his great love for Onesimus, and his impending visit. The *crux interpretum* is v. 16. Does Paul intend for Philemon to manumit Onesimus? Or is Paul simply telling Philemon to treat Onesimus not just as a slave, but also as a Christian brother (and thus not to pursue legal recourse against him)? The history of interpretation is mostly a record of scholarly grapplings with this question.

History of Interpretation

As early as the fourth century CE, Philemon had become a battleground for the dispute over abolitionism. In theological battles with the gnostic Carpocratians, as well as the Eustatians and the Donatist Circumcellions— all abolitionists—Chrysostom, Jerome, and Theodore of Mopsuestia used Philemon to defend slavery. Likewise, Luther and Grotius held that Paul was not advocating the abrogation of slavery, but the reconciliation of a slave and his master. This interpretation held sway, with notable dissenters (e.g., Calvin), until the nineteenth century, when abolitionists again read Philemon as urging Onesimus's manumission, or at least sowing the seeds of slavery's destruction.

The twentieth century witnessed a bewildering number of new interpretations. J. Knox, for example, questioned the traditional reading at almost every point. He argued that Archippus, not Philemon, was actually the owner of Onesimus, and that the Letter to Philemon is to be identified with the Letter to Laodicea mentioned in Col. 4:16. Paul's purpose in writing to Archippus, Knox contended, was to secure Onesimus's release in order that he might accompany Paul in his labors. Paul was successful, and Onesimus later became bishop of Ephesus (cf. Ignatius of Antioch, who mentions an Onesimus in this connection; *Eph.* 1.3). Philemon's inclusion in the canon was engineered by the grateful Onesimus, who collected the correspondence on his hero, Paul.

While Knox's contributions have met with considerable skepticism, many have followed him in radically rethinking the traditional interpretation. Some have suggested that Onesimus was not a runaway, but may simply have overstayed a leave of absence. Perhaps Philemon had commissioned Onesimus to carry out business in Rome, and Onesimus had failed to return promptly when his task was completed.

Both P. Lampe and B. Rapske have made the case that Onesimus sought out Paul to serve as *amicus domini* and arbitrate a dispute between Onesimus and his master—a common practice in Roman slavery. This view has garnered many proponents among recent commentators (Dunn; Fitzmyer; Bartchy). S. Winter theorizes that Onesimus was sent as a messenger from the Colossian congregation and was converted during his stay with Paul, where he proved to be quite useful, and that Paul therefore wrote Philemon to request Onesimus's continued service. Others have questioned whether Onesimus was a slave at all (Callahan).

Also influential in recent interpretation has been careful historical research into the nature of slavery in the first century (Bartchy). Roman slavery was by no means equivalent to that of nineteenth-century America. Roman slaves varied widely in their social status, their treatment, and the tasks they performed. Manumission was commonplace, so much so that laws were passed in order to limit and regulate the influx of freed slaves into the economy.

Reading Philemon Theologically

Philemon addresses such a particular historical situation that one might legitimately question whether the letter has any contemporary theological significance. While Philemon is hardly a doctrinal treatise or a sustained theological argument, beneath its surface lies a profound conception of Christian community.

Although the letter is primarily for Philemon, it is also addressed to the church in his house, an indication that Paul saw the situation not merely as a private matter, but one that involved the larger church body, who would in turn encourage Philemon to carry out Paul's wishes. Paul stresses this relational dynamic by identifying Onesimus as his "child" (v. 10 NRSV) and his own heart (v. 12), as well as appealing to his *koinōnia* with Philemon (vv. 7, 17).

If the believing community is to be so integrally connected, it must be characterized, as a reflection of its Lord, by reconciliation and forgiveness. Paul encourages Philemon to go the second mile in receiving Onesimus back (v. 21). As an imitator of Christ, Paul offers to pay Onesimus's debts, if necessary, to effect reconciliation, but it is clear that he expects Philemon also to renounce his rights and make no such demands.

Most importantly, Paul manifests his conviction that, as a new society called forth by God's redemptive act in Christ, the church is to be markedly different from the surrounding society, most notably in the importance commonly attached to social and legal status. Paul's appeal in v. 16 is a natural corollary to his pronouncements elsewhere (Gal. 3:28; Col. 3:11). Within the body of Christ, social distinctions are radically relativized in the light of a common relation to Christ.

The troubling question remains: if Paul held to such a rigorous view of Christian community, how could he have failed to request Onesimus's manumission? Some scholars would argue that he does, in fact, make such a request, pointing to the "even more" of v. 21, as well as the seeming contrast between "brother" and "slave" in v. 16. But even if that is the case, such manumission would be limited to Onesimus and would be specifically in order that Onesimus could return to work with Paul (as Col. 4:9 suggests happened). Philemon was hardly intended to be a manifesto on slavery.

It is evident from Paul's other letters that he did not see ownership of slaves as intrinsically sinful at that moment or inimical to Christian fellowship and community (cf. 1 Cor. 7:21–24; Col. 3:22–4:1), so there would be no ideological reason for him to request Onesimus's manumission. Indeed, Paul's response to the situation can rightly be called "a practical outworking" of the household codes in his other epistles (Barth and Blanke 153).

For the believer, who accepts the letter to Philemon as the word of God, neither a tendentious reading of Paul as an egalitarian hero nor a facile dismissal of Paul as a culture-bound bigot will suffice. Some criticize Paul for shortsightedness or a lack of nerve in not applying his prior magnificent statement of Christian equality (Gal. 3:28) to the situation of Onesimus, but perhaps they have derived their fundamental convictions more from the Enlightenment than from the Scriptures. Such an attempt to be more Pauline than Paul is misguided.

In the final analysis, a focus on slavery has obscured the true theological message of Philemon: The church is to be a radically new society, where divisions founded upon race, gender, and social status are overcome by unity in Christ. In the church the reconciliation and forgiveness modeled by the Lord is manifested in a spirit of agapeic servanthood. Without dispute, this is a message the church in every age needs to hear.

Bibliography

Bartchy, S. *Mallon Chrēsai*. SBLDS 11. Scholars Press, 1973.

Barth, M., and H. Blanke. *The Letter to Philemon*. ECC. Eerdmans, 2000.

Callahan, A. *Embassy of Onesimus*. NTC. Trinity, 1997.

Dunn, J. *The Epistles to the Colossians and to Philemon*. NIGTC. Eerdmans, 1996.

Fitzmyer, J. *The Letter to Philemon*. AB 34C. Doubleday, 2000.

Knox, J. *Philemon among the Letters of Paul*. University of Chicago Press, 1935.

Lampe, P. "Keine 'Slavenflucht' des Onesimus." *ZNW* 76 (1985): 135–73.

O'Brien, P. *Colossians, Philemon*. WBC. Word, 1982.

Rapske, B. "The Prisoner Paul in the Eyes of Onesimus." *NTS* 37 (1991): 187–203.

Winter, S. "Paul's Letter to Philemon." *NTS* 33 (1987): 1–15.

19

Hebrews

JON C. LAANSMA

The writer of Hebrews is one of the great pastoral theologians of the apostolic period. In spite of its persistent historical and theological difficulties, this summons to a faithful response to the divine voice sounds a clear note to a people that has here no abiding city.

History of Interpretation

By the second century CE the Eastern church, with its emphasis on the pilgrimage of the soul to God, had embraced Hebrews and considered it Pauline (on the history of interpreting Hebrews, see Koester 19–63; Hagner; Greer; Hagen, *Testament*; Hagen, *Commenting*; Demarest). The Western church, however, which boasts the earliest use (*1 Clement*; ca. 95 CE), was more concerned with questions of church order and either ignored Hebrews or disputed its Pauline authorship and authority. A consensus emerged during the christological debates of the fourth and fifth centuries. From texts such as 1:4 and 3:1–2 the Arians argued that the Son was created and *became* greater than the angels; on the other hand, Athanasius (d. 373) found affirmations of the Son's divinity in passages such as 1:3 and 13:8. The latter view won out, though subsequent readings continued to use

Hebrews to support differing views of the relationship between Christ's humanity and divinity. At the same time Ambrose (d. 397) argued that 6:4–6 forbids only the *rebaptism* of repenters, solving what had been a key problem for the Western church. Within this consensus the West gradually came to embrace Pauline authorship, although the book's position in lists and collections reflects the view that it stands on the outer margin of Paul's writings. Also during the earliest centuries, the church's leaders had come to be called "priests," and the Mass had come to be understood in terms of a sacrifice; both of these developments drew on and influenced the interpretation of Hebrews.

The disruptions of the sixteenth century affected the reading of much of Scripture, including Hebrews. The humanists reopened questions of authorship—doubts grew about the ascription to Paul—and shifted their attention from the Vulgate to the original languages. Erasmus (d. 1536) believed that Hebrews represented a movement from a lower order of religiosity (the OT) to a higher spiritual and moral order (the New). Luther (d. 1546) suggested Apollos as the author and placed Hebrews after 3 John; his heirs continued to debate its canonical status. Based on Heb. 9:16–17, Luther came to construe the Mass not as a sacrifice offered to God, but as a *testament* that Christ offers to his people, which is received by faith alone. Among the other Reformers, while some affirmed Paul's authorship, Calvin (d. 1564) argued against it but affirmed the book's place among the apostolic writings. For some, the conviction that the Holy Spirit was ultimately responsible for the book made questions about the human author of lesser consequence. All the Reformers argued strongly that Christ's once-for-all sacrifice precluded any notion of the Mass as a sacrifice. In response, the Council of Trent included Hebrews among the letters of Paul and, using Hebrews in support, reaffirmed that the Mass is a propitiatory sacrifice offered in an unbloody manner by Christ's disciples, whom he established as priests.

With the rise of modern historical criticism in the seventeenth and eighteenth centuries, work focused with ever-increasing intensity on questions surrounding the book's original situation vis-à-vis the historical rise of Christianity.

Answers for such questions can be luminous for interpretation, but in the case of Hebrews evidence is limited. The *author* remains unknown. Suggested names, either as author or editor/translator, include Paul, Clement of Rome, Luke, Barnabas, Apollos, Silas, and Priscilla and Aquila. For centuries it was assumed that the *addressees* were Jews (cf. the book's title, dating to the second century) and their *location* was in Palestine. Many, however, have argued for a Gentile audience. On balance it was probably a mixed audience (Ellingworth 21–27), and the book's single geographical hint (13:24) favors Italy and possibly Rome as the destination (see further Lane 1:liii-lx).

Involved in these decisions are questions of *date* and *occasion*. A date following 70 CE is possible but, taking the internal and external evidence together, a date not long before Nero's persecutions took hold works best (64–65). As to the *problem* being addressed, what we must allow for is the possibility of a complex mix of issues related to the community's history and social setting. In part, it may have been this community's felt need of a cultic means of addressing the consciousness of postbaptismal sins that called forth this address (Lindars 4–15). There appears to have been willingness to trade off true endurance for a compromise with their antagonistic world. It is maintained by many that there was a return—in actuality or spirit—to the temple or synagogue. From the writer's point of view, there has been a failure to grasp the implications of confessions they had made, teachings they had received, and examples they had witnessed. In any event the single most *identifiable* impediment to this community's progress is reluctance to do precisely what the writer repeatedly urges them to do. Through Christ, they need to draw near to God, to "hold fast to" their Christian hope based on God's promise, and to do this in close, daily fellowship with one another (e.g., 10:23–25 NRSV).

Over the last century much of the work done on Hebrews has focused on *backgrounds*, its *use of the* OT, and *literary-rhetorical* analysis.

Hebrews contains substantial parallels with Paul, with the Stephen traditions of Acts 7, and with 1 Peter; there are also allusions to Jesus' earthly career (for the latter, Hughes 75–100; Koester 106–9). Although none of these can make a claim for dependence in literary terms, they evidence the participation of Hebrews in broader currents of apostolic proclamation. In particular, Manson's thesis that Hebrews stands in the stream represented by Stephen and the "Hellenists" has been corrected and refined but has continued to receive support (Hurst 89–106; Lindars 120–21, 124–25; Barrett, "Christology").

Religio-historical work has not only uncovered parallels to isolated elements, but has also endeavored to bring into focus the conceptual background of Hebrews. That Hebrews' imagery and argument involve *both* a vertical, spatial duality of earth and heaven *and* a horizontal, temporal duality of this age and the age-to-come is patent, though the nature of the duality and which orientation (vertical or horizontal) is controlling is not. The very definition of terms is highly problematic, yet the options for

Hebrews' pre-Christian background have clustered around Philo, Gnosticism, Qumran, apocalyptic writings, and *merkabah* (throne-chariot) mysticism. On the whole, Hebrews best fits within the Christianized "already–not yet" version of the linear-apocalyptic (Hurst 11) outlook encountered elsewhere in the NT (Barrett, "Eschatology"). Yet the impression remains that the writer had some exposure to the philosophical categories and uses of language that also appear in Philo, and that this has contributed to his manner of expression.

The major *explicit* source of the writer's thought is the *OT*. It is apparent that all of Hebrews' citations are drawn from a Greek *Vorlage*; there is no compelling evidence that he made use of a Hebrew source. Hence, work has proceeded to explore the canonical (and extracanonical) scope of the writer's quotations and allusions, the form of the LXX used, the alterations of the wording of the OT texts, the rationale behind the changes, the rhetorical deployment of the citations within the argument, the exegetical methods employed, and the underlying hermeneutics.

Finally, the *genre* of Hebrews can tentatively (Koester 81) be described as a homily. *Rhetorical* analysis has clarified the high level of skill in the use of the Greek language and in the art of persuasion represented, though the book has finally resisted easy classification according to ancient models of epideictic or deliberative rhetoric. The dominant models employed for understanding the *literary structure* of Hebrews have been structural agnosticism, conceptual analysis, rhetorical criticism, literary analysis, and linguistic analysis. In his text-linguistic analysis Guthrie has argued that by separating the exhortatory units from the expositional, it is possible to identify the distinctive manner in which both of these series of units proceed toward the same pastoral goal.

Hearing the Message of Hebrews

Hebrews is a pastoral theologian's rhetorical effort to shore up the faith of this church and the only work we have from his hand. Judgments about its theology (or theolog*ies*) must therefore be made carefully and only as viewed through the lenses of the book's structure and the writer's pastoral-rhetorical interests (Lindars 1–3, 26–29). Such a reading includes taking seriously its cultic language (e.g., sacred space, blood; see Dunnill) and temple imagery as well as the argument's appeals to emotion (Koester 89–91).

The book unfolds along the parallel tracks of exposition and exhortation (for the present analysis of the book's structure, see Guthrie). The *expository* track has two parts: 1:1–4:13 and 4:14–10:25. Along the way (2:1–4; 3:1–4:13; 5:11–6:20) and following 10:25 (10:26–13:25) the writer drives home the point for this community through direct *exhortations*. These two tracks, though they converge on the same goal, are structured quite differently.

The Goal: Exhortation

The hortatory units, rather than following a logical development, achieve their goal by means of a largely emotional appeal that reiterates key ideas (e.g., sin, faith, endurance, word of God, enter); through these the readers are challenged to persevere.

The series of exhortations as a whole operates within a view of history that locates this audience in the climactic epoch (1:2) of creation's story. In this story the Son is the eschatological heir of all things and the one through whom all things were made—a story whose end is imminent. In this way the readers are made to see that all that has gone before has been oriented to salvation wrought through the Son. To turn away from this salvation is therefore to abandon all hope and worse. And the divine word, having explicitly spoken to this salvation in advance, has also fashioned for them patterns—types—that both instruct and exhort with respect to this salvation.

The writer's concern is ultimately with the fate of the entire community, in keeping with the larger vision of the book, which sees the people of God, past and present together, awaiting the fulfillment of the divine promises. Thus, in 3:7–4:13, the drama within which the readers are to see themselves is that of Num. 14, wherein the apostasy of a *few* led to the apostasy of the *entire* community (cf. Heb. 12:15). Accordingly, though Hebrews does not give expression to a developed ecclesiology, the strategic role of *daily* gatherings (3:13; 10:25) for the community's existence must be noticed.

Salvation itself is projected in local terms, as the "world to come," a resting place, the Most Holy Place, a city, a heavenly homeland, Mt. Zion, even the region *outside* of a sphere (13:13). These images draw heavily on the audience's instinctive understanding of sacred space and its dangers for those to whom sin clings. On the other hand, free entrance into the space of God's presence is an almost indescribable joy, giving them on earth a share in the holiness (12:14) of the temple. Here too, the communal gatherings play a critical role (Lindars 105). This salvation, which they already enjoy in part (6:4–5, 19–20), for the present remains in the form of "promise," and the community is portrayed alternately as a *waiting* (e.g., 10:25) or a *pilgrim* people.

In view of Christian existence as a sojourning and taking for granted the hostility of sinful humanity (12:3), suffering is viewed as the corollary of this faith (e.g., 10:32–39; 11:25–26; 13:11–14) and a universal means of perfecting God's sons and daughters (2:10–11; 5:7–10; 12:4–11). The world external to the church is the inhospitable location within which it sojourns; by going forth *out* of the world (13:13), they are *in* it but not *of* it. The fundamental sin is that of unbelief (= disobedience), and God's enemies (1:13) are those who reject his promise. Apostasy begins where faith falters (2:2; 5:11–14). Full apostasy is presented as a genuine possibility even if the writer believes that his audience is destined for better things. Probably we should read the warning of 5:11–6:12 in the light of the notion of sacred space and corporate conceptions of salvation, such that those who are baptized into the community are viewed as genuinely participating in the realities of salvation. Their subsequent renunciation of faith in full knowledge and understanding of what they are doing (6:6; 10:29) leaves them no possibility of repentance (cf. 12:17). There is likely some connection with Mark 3:29 (Matt. 12:32) and 1 John 5:16–17, though all of these are difficult texts (cf. also 1 Tim. 1:13). In any event it is doubtful that the writer foresees a situation within which the church itself would enact rules to *enforce* 6:4–6.

The types of exhortations given are both "static" ("hold fast") and "dynamic" ("approach"; "go forth") in nature, and receive their focus in the exhortation to be *faithful* (Attridge 21–22). The description (11:1) and portrayal (11:2–12:3) of faith—the object of which has never changed—presents it as the capacity for the readers to conduct themselves steadfastly in their present world-order and life-situation, even to the point of death. They do so in accordance with a heavenly and yet unseen reality, simply because it is held forth to them in God's word. Their high priest is himself the leader and perfecter of this faith (12:2–3; 2:10; cf. 6:20). A positive agenda of earthly, societal righteousness is the largely unexpressed entailment of this faith; this is not escapist or isolationist.

The Means to the Goal: Exposition

If the hortatory units work together through the reiteration of key motifs, the expositional track of the argument develops along both spatial and logical lines (Guthrie 121–27).

It is likely that the expositional material in 1:1–4:13 is in its core largely traditional and familiar to the readers, even if the writer is giving it a fresh expression. Thus, the use of Pss. 2, 8, and 110; the wisdom Christology of 1:1–3 (Dunn 51–56, 206–9); and the christological descent-ascent pattern are all strongly paralleled elsewhere (e.g., John 1:1–18; Phil. 2:5–11; Col. 1:15–20). It is with 5:1–10:25 that the argument advances into new territory.

Son: 1:4–4:13

On one level, the common thread in this section is the need properly to receive the revelation (word) of God in the Son. Thus, statements of the preexistent and exalted Son's superiority to the prophets, angelic mediators of the old covenant (2:2), and the lawgiver Moses are capped by an extended appeal to receive God's word of promise in obedient faith (3:7–4:11), and finally by a most emphatic affirmation of the ineluctability of God's judging word (4:12–13). All of this summons the readers sharply to attentiveness before the fresh teaching of 5:1 and following.

At the same time this section is channeling all this in the direction of the high priestly teaching. This is done both explicitly (1:3; 2:17–18; 3:1) and indirectly, especially through the sonship idea. In diverse ways Christ—in his nature, status, and history as Son—uniquely and for all time fills the role of high priest. The one identity is metamorphosed into the other through both an internal consistency and an inner textual move: Ps. 110, already in wide currency for the christological implications of its first verse, had also made the pronouncement of verse 4.

High Priest: 5:1–10; 7:1–28

Bookended by the major inclusion of 4:14–16 and 10:19–25, and bracketing out 5:11–6:20, the exposition of Christ's high priesthood runs from 5:1 through 10:18—which divides into two movements, with a brief summary statement in between (8:1–2). Thus, the writer first establishes that Jesus is our high priest (5:1–10; 7:1–28), then develops further implications from his priestly work in the heavenly temple (8:3–10:18).

Taking together 4:14–16 with 5:1–10, the *fact* of Christ's priesthood is substantiated by his history as Son and, most pointedly, by the oracular fusion in 5:5–6 of Pss. 2:7 and 110:4 (109:4 LXX). All of this is correlated and contrasted with human high priesthoods, especially the Aaronic. In the same sentences Christ's priesthood is held forth to the community as a *normative example for them* of faith(fulness) in hardship, as utterly *removed from sin*, and as the *promise* of a *sympathetic* priest by virtue of his total (yet without sin!) identification with them in worldly existence. All these features are pregnant with paraenetic implications.

Hebrews 7:1–28 advances by further developing the nature, need, and benefits of Christ's priesthood, beginning with a discussion of Melchizedek. Melchizedek remains for Hebrews a human figure; what is said represents a christological-typological reading of the canonical *texts* of Gen. 14 and Ps. 110. The point is to define the nature of the priestly "order" to which Ps. 110 makes reference. This exegesis implies that the *type* of Gen. 14:18–20 anticipates Ps. 110:4, that Ps. 110:4 invites such reflection on Gen. 14, and that the orientation of both will come to light in the historical rise of the Son of God. It likewise matters that this priesthood preceded Levi's and that the historical figure of Abraham encountered and acknowledged it; all this anticipates Heb. 11.

If 7:1–10 looks back to Gen. 14, then verses 11–19 (1) note that Ps. 110:4 itself anticipated a new priestly order, and (2) turn their attention forward to the correlative fact of the appearance of the Son. The upshot is that the manifest change of priesthood has brought a change of *law/covenant*, through which *perfection* has come.

The idea of "perfection" is prominent throughout Hebrews. Christ is "perfected"—with respect to vocational fittedness rather than moral development—and is the "perfecter" of faith. The beneficiaries of a covenantal arrangement can also be said to have been or not been "perfected." Ultimately, perfection is everything involved in effecting arrival at the goal of creation's and salvation's history: the approach through Christ to God. Thus, rather than speaking of the "fulfillment" of the OT, Hebrews prefers to show how the imperfect anticipated that which alone brings us to the goal, the perfect (cf. 1:1–4).

This perfection is a function of a change of law. Law is subsumed in *covenant*, the core feature of which is the relationship of this God and his people, and most centrally the right of entrance into the divine presence. In effect the Mosaic law *asserts* the postponement of the revelation of the promised access even as it symbolizes it. With the historical inauguration of the "eternal covenant" (13:20), the goal has been reached. How this writer views the revelatory function of the first covenant is implied by the way in which he uses it to explicate the *perfect* high priesthood of the Christ; discontinuity and continuity thus converge in the notion of perfection. Further, if Ps. 110 ordains a change of priesthood, then we should expect to find that the Scriptures anticipated a change of law/covenant. Of course, they do so in a famous passage (Jer. 31), and the writer will cite it shortly (8:8–12). Thus Jer. 31, which again bespeaks discontinuity *and continuity*, is made to serve the argument of Ps. 110:4, and the scriptural pieces interlock perfectly in the Son (1:1–2).

Finally, before summarizing the argument thus far (7:26–28), it is further supported by focusing on the implications of the divine oath and the inherent weakness of the human priests (vv. 20–25). Merely human priests are not able to usher humanity through eschatological divine judgment and death to the "world to come." Thus, the Son by virtue of his resurrection life "is able to save forever [or, to the uttermost] those who are drawing near to God through him, because he always lives to intercede for them" (v. 25 AT; cf. 2:14–15).

Priestly Ministry in the True Tent (8:1–10:18)

If the argument of 5:5–6 proceeded by slipping from Ps. 110:1 down to v. 4, then the direction is reversed in 8:1–2, the hinge text between 5:1–7:28 and 8:3–10:18. The fact of the high priesthood having been established through Ps. 110:4, we follow the lead of Ps. 110:1 into the location and nature of Christ's ministry.

First, it is established that the Melchizedekian order must involve a sacrifice in a temple, and that it must be the "true" sacrifice and temple to which the earthly sacrifices and tabernacle/temple *corresponded* (an ancient and widespread notion, native to the OT) and which they *foreshadowed* as an eschatological reality. All this was indicated by the Scriptures themselves. As to the day of inauguration, Christ's earthly ministry before the cross served to prepare and qualify him vocationally. But his entrance into the office appears to have comprised everything from the cross onward, such that the cross is an aspect of the *heavenly* offering (Milligan 127–33; Peterson 191–95; contra Westcott 227–30).

Having established that Christ, as our high priest (5:1–7:28), has obtained a ministry within the "true tent" superior to that of the Levitical priesthood (8:1–13), the exposition proper concludes with an extended and involved description of that ministry (9:1–10:18). To understand Christ's service, this description proceeds along the lines of a broad utilization of the Levitical priestly service. The centerpiece is going to be the annual Day of Atonement (Lev. 16; cf. 23:26–32; Num. 29:7–11), quite naturally, since the ultimate point of either system is the approach to God, quintessentially expressed in the entrance into the Most Holy Place. Yet the argument slides with ease from there to the daily service and the covenant inauguration ceremony and back, allowing these cultic actions to merge somewhat. Ultimately, the argument is that the *entire* integrated Mosaic cultus (the law) possesses the "shadow of the good things that are coming, and not the very embodiment [or, actual presence] of the realities" (10:1 AT; cf. 8:5). Thus, while the law corresponds to and thus reveals Christ's ministry, providing the categories through which Christ's ministry is to be imagined and understood (continuity), it must be clearly seen that it is *not* the reality and stands in contrast to it (discontinuity).

What should be noticed in this is that the logic of the argument does not work on the basis of a simple material versus immaterial opposition. It is finally the *blood and body* of Christ as fully human that replace the sacrifices of the old covenant. Just exactly what blood signified for the writer is never articulated (cf. Ellingworth 471–74; Attridge 248); likely it was accepted by writer and readers alike as a polyvalent symbol from the OT. Within this argument, Christ's blood alone effects *true* cleansing, forgiveness, and sanctification; certainly the opening chapters of Scripture are never far from the writer's mind, suggesting that he views all of this as the answer to the defilement, death, and expulsion of Gen. 3. This in turn assumes a broader understanding of a substitutionary atonement (2:9; 10:12). For this reason, Christ's sacrifice was effective for all sins *from the foundation of the world* (9:15, 26).

Hebrews 10:1–18 constitutes a four-shot finishing salvo, summarizing the general perspective on the law (10:1–3) and underscoring it with three scriptural appeals: Ps. 40:6–8 (39:7–9 LXX, in Heb. 10:4–9); Ps. 110:1 (109:1 LXX, in Heb. 10:11–14); Jer. 31:33–34 (in Heb. 10:15–18). The closing words of 10:18, masterfully chosen, contain within them both promise (10:19–25) and warning (10:26–31).

Hebrews and the Canon

The question of canonization was dealt with above (on what follows, in general see Lindars 119–27). Certainly there are NT parallels to elements within Hebrews' theology (e.g., Attridge 30–31, 102–3; Koester 54–58). Yet, in spite of the call to hold fast to "our confession" of Jesus being "high priest" (3:1; 4:14; 10:23), only in Hebrews is Christ directly called the "high priest" (= "great priest" in 10:21) or even a "priest." Nowhere else in the NT is Melchizedek or his priesthood mentioned or Ps. 110:4 taken up. Moreover, the convergence of sonship (not merely a royal idea in Hebrews) and priesthood, on the one hand, and priesthood and kingship on the other (6:20–7:1) is provocative against the OT background. Unique also is the way in which Hebrews portrays the heavenly cultus, especially in line with the Day of Atonement. All these points, with the exception of kingship, are basic to Hebrews' entire argument.

It has been said of Hebrews' Christology that it provides some of the clearest statements in the NT supporting *both* preexistence *and* adoption (Dunn 52). Related to this, the depictions of the Son's inclusion in the divine identity *and* his full participation in human "blood and flesh" (2:14 AT)—yet without sin—are among the strongest anywhere. Moreover, Hebrews does not hold back from drawing out the implications of the Son's humanity as the leader and perfecter of faith (2:10, 17–18; 4:15; 5:7–10; 12:1–3). Hebrews' definition and illustration of faith itself develops much more richly than James (2:14–26), and in a distinctive fashion develops an aspect of faith that Paul only alludes to (e.g., Gal. 5:6). In its strong warnings against unbelief, Hebrews' "rigorism" (5:11–6:20; 10:26–30, 39; 12:17) has challenged readers since the earliest centuries. Themes such as the word of God, angels, promise/oath, resting place, the new covenant, perfection, and divine discipline receive distinctive treatment here.

Certainly, Hebrews' use of the OT signals a deep investment of this writer's argument in the Scriptures. This facet of the book not only provides one of the chief NT examples of apostolic exegesis; it also represents a highly developed theology of the divine Word in history (Hughes). His approach to the OT takes seriously its historical nature but insists that it speaks directly to the Christian context, sometimes even consisting of words spoken by Christ himself (e.g., 2:12–13; 10:5–7); carefully understood, there is nothing naive or manipulative in his work. Consistent with this is the strategy to show how the OT Scriptures themselves indicate their incompleteness and anticipate the perfect yet to come (Caird, "Exegetical"). The result is that both deep-running *continuity* and sharp *discontinuity* cut across the entire fabric of usage. Certainly this strategy is informed and guided by the writer's Christology, and there can be no question that the Scriptures came to this writer as already interpreted. Yet he gives every indication of conducting an independent, fresh reading of the OT, which is finally to be measured by the implicit claims that this is *truth*. It is true both in terms of what the Scriptures were/are saying (from his own perspective, he is simply articulating the meaning that is in fact *there*, in the text) and in terms of how things are with God and the world, "yesterday and today and forever" (13:8).

Hebrews and Theology

There is something fascinating and unsettling about this book that names neither author nor audience. It cannot have come from any of the disciples, and it has no claim to have been Paul's, yet it represents one of the leading theological voices of the apostolic age. The most "Hellenistic" of NT books, yet known as "to the Hebrews," intensely pastoral and theologically creative, a heavenly summons to a very earthly holiness—it has spent much of its existence on the margins. Its glimpse into the abyss of apostasy has kept the church off balance from the beginning till now. Its cultic logic has puzzled a Gentile-dominated church, derogating the blood sacrifices of animals by insisting on the blood sacrifice of the Son of God and pronouncing obsolete the Mosaic cultus while leaving no alternative but to view Christ's work, encompassing all of creation's story, through the cultic world of Israel's story. In Christ's work, finally, the voice of God has been heard, the gospel of Jesus Christ, the Son of God, our great high priest. As certainly as Hebrews contemporizes the OT Scriptures in the mouth of the Holy Spirit, so also in it the Spirit speaks, as the church has acknowledged.

Without looking over its shoulder, Hebrews has passed beyond questions of Jew-Gentile boundary markers and ethnic derivation to the one God who has spoken to his one historic people, past, present, and future, formerly and incompletely in the prophets, consummately in these last days in the Son. *All* of the readers—presumably Gentiles too—are Abraham's seed (2:16) and heirs of the promise to him (6:13–20). Again, this writer has not been shy to make explicit what was latent in the inherited confession. He fearlessly works out the implications of the Scriptures and thus reveals—not constructs—for the church a wider and clearer vision of a priestly sacrifice and intercessory ministry than is given anywhere else in the canon (regarding the Eucharist, in general and as a sacrifice, and the Christian priesthood, see Koester 127–29; Lindars 136–42).

Centrally, Hebrews is a summons to faith. That its salvation is by divine grace is explicit, and in the world projected by this writer's theology, it could not possibly be otherwise than through faith. That this is a faith with deeds, a faith expressing itself through love, is assumed. But what matters here is that ours is a faith that is "the reality of things hoped for, the proof of things unseen" (11:1 AT). This faith was pioneered and perfected by Jesus Christ, so that through his work authentic faith embodies *his* agonistic story of salvation.

Remarkably, given the nature of its argument, this discourse with studied care avoids a restriction of its challenge to Jewish readers tempted to return to the religion of the temple. Certainly, as Lindars has emphasized (101–18, 134), there is an effective program offered for those who feel the need "to do something practical so as to objectify their inner conflict of emotions" concerning guilt. Yet if, when Hebrews says that "we have here no enduring city" (13:14), this applies to Jerusalem, then, a fortiori, it applies to Rome—or to Kampala—as it does to Jerusalem. Nothing finally requires us to think that the writer's concerns were limited to a threatened return to Judaism; his thoroughgoing appeal to the OT law is due more to his theology of the Word than to the orientation of his audience. His real concern is that his readers "show the same zeal" that they had earlier demonstrated "until the end"—that they continue to stand their ground "in a great contest with sufferings," accepting the seizure of their possessions, because they know that they have a "better and lasting possession."

What this sermon's effect was on the house church for which it was written cannot be known. But for the church catholic this "word of exhortation" has done exactly what it set out to do: encourage and embolden to a faith that will go outside the camp, bearing the disgrace Christ bore. Countless thousands have enacted such a form of existence "to the point of shedding blood," based precisely on this firm demonstration and revelation of the high priestly work of Christ. They did not shrink back.

Bibliography

Attridge, H. *The Epistle to the Hebrews*. Hermeneia. Fortress, 1989.

Barrett, C. K. "The Christology of Hebrews." Pages 110–27 in *Who Do You Say That I Am?* ed. M. A. Powell and D. Bauer. Westminster John Knox, 1999.

———. "The Eschatology of the Epistle to the Hebrews." Pages 363–93 in *The Background of the New Testament and Its Eschatology*, ed. W. D. Davies and D. Daube. Cambridge University Press, 1954.

Blackstone, T. "The Hermeneutics of Recontextualization in the Epistle to the Hebrews." Diss., Emory University, 1995.

Bockmuehl, M. "The Church in Hebrews." Pages 133–51 in *A Vision for the Church*, ed. M. Bockmuehl and M. B. Thompson. T&T Clark, 1997.

Caird, G. B. "The Exegetical Method of the Epistle to the Hebrews." *CJT* 5 (1959): 44–51.

———. "Son by Appointment." Pages 73–81 in vol. 1 of *The New Testament Age*, ed. W. C. Weinrich. Mercer University Press, 1984.

Demarest, B. *A History of the Interpretation of Hebrews 7,1–10 from the Reformation to the Present Day.* Mohr/Siebeck, 1976.

Dunn, J. D. G. *Christology in the Making.* 2nd ed. SCM, 1989.

Dunnill, J. *Covenant and Sacrifice in the Letter to the Hebrews.* SNTSMS 75. Cambridge University Press, 1992.

Ellingworth, P. *The Epistle to the Hebrews.* NIGTC. Eerdmans, 1993.

Grässer, E. *Der Glaube im Hebräerbrief.* MTS 2. Elwert, 1965.

Greer, R. *The Captain of Our Salvation.* Mohr/Siebeck, 1973.

Guthrie, G. *The Structure of Hebrews.* NovTSup 73. Brill, 1994.

Hagen, K. *Hebrews Commenting from Erasmus to Bèza, 1516–1598.* Mohr/Siebeck, 1981.

———. *A Theology of Testament in the Young Luther.* Brill, 1974.

Hagner, D. *The Use of the Old and New Testaments in Clement of Rome.* NovTSup 34. Brill, 1973.

Hughes, G. *Hebrews and Hermeneutics.* SNTSMS 36. Cambridge University Press, 1979.

Hurst, L. D. *The Epistle to the Hebrews.* SNTSMS 65. Cambridge University Press, 1990.

Käsemann, E. *The Wandering People of God,* trans. R. A. Harrisville. Augsburg, 1984.

Koester, C. *Hebrews.* AB 36. Doubleday, 2001.

Laansma, J. *"I Will Give You Rest."* WUNT 2.98. Mohr/Siebeck, 1997.

Lane, W. *Hebrews 1–8* and *Hebrews 9–13.* WBC 47A–B. Word, 1991.

Lindars, B. *The Theology of the Letter to the Hebrews.* NTT. Cambridge University Press, 1991.

Loader, W. R. G. *Sohn und Hoherpriester.* WMANT 53. Neukirchener Verlag, 1981.

Manson, W. *The Epistle to the Hebrews.* Hodder & Stoughton, 1951.

Milligan, G. *The Theology of the Epistle to the Hebrews.* T&T Clark, 1899.

Peterson, D. *Hebrews and Perfection.* SNTSMS 47. Cambridge University Press, 1982.

Westcott, B. F. *The Epistle to the Hebrews.* Macmillan & Co., 1892.

20

James

WILLIAM R. BAKER

James, disparaged by Luther and broken into context-less pieces by Dibelius, has struggled for its theological voice to be heard by the church. Today, as theology is being turned on its head into action items for faithful Christians, James's "wisdom" comes across as theologically cutting edge for people who desire a dynamic relationship with God.

History of Interpretation

The clearest early use of James comes from the Eastern church, specifically from Origen, in the third century, who cites it thirty-six times. Employment of similar language, such as "double-minded" (a term unique to James in the NT), suggests possible knowledge of James in early Western writings, such as *1 Clement*, Shepherd of Hermas, the *Didache*, and the *Letter of Barnabas*. Eusebius reports that Clement of Alexandria, Origen's predecessor, wrote an entire commentary on James, though Clement never cites James in other extant writings.

Despite its early favor in the Alexandrian school, James was not allegorized. More common was quoting statements from James, without regard for their contexts, in support of various teachings. Cyril of Alexandria, who cites James 124 times, for example, isolates James 3:2 ("We all stumble in many ways") from its context about teachers, as support for general human frailty. He also, among many others, promoted 1:17 ("Every good and perfect gift is from above") as a proof for the divinity of Christ.

Chief interest in James—both in the West and in the East throughout the early centuries of teaching and preaching, beginning as early as fourth-century Hilary of Poitier but including Augustine—focused most heavily on the latter half of 1:17 ("who does not change like shifting shadows") as crucial biblical support for God's immutability. Another focal interest was James's intersection with the cosmic struggle of God and the devil in temptation of the believer. Augustine wrote an unrecovered commentary on James, and his respect for James, shown in his sermons, helped vault it from obscurity in the West. He was interested in the moral teaching of James, especially with regard to speech.

The Venerable Bede, eighth-century author of the best, most influential early commentary on James, carefully explicates 1:13 by explaining that God does test people with "external" temptations, but only the devil tempts with "internal" temptations, which attack the soul. This also helps explain Jesus' temptation, which troubled the early church in light of this verse. Bede, more like commentaries centuries later, combines exacting exegesis with insightful theology and application.

Eleventh-century Theophylact, who is almost certainly dependent on Didymus the Blind and Oecumenius, curiously identifies the "righteous man" of 5:6 (KJV) not only with Christ but as a prophecy of the author's (understood as James, Jesus' brother) own political execution.

Attention did not focus on faith and works in 2:14–26, though the contrast with Paul is recognized. A seventh-century monk, Andreas, is typical in explaining that "faith" in Paul is prebaptismal, whereas "faith" in James is postbaptismal. Augustine proclaims that James explains how Paul should be understood, that good works are to result from justifying faith. Origen and Cyril of Alexandria both similarly bring James into their commentaries on Romans.

In the Reformation era, Luther disdained James's teaching on faith, lack of any teaching about Christ, exaltation of the law (his understanding of "law of liberty" in 1:25 KJV), and lack of logical order. This led him to the dogmatic conclusion that it was not written by an apostle but by a second-generation believer, probably Jewish, who carelessly wrote down some apostolic teaching he had heard but packaged this with his own nonapostolic, even anti-Christian ideas. Even in the early church, the authorship of James was a question mark on its authority, and Eusebius recognized it as a "disputed" book. Origen's connecting it to James, the Lord's brother, had settled the question for most. Though concern over James's authorship troubled others of Luther's era, like Erasmus and even Luther's disputant, Cardinal Thomas de Vio (Cajetan), Luther's radical solution was unique.

None of the other Reformers, such as Tyndale, Zwingli, Calvin, or even Philipp Melanchthon, were influenced to adopt this extreme position, which strikes many as a much-too-convenient way for Luther to subordinate James's theology of faith to salvation by faith alone. The fact that 2:26 was used against Luther in his Leipzig Debate and that 5:14 was the Roman Catholic proof text for the sacrament of extreme unction may be historical factors that prejudiced Luther against James.

In his commentary, Calvin explicitly rejects Luther's unwise precedent, cautioning against imposing uniformity and upholding the value of diversity in the canon. Calvin underscores this by asserting that Paul and James apply faith to different, legitimate facets of justification, Paul to acceptance by God, James to a reality that requires evidence. In fact, a person can even be said to be justified by works in that works are a necessary evidence of saving faith. Calvin makes no mention of divine immutability in 1:17 and Christ in 5:6 and rejects extreme unction in 5:14 on the basis that the gift of healing was a temporary apostolic gift.

Despite the fact that Luther's canonical subordination of James and conjectures about authorship were but a ripple that seemed to disperse quietly in his day, they erupted again like a geyser in the era of critical scholarship and continue to moisten the air of James scholarship. Efforts to resolve the issue of authorship and the related issue of James's relationship to early Christianity occupied nearly all scholarly resources from the mid-1800s to the late twentieth century.

The quest to find historical solutions began with Herder, who postulated that Paul and James had a personal relationship, understanding each other's view of justification and faith. Historical criticism proper began with Kern and De Wette, who, interacting with each other's publications, propelled the notions that Paul and James are totally incompatible on justification (Luther redivivus). They counted James as the pseudonymous voice of a radical, Ebionite, Jewish Christianity of the second century, which opposed domineering Gentile Christianity, and as devoid of any coherence or valuable theological perspective.

This low opinion of James was magnified by those connected to the Tübingen School and reached its pinnacle at the end of the nineteenth century. Then Massebieau and Spitta independently proclaimed James to be a

Jewish document, covered with a veneer of Christianity by the introduction of Jesus Christ to 1:1 and 2:1. At the same time, in contrast, Mayor, and also G. Kittel, believed historical-critical methodology implicated James, written by Jesus' brother, legitimately to represent earliest Christianity, pre-apostolic council (49 CE), still heavily flavored with Jewish thought. They even raised evidence to suggest that Paul responds to James on faith and not vice versa.

As the twentieth century began, two scholars focused on the literary aspects of James but with strikingly different conclusions. Ropes, postulating a pseudonymous Palestinian author writing post-70 CE, recognized James's indebtedness to Jewish and Christian thought, and also Jewish Wisdom literature, but nevertheless advocated that the controlling influence is the fourth-century BCE Greek moral form of address, "diatribe." Ropes also recognized James's intelligent use of Greek to create catchwords, particularly in chapter 1. Unlike Ropes, who believed the somewhat isolated units show progress in thought, Dibelius, operating from a form-critical perspective, put feet on Luther's earlier criticism. He determined that the organization of the pieces in James is totally ad hoc and superficial, that the book is the best NT representative of paraenetic literature throughout, and that each unit must be interpreted independently from its context because no authorial intention holds the book together. All of this leads to his conclusion that James has no theology of its own, only thoughts ripped from other contexts and meaninglessly pieced together.

Nearly all twentieth-century study has attempted to breathe life into James after Dibelius's near deathblow to it. Adamson specifically focuses his commentary on demonstrating the coherence and relevance of James to Christian life. Laws boldly unveils integrity of human character, akin to God's own singleness, as the underlying theological conviction of the book. Davids advanced the study of Francis, and Martin built on the work of Davids, taking the epistolary character of James to its penultimate and contending for an intricate cycle of patterning within. Cargal and Johnson find cohesiveness through rhetorical criticism. Moo suggests that James be approached as a sermon and defended as a theological document.

The Overall Message

Dibelius's charge of incoherence has quite rightly been set aside as exaggerating the scissors-and-paste construction of James and drawing unfounded conclusions regarding the paraenetic genre. Even if James results from the work of an editor or even a collector, its purpose and intent are communicated at least by the arrangement of the material.

Despite the lack of a direct statement of purpose or a clear statement of its intended audience, James does base its teaching on the author's intimate and authoritative knowledge of a specific community to whom he writes. Yet, exactly how wide or narrow the community is cannot be determined very far. They are Hellenistic Jewish Christians, but as to where in the early Christian Mediterranean world, only conjectures may be offered.

What is clear is that James fits more into a wisdom genre than into the polemics of philosophy or theology. James leads with behavior and relationship to God, for which theological values form an oft-assumed base. James is concerned that his readers live well and more successfully than they currently are. This is the typical concern of Wisdom literature, like Proverbs, or Job, or Sirach.

The general problem the author of James perceives for his readers is that their spiritual development is being hindered by various forces: their own economic and social condition, lack of conviction, poor choices, overconfidence in the security of their position with God, injustices inflicted on them, and the influence of the world around them. The solution is to repent, to turn back from their spiritual wasteland of wandering before it is too late and Christ comes in judgment. The author's overall goal is for his readers to become one in person, in community, and in relationship with God. The proof of this new and continuing orientation is in their behavior with respect to God and others, in and outside the church. The means for this is for them to hear God immediately through the epistle itself, and daily through prayer, worship, and the church.

James's focus on hearing God comes from recognizing the significance of the proverb of 1:19, "Let everyone be quick to hear, slow to speak, and slow to anger" (NRSV), in relationship to the entire epistle. It is commonly recognized that the three parts of this proverb are unpacked in the paragraph that follows: "slow to anger" (1:20–21), "quick to hear" (1:22–25), and "slow to speak" (1:26–27). What is not so often observed is that these three parts of the proverb, broadly conceived, are also developed in the ensuing chapters: correctly hearing the word (ch. 2), the difficulty of controlling the tongue (ch. 3), and the damaging effect of angry speech (ch. 4). The positive effect of hearing God reverberates through every negative issue the author takes up, right through to enabling a wandering believer to hear and respond to the truth of God in 5:19.

Contribution to the Canon

Despite its current location at the back of the NT canon among the "non-Pauline" collection of epistles, reflecting the Western (Roman) ordering, in the Eastern order (also reflecting Athanasius's order in his Festal Letter of 367), James heads the General Epistles, which follow immediately after Acts, before the Pauline Epistles.

How might reading James this far up in the NT canon affect our interpretation of it? First, it would be more obvious that James is a trustworthy representative of Jesus' teaching, particularly the Sermon on the Mount, as also found in the Gospels. Second, it would be more apparent that James showcases concerns of the church in its earlier, pre-Gentile days as seen in the earlier chapters of Acts. Third, it might make it easier to see that Paul, not James, is the innovator in the early church and the one whose teaching requires careful scrutiny and patient explaining.

Deppe documents that while as many as 184 sayings in James have been purported to be allusions from the Synoptic Gospels, those that are most assuredly legitimate (though many others are probable allusions) narrow to eight: James 1:5 and 4:2c–3 (Matt. 7:7; Luke 11:9); 2:5 (Luke 6:20b; Matt. 5:3); 5:2–3a (Matt. 6:19–20; Luke 12:33b); 4:9 (Luke 6:21, 25b); 5:1 (Luke 6:24); 5:12 (Matt. 5:33–37); 4:10 (Matt. 23:12; Luke 14:11; 18:14b). While James never quotes Jesus or one of the Gospels, it showcases how many early Christian teachers may have freely incorporated the very language of Jesus' teaching as they understood it. This allows that teaching to be applied to new situations, as when showing favoritism to the powerful and neglect to the marginal becomes a violation of neighbor love (2:1–4).

James provides a peek into the early church. Whether or not its date is pre-Gentile, its orientation is Gentile-less, with no mention of circumcision or issues of how Jewish law applies to those beyond Jews. It speaks of the assembly of believers as a "synagogue" (2:2 Greek), implying that the church began organizing itself on this Jewish model. It suggests that non-believers at times frequented these synagogues (2:2–4). It shows that elders, apparently at least two, provided spiritual leadership, that they visited the sick and sought their spiritual and physical healing through prayer. It also shows that people in the church had spiritual obligations to care for one another through times of nagging sinfulness and even apostasy (5:13–20). Recognition that James draws upon three of the same OT passages as 1 Peter but for different purposes (Isa. 40:6–8//James 1:10–11//1 Pet. 1:24; Prov. 10:12//James 5:20//1 Pet. 4:8; Prov. 3:34//James 4:6//1 Pet. 5:5) suggests that early Christian teachers worked freely from common resources.

With Paul, James shared a desire that people be justified before God through Christ. Yet, James was not concerned about those entering justified status so much as those exiting by default or intention. James would probably have agreed with Paul's adamant position that keeping Jewish traditional laws and rituals has nothing to do with justification in Christ. Nevertheless, he was probably intentionally cautionary about how Paul's teaching on this subject could be easily misused.

However the canon is organized, James stands as an important balance to Paul's presentation of justification, and a needed caution. James has value as the only NT epistle that marshals a theological defense of the poor, a sustained concern about speech-ethics, and reflection on numerous and various aspects of prayer. This makes its canonical weight proportionally much heavier than its slim size.

Theological Significance

James's thoughts about God are typical of anyone raised in a Jewish home in the early first century, and the author assumes his readers share these convictions with him. They rest comfortably beneath the surface of his main points. When 1:17 says that God supplies the good things in people's lives, the author shows his trust that God knows what is good for us and who we are personally, and that he is powerful enough to harness the forces of the universe to our well-being. When 4:3 says that people do not receive everything they pray for because of sinister desires, the author reveals his belief that God knows our motives, good and bad—that we cannot hide anything from him.

Many other ideas about God can be discerned. He is the Creator (1:17–18), making people in his own image (3:9), and his word is powerful enough to give people rebirth (1:18). His character is constant in that he never cavorts with evil (1:13, 17), always keeps his promises (1:12), and has a watchful, discerning eye on the poor and how the powerful treat them (1:9–11; 2:1–7; 5:1–6).

No doubt, James is far more God- than Christ-centered, though what is said about Christ has to count as a quite high Christology. Jesus shares the titles "Lord" (1:1; 2:1; 5:7–8, 14–15) and Judge (5:9) with God; his very name, like God's, is powerful enough to heal (5:14) and significant enough to be blasphemed/slandered (2:8); to him is possibly attributed the Shekinah glory of God (2:1). Christ's return to judge on God's behalf is also pending (5:7–9).

James emphasizes that the fundamental point of human life is to find God, respond to his voice, and relate to him successfully and robustly, now and eternally. As essential as Christ is in this enterprise, James reminds us of something Christianity understandably quite easily forgets, that Christ is the means, perhaps the agent, but not the end of our quest. Our goal is God and a successful relationship with him. To focus solely on Christ in worship is to miss Christ's own purpose of bringing us to God. In this way, James should be prized and heard in the church. Though written to believers, James speaks to Christians first as people, and second as those who believe in Jesus. Thus, it can speak to people beyond the church. James functions as a guide to everyone in their most basic need, to be integrated with others, God, and themselves. James tells us that we can each, like Abraham, be God's friend, and he ours. No message is more needed for the world or for the church than this.

Bibliography

Adamson, J. *The Epistle of James*. NICNT. Eerdmans, 1954.

Baker, W. "Christology in the Epistle of James." *EvQ* 74 (2002): 47–57.

———. *Personal Speech-Ethics in the Epistle of James*. WUNT 2.68. Mohr, 1995.

Bauckham, R. *James*. New Testament Readings. Routledge, 1999.

Bray, G., ed. *James, 1–2 Peter, 1–3 John, Jude*. ACCSNT 11. InterVarsity, 2000.

Calvin, J. *Commentaries on the Catholic Epistles*. 1551, trans. J. Owen. Eerdmans, 1948.

Cargal, T. *Restoring the Diaspora*. SBLDS 144. Scholars Press, 1993.

Chester, A., and R. P. Martin. *The Theology of the Letters of James, Peter, and Jude*. Cambridge University Press, 1994.

Davids, P. *Commentary on James*. NIGTC. Eerdmans, 1982.

Deppe, D. *The Sayings of Jesus in the Epistle of James*. Bookcrafters, 1989.

De Wette, W. M. L. *Historical-Critical Introduction to the Canonical Books of the New Testament*, trans. F. Frothingham. Crosby & Nichols, 1858.

Dibelius, M. *James*. Revised by H. Greeven. Hermeneia. Fortress, 1976.

Francis, F. "The Form and Function of the Opening and Closing Paragraphs of James and I John." *ZNW* 61 (1970): 110–26.

Herder, J. G. *Briefe zweener Brüder Jesu im unserm Kanon*. Meyer, 1775. Herders sämmtliche Werke 7, ed. B. Suphan. Weidmann, 1884.

Johnson, L. T. *The Letter of James*. AB. Doubleday, 1995.

Kern, F. H. *Der Brief Jakobi untersucht und erklärt*. Fues, 1838.

———. "Der Charakter und Ursprung des Briefes Jacobi." *TZTh* 8 (1835): 3–132.

Kittel, G. "Der geschichtliche Ort des Jakobusbriefes." *ZNW* 41 (1942): 54–112.

Luther, M. *Luther's Works*, vols. 35–36, 54. Fortress, 1959.

Martin, R. P. *James*. WBC. Word, 1988.

Massebieu, L. "L'épître de Jacques: est-elle l'oeuvre d'un chrétien?" *RHR* (1895): 249–83.

Mayor, J. *The Epistle of St. James*. 1913. Zondervan, 1954.

Moo, D. *The Letter of James*. Pillar. Eerdmans, 2000.

Ropes, J. *The Epistle of St. James*. ICC. T&T Clark, 1916.

Spitta, F. *Zur Geschichte und Literatur des Urchristentums*. Vol. 2, *Der Brief des Jakobus*. Vandenhoeck & Ruprecht, 1896

Wall, R. *The Community of the Wise*. NTC. Trinity, 1997.

21

1 Peter

PETER R. RODGERS

The First Epistle of Peter purports to be a letter from the apostle Peter to scattered Christians in Asia Minor, who are suffering for the name of Christ. Peter writes to remind them of their redemption through the death of Christ, their living hope through his resurrection, and their new status as God's own people. He encourages them to follow Christ's example and to maintain love for one another and good conduct toward outsiders. Most modern and postmodern commentators have challenged this picture, while some have continued to adhere to it in some form. Theological interpretation may offer a way through this interpretative impasse.

Recent Interpretation

Around the middle of the twentieth century, two important commentaries appeared that set the terms for subsequent interpretation of 1 Peter. E. G. Selwyn's commentary, with extensive additional notes, argued that the apostle Peter authored the letter, with Silvanus (5:12) as the amanuensis. Numerous similarities with other NT documents in catechetical and paraenetic material were presented as evidence that the letter represented mainstream apostolic Christianity at its formative period. For Selwyn, the likely situation that called forth the letter was the fire in Rome and the ensuing persecution of Christians by Nero (63–64 CE).

F. W. Beare, on the other hand, argued that the background to the letter is to be found in the situation described by Pliny the Younger, governor of Bithynia in 112, who wrote to the emperor Trajan about the policy of the empire concerning Christians. Beare saw the letter as a literary fiction, written in the name of the apostle to scattered suba-postolic churches in Asia Minor. Beare's thorough textual, lexical, and background studies added weight to his arguments. Subsequent study has lined up behind one or the other, with the majority of commentators positing a pseudepigraphical work written toward the end of the first century (Goppelt; Michaels; Achtemeier; Elliott). Even J. H. Elliott's recent landmark commentary (AB), which posits a date between 73 and 90, does not offer a way beyond the stalemate.

Recent Studies

Compared to the Gospels and the Pauline Letters, 1 Peter has suffered rela-tive neglect. Only a few important commentaries and studies have appeared since 1950. In the last half-century, studies in 1 Peter have demonstrated both the necessity and the opportunity for theological interpretation.

F. L. Cross

Cross argued that 1 Pet. 1:3–4:11 constituted the celebrant's portion of a baptismal rite, and that the actual initiation takes place after 1:21. Cross's view has not been widely accepted, due to forced exegesis and examples drawn from a later date (e.g., the *Apostolic Tradition* of Hippolytus). But his focus on the theme of exodus and Passover as a major emphasis in the letter has not been sufficiently explored. The paschal references in 1 Pet. 1 need to be placed in the context of developing Jewish exegesis of this most important text (Exod. 12) and event in the story of God's people.

J. H. Elliott

Chief among contributors to the study of 1 Peter has been J. H. Elliott. Elliott's *The Elect and the Holy* examines the term "royal priesthood" or "a kingdom of priests" (2:9, citing Exod. 19:6). Elliott concludes that the expression refers not to believers as individual priests, but only to the believing community as community. If Elliott's exegesis and conclusions are sound, 1 Pet. 2 may not be used to support the notion of a priesthood of all believers. However, to insist on a corporate interpretation to the exclusion of an individual one is to miss a narrative element of fundamental importance. No OT passage is more formative for the narrative theology of 1 Peter than Ps. 34. A long quotation from the psalm occurs in 1 Pet. 3, and there are a number of allusions. A citation from Ps. 34:8 immediately precedes the relevant section (2:4–10). A curious and instructive feature of this psalm (and others, notably 130, 22, 69) is the interplay of the individual and the community (Ps. 34:1 "I will bless . . ."; v. 3 "Let us exalt . . ."). The individual righteous sufferer who cries to God for help finds that he or she is not alone. In the narrative movement of Ps. 34, both the individual and the community are distinctive and important. Both are in focus in the story told by the author of 1 Peter, who has meditated deeply on Ps. 34.

The last two decades of the twentieth century have witnessed the rise of social-scientific study of the NT. A pioneering study in 1 Peter has been Elliott's *A Home for the Homeless*. He applies new insights from sociology to the letter, contending that the recipients' strangerhood, their condition of estrangement and alienation, remains social rather than cosmological. Their predicament as "resident aliens and visiting strangers" is contrasted not to having a home in heaven, but to having a home within the Christian community. The reference is more sociological than theological. The trials refer not so much to official persecutions from Rome, but more to local ostracism and pressure due to their strangeness as a new social group. Still, there are important grounds for retaining the NRSV translation "exiles" rather than Elliott's "strangers" in 1:1. N. T. Wright has argued persuasively that the exile is a governing element in the metanarrative all Jewish groups shared in the NT era. The story of deliverance from exile, informed as that story itself is by the foundation of the exodus, is the theological backdrop of the Christian claim that through the death and resurrection of Jesus, Christians have been delivered from bondage into freedom. For early Christians, and especially the writer and recipients of 1 Peter, that deliverance was articulated in terms of Scriptures like Pss. 34 and 39 (v. 12, cited in 1 Pet. 2:11) and Isa. 52–53. Not only the language but also the logic of these passages shaped the theology of the letter. Thus, we must look to its varied use of the OT for an indication of its metanarrative and theology.

W. J. Dalton

Dalton's important monograph, *Christ's Proclamation to the Spirits*, argues that Christ's journey to "preach to the spirits in prison" (3:19) refers not to his "descent into hell," which has been a common assumption from patristic times onward, but to Christ's ascension. During his ascension Christ proclaimed triumph over the rebellious angels, imprisoned in the third heaven of intertestamental Jewish cosmology. Dalton's view has found wide acceptance among commentators. The ascension is certainly fundamental to the whole passage (3:18–22); verse 22 says that Jesus Christ "has gone into heaven, and is at the right hand of God, with angels, authorities, and powers made subject to him" (NRSV). Dalton rightly notes that the influence of Ps. 110:1 is paramount, but he does not develop this line. Psalm 110:1, the most frequently cited OT text in the NT, is probably a conscious echo in 3:22 and fundamental to the theology and ethics of the letter. The same word for the subjection of hostile powers is used to urge slaves and wives to submit, in the household codes. Further study along this line would be fruitful for understanding the theology and ethics of the letter, and elsewhere in the NT.

L. Goppelt

In his commentary, Goppelt, like Elliott, pioneered a social-scientific approach. Surveying the household codes in their cultural setting, he concluded that they represent not the application of an OT and Jewish tradition, but the reworking of a Hellenistic ethos on the basis of principles developed by Jesus and Paul. But such a claim fails to reckon with the theological reflection on Scripture in 1 Peter. The ideas of good behavior are drawn directly from Scriptures like Ps. 34 and Prov. 3. Psalm 34:14 may even have contributed to the unique vocabulary of 1 Peter. His NT *hapax legomenon* for doing good (*agathopoiia*) is probably his own coinage, resulting from meditation on Ps. 34.

D. L. Balch

Balch studied the domestic codes in 1 Peter in the context of attitudes toward husbands and wives in Greco-Roman culture and Hellenistic Judaism. His work, however, does not take sufficient account of the importance of the OT and its interpretation (despite his references to Philo) as the primary influence on the thought and shape of 1 Peter. His Scripture index does not even list Isa. 3:18–24 (as do most commentaries). Epictetus or Seneca may indeed have influenced the argument, but how much more the OT! So with Gen. 18:12 cited at 3:6. Hardly a proof text, this echo may offer some new clues to the background of the letter.

W. L. Schutter

Schutter's *Hermeneutic and Composition in 1 Peter* takes an important step forward. His sustained attention to the hermeneutical presuppositions, methods, techniques, and assumptions in the letter's use of the OT points the way for further study. Especially valuable is Schutter's focus on the OT as a formative influence. The section 1:13–2:10 he takes as a "homiletic midrash," and he offers several parallels from Philo and rabbinic literature for comparison. A sustained study of the use of the OT in 1 Peter, following the lines laid out by Schutter, is certainly needed, and it is likely from this direction that the most valuable work on 1 Peter will emerge in the future.

Theology and OT Hermeneutics

A thorough study of the use of the OT in 1 Peter will concentrate on at least the following six areas:

Form

Careful attention must be paid to places where the text form of the OT citations differs from the MT or LXX. The differences, sometimes slight, have been explained as stylistic, use of a different version, quotation from memory, or targumizing. A special focus on the textual variations within quotations should prove fruitful, especially where the change may be theologically motivated (e.g., 3:14–15 using Isa. 8:12–13; did 1 Peter write "God" or "Christ"?). The reading *Christos* at 2:3 in Papyrus 72 may reflect an important interpretative tradition.

Introduction

First Peter contains both OT texts introduced with a formula (1:16; 2:6) and also passages without them (1:24–25, citing Isa. 40; 3:10–12, citing Pss. 34; 2:21–25, citing Isa. 53). The presence or absence of an introductory formula may indicate the degree of familiarity of writer and readers with the OT and something about background. A study of the formulas, or their absence, would indicate that both writer and recipients were more Jewish than is usually allowed. The echoes of Scripture abound in 1 Peter, and fragments of the OT have been woven artfully into the literary framework. In identifying echoes the interpreter will benefit from applying the criteria developed by R. Hays, which include availability, volume, recurrence, satisfaction, and thematic coherence.

Selection

Listed together, the OT texts in 1 Peter appear as a random selection of quotations. Is there any discernible logic to their selection? Here greater attention is needed to the purpose of 1 Peter as a treatise intended to encourage God's people undergoing persecution for their faith. Special attention to 4 Macc. 18:10–19 (a Jewish persecution document that features both Ps. 34 and Prov. 3) will prove fruitful. This passage holds a number of keys to understanding the letter. In addition, the exegete will ask why several verses were cited from Ps. 34, but surprisingly not 34:20: "He keeps all their bones; not one of them will be broken" (NRSV).

Application

Some OT texts used in 1 Peter are found elsewhere in the NT, where they are applied to other features of the Christian story. For example, phrases from Isa. 53 are employed in 1 Pet. 2:18–25 to encourage Christians to follow the example of Jesus' patient endurance of suffering. Both in 1 Peter and elsewhere in the NT, the passage is applied to the death of Christ and to his healing ministry.

History

OT texts in 1 Peter should be studied in the context of the developing exegesis in the Judaism of the period. Isaiah 28:16, for example, is combined with Isa. 8:14 by both 1 Peter and Paul (1 Pet. 2:3–10; Rom. 9:32–33). But the text has a developed exegetical history before its use by NT writers. It is found in the Qumran texts (1QS 8.7). So 1 Peter is participating in a developed exegetical tradition. This will also be true in the case of the allusions to Exod. 12 (and the probable allusion to Gen. 22 at 1:20).

Function

Often the OT is assumed to play a supportive or confirming role for the argument of 1 Peter. Texts are brought in, it is argued, as "proof texts." However, careful study demonstrates that the OT has had a much more creative role in the theology of the letter. For 1 Peter, Scripture is not so much plundered as pondered. This proves to be as true for the quotations as for the allusions and echoes of the OT. Elliott has noted the "important and creative role" of Isa. 52–53 for the theology of the letter. Commenting on 2:18–25, Elliott writes, "In its fusion of biblical themes and motifs, kerygmatic formulas, and extensive use of Isaiah 52–53 this passage illustrates both an independence from Pauline thought and a theological formulation that is as creative as it is singular in the NT" (*1 Peter*, 504).

Elliott has called 1 Peter an "exegetical stepchild." Perhaps its relative neglect can now work to its advantage. Sustained study of 1 Peter will bring fresh theological and practical perspective to a discipline that has concentrated primarily on the Gospels and Pauline writings. The letter, which contains more OT relative to its size than any other NT document, except perhaps Revelation, may have much to contribute at a time of renewed interest in the theological interpretation of Scripture.

Bibliography

Achtemeier, P. *1 Peter*. Hermeneia. Fortress, 1996.

Balch, D. L. *Let Wives Be Submissive*. SBLMS 26. Scholars Press, 1981.

Beare, F. W. *The First Epistle of Peter*. 3rd ed. Blackwell, 1970.

Cross, F. L. *1 Peter*. Mowbray, 1954.

Dalton, W. J. *Christ's Proclamation to the Spirits*. 2nd ed. Pontifical Biblical Institute, 1989.

Elliott, J. *The Elect and the Holy*. NovTSup 12. Brill, 1966.

———. *1 Peter*. AB 37B. Doubleday, 2000.

———. *A Home for the Homeless*. Fortress, 1981.

Goppelt, L. *A Commentary on 1 Peter*, ed. F. Hahn. Eerdmans, 1993.

Hays, R. *Echoes of Scripture in the Letters of Paul*. Yale University Press, 1989.

Michaels, J. R. *1 Peter*. WBC. Word, 1988.

Schutter, W. L. *Hermeneutic and Composition in 1 Peter*. WUNT 2.30. Mohr/Siebeck, 1989.

Selwyn, E. G. *The First Epistle of Peter*. 2nd ed. Macmillan, 1947.

Wright, N. T. *The New Testament and the People of God*. Fortress, 1992.

22

2 Peter

PETER H. DAVIDS

Often seen as one of the "ugly stepchildren" of the NT, 2 Peter has suffered neglect in the modern period. However, 2 Peter makes a significant contribution to help us understand the relationship of eschatology and ethics, and recognize the enculturation of the Christian message in a different culture than the one in which it arose.

History of Interpretation

Second Peter has had a mixed reception in the church. Origen, the first expressly to cite it, had his doubts about the work, as did Eusebius, who said that the church in the East did not consider it canonical. As late as the end of the fourth century, Didymus of Alexandria could cite it as a forgery. On the other hand, it is clear that the work was circulating by the mid-second century, and it does appear along with 1 Peter in the Bodmer papyri. More importantly, not only did Jerome defend it, but also a number of the later church fathers used it, including Chrysostom, Augustine, Hilary of Arles, and Bede. However, for the most part these are brief citations, mined in the service of the teaching or controversies of the time. Martin Luther likewise quoted from the work, and Calvin, as usual, wrote a commentary on it, but for both men Paul was central and 2 Peter of peripheral interest. After the rise of biblical criticism, 2 Peter fell even more out of favor, because the work was viewed as early catholic and because of a rejection of its apocalyptic eschatology. Only in the last two decades of the twentieth century did 2 Peter come into its own as scholars began to appreciate its rhetoric and its theological contribution.

The Message of 2 Peter

The concern of 2 Peter is with licentious teaching that has arisen within certain house churches in one or more city churches of the Christian movement. This licentiousness was being supported by a denial of the parousia and the concomitant final judgment. Ethics and eschatology were going hand in hand negatively. It is also likely that they were using Paul's doctrine of grace to support their licentiousness, claiming that freedom from the law means freedom to break moral boundaries.

Second Peter points out, first, that when called by God to know him, one is freed from the power of desire and made a participant in the divine nature, which should work itself out in increasing virtue. This confirms election and makes one's eschatological hope secure.

Second, the parousia is a secure doctrine in that its prophetic announcement has been confirmed by the proleptic vision given in the transfiguration. Any claim that delay indicates nonreality is negated by the evidence of the flood, where there was also delay before judgment, and an appropriate knowledge of God's nature. His view of time and therefore his patience are not the same as the finite human view of time or human patience. God is patiently waiting, because it is his will that everyone be saved (3:9; yet 2 Peter clearly implies that God will not realize this desire). The end will come, the world will be destroyed, the judgment will happen, and a new and totally righteous heavens and earth will be created (3:10, 12–13). This eschatological hope should motivate believers to moral earnestness (3:11).

The teachers of licentiousness, however, are apostates, for by their pursuit of sex, money, and power they have rejected the teaching of the very Master who bought them. Their doom is sure, as numerous OT examples show. In fact, it would have been better for them never to have been freed by Christ, for having experienced the freedom from desire referred to at the beginning of the letter, they have turned back and have become reenslaved, their last state being therefore worse than their pre-Christian state.

Second Peter and the Canon

Second Peter demonstrates conscious intertextuality within the NT. First, the author is aware of more than one of Paul's letters, which he classes with the "other scriptures" (likely including Pseudepigrapha and early Gospels as well as the canonical OT), demonstrating that Paul's writings have become influential in the church among both the "orthodox" and the "unorthodox." Second, 2 Pet. 2 incorporates most of Jude, but does so by editing the work so as to remove explicit references to the Pseudepigrapha (but not the content drawn from those references, for example, the imprisonment of the fallen angels of Gen. 6) and by expanding some of the other narratives. Thus 2 Peter shows both canon formation and intracanonical interpretation, although both are happening before there is a developed canon consciousness.

Second Peter also witnesses to intertextuality between NT and OT writers. That is, it shows the nascent Christian movement interpreting and applying the Hebrew Scriptures and largely doing so through the lens of Second Temple Jewish tradition, traditions we know from apocalyptic works like *1 Enoch* and *Jubilees*.

The writer's contribution to canonical teaching is largely twofold. First, he explains the nature of the final judgment in different images from those found elsewhere. Second, he explains the idea of salvation as release from control by desire and a participation in the divine nature, which enables virtue. Despite its origin in the call of God, this release is apparently conditional, for one can turn from it and return under the control of desire. This complements teaching found in Paul.

Finally, 2 Peter reveals an early Christian translating received theological concepts into a Greek cultural context, which complements the more non-Hellenistic Jewish conceptual world of works such as Matthew and James.

Theological Significance of 2 Peter

Second Peter underlines the position found in James and Paul that traces the roots of the human predicament to desire. But given the Hellenistic tone of 2 Peter, one suspects that desire has shifted from the Jewish *yetser* (inclination) of the other two writers, which is evil only in that it has no boundaries, to the rejection of desire per se, as found in the Hellenistic world.

God is viewed as good and gracious, so he rescues believers through his promises, by which he makes them participate in the divine nature; this new nature makes human beings now capable of moral growth, since they are freed from the power of desire.

Such freedom is, however, conditional, for if someone fails in moral growth, which would confirm their election by God, he or she may stumble; that is precisely what the teachers 2 Peter condemns have done. Despite having once enjoyed the same freedom and cleansing from sin that the majority in the church still enjoy, these people have turned back to sin and are in a worse state than they were before they got to know Jesus. This conditionality is reminiscent of Hebrews and some teaching of Jesus.

Second Peter's author contributes to a high Christology with his reference to "our God and Savior Jesus Christ" (1:1), although for the most part he refers to Jesus as Lord, as in the parallel expression "our Lord and Savior Jesus Christ" (twice: 1:11; 2:20). This authority of Christ is underlined by his use of "Master," a term that in the NT outside of the *Haustafeln* (household codes) normally refers to God, but that 2 Peter follows Jude in referring to Jesus. While this "Master . . . bought" believers (including the apostate teachers; 2:1 NRSV), the atonement is not otherwise referred to, showing that it was possible in the early church to speak about rescue and redemption without direct reference to the crucifixion.

While the focus of 2 Peter is avoidance of the licentiousness that Peter attributes to the teachers he opposes, his argument revolves around eschatology. Although parousia delay (Christ not returning during the first generation of Christians) is not the main issue, the teachers were using this delay as evidence that there was no final judgment and thus actions done in this world did not have a recompense in the coming one. Second Peter discusses the apparent delay in terms of God's patience. While God does not entirely have his purpose fulfilled (it is clear to 2 Peter that at least the apostate teachers are going to hell), his will is that no one should perish, but that all come to salvation (3:9). Furthermore, picking up on a theme found repeatedly in the OT, 2 Peter observes that God's sense of time is not equivalent to the human perception. The end will come, it will come unexpectedly (like a thief), and when it comes the world will be destroyed by fire. The elements themselves will melt (one cannot be sure whether the elements are earth, air, fire, and water, or whether, like Democritus, he thought in terms of some type of atoms). In this process all hidden things will be revealed: nothing will be shielded from judgment. Some, like the teachers 2 Peter refers to, will go to destruction (the nature of this state is not discussed), while the righteous will receive the new heavens and earth.

Because nothing in this world is lasting, it therefore makes sense for the believers to live for the coming age and its values. Eschatology determines ethics.

It should be noted that in 2 Peter there is no reference to an intermediate period between the destruction of the world by fire that ends this age, and the establishment of the age to come. Thus, unlike Revelation, he has no millennium (however one interprets that symbol). His focus is on the destruction of this world (which the teachers apparently think is eternal) and the coming of the new.

Significant is the virtual absence of pneumatology in 2 Peter. While believing human beings participate or share in the divine nature, neither this nor the sanctification that it enables is attributed to the Spirit. The Spirit is mentioned, however, when 2 Peter mentions prophecy. In 2 Peter prophecy is probably OT prophecy, so long as one includes *1 Enoch* and other similar literature along with the canonical OT (since 2 Peter accepts the content that Jude derives from *1 Enoch*). This prophecy is the product of the Holy Spirit rather than human will, and thus it must be interpreted accordingly, which perhaps indicates that 2 Peter does believe that the Spirit is present in the teaching of the church. What is clear is that his other source of authority is the teaching of Jesus and his apostles, including the church's witness to the life of Jesus. There is no evidence in 2 Peter that he knows written Gospels, but it is clear that he knows of several Pauline letters. These he groups with "the other writings," which is a term that 2 Peter uses for the writings that we call the OT (understanding that he likely includes other books that we would not include in this category). These writings, including Paul, are a means of revelation, but they can be twisted (the specific reference is probably to Paul's teaching on grace and freedom from the law), resulting in the destruction of those who do so, not because they twist the meaning of Scripture, but because this twisted meaning leads to behavior that destroys them.

Bibliography

Bauckham, R. *Jude, 2 Peter*. WBC 50. Word, 1983.

———. *Jude and the Relatives of Jesus in the Early Church*. T&T Clark, 1990.

Bray, G., ed. *James, 1–2 Peter, 1–3 John, Jude*. ACCSNT 11. InterVarsity, 2000.

Charles, J. D. *Virtue amidst Vice*. JSNTSup 150. Sheffield Academic Press, 1997.

Chester, A., and R. Martin. *The Theology of the Letters of James, Peter, and Jude*. NTT. Cambridge University Press, 1994.

Kelly, J. N. D. *A Commentary on the Epistles of Peter and Jude*. BNTC. Baker, 1981.

Kraftchick, S. *Jude, 2 Peter*. Abingdon, 2002.

Neyrey, J. *2 Peter, Jude*. AB 37C. Doubleday, 1993.

Vögtle, A. *Der Judasbrief der zweite Petrusbrief*. EKKNT 22. Benziger/Neukirchener Verlag, 1994.

Wall, R. "The Canonical Function of 2 Peter." *BibInt* 9, no. 1 (2001): 64–81.

Watson, D. *Invention, Arrangement, and Style*. SBLDS, 104. Scholars Press, 1988.

23

Johannine Epistles

I. HOWARD MARSHALL

Second and 3 John are two short letters from a person who simply calls himself "the elder" to "the elect lady and her children" (either a Christian community or possibly a Christian family) and to his friend Gaius respectively. The letters praise them for their spiritual progress, encourage them to follow love and truth, and urge them to be hospitable to traveling Christian teachers but not to those who do not confess that Jesus Christ has come (or possibly will come) in the flesh. They shed an interesting light on local church life, probably around Ephesus, in the late first century. The unnamed author is known to early tradition as "John," but whether this is John the apostle or another person is not entirely clear.

First John (our focus in the remainder of this article) develops much more fully the theological teaching in these two letters, but it is a tract or written discourse and lacks the form of a letter (including any indication of authorship). The close similarities in style and theological idiom make it most likely that it is by the same author. It is related in the same kind of way to the Gospel of John and is either by the same author (the traditional view) or by somebody in the same Christian circle (an increasingly widely held view). Most hold that it was written subsequent to the Gospel.

History of Interpretation

First John has traditionally been understood as a letter to an unknown group of believers in danger of various problems and errors. These include (1) the danger of claiming freedom from sin; (2) the failure to recognize that Christian love must include not only God but also one's fellow Christians, and must be a matter of deeds as well as words; (3) the problems caused by a group who have left the congregation and denied in some way that Jesus was the incarnate Son of God, the Christ (their thinking resembled that of Cerinthus, a first-century heretic, who claimed that a divine power came upon Jesus at his baptism and departed just before his crucifixion, so that it was only the human Jesus who suffered and died [since a divine being could not do so]); and (4) the difficulty of knowing whether the messages given by prophets claiming inspiration from the Holy Spirit were genuine or otherwise.

These may be identified as the major problems. Side by side with them the author deals with some issues common to any group of Christians: failure to seek forgiveness for sin, the danger of loving sin, uncertainty regarding whether they had true knowledge of God, the danger of assuming that Christians may continue in sin, self-condemnation rather than confidence in approaching God in prayer, problems in pastoral concern for sinful members of the congregation, and the attractions of idolatry. Much of this may be seen as a lack of Christian confidence, and the readers needed encouragement rather than blame. This is what the letter provides; it is meant to strengthen in faith, love, and hope.

Modern critical discussion has raised a number of issues:

1. The identification of the false teaching. It is not identical with that of Cerinthus, and closer parallels have been sought in the teaching opposed by Ignatius or simply in Judaism, denying that the Messiah was Jesus (Griffith). Or it has been argued that there is no other heresy known to us with which it completely corresponds.

2. The relationship of the letter to the Gospel. In various forms it is suggested that the letter endeavors to correct false ideas that may have been held by the readers of the (earlier) Gospel. The problem is complicated by the tendency of some scholars to see various stages in the composition of the Gospel by editors with different agendas and the consequent need to determine where the letter fits into the history of a so-called Johannine community (Brown). Some hold that the letter is more "orthodox" than the Gospel and represents a later,

more "ecclesiastical" stage in the development of the community. Such a theory assumes that the authors of the Gospel and Epistles were different. More recently, there have been strong criticisms of the whole idea of reconstructing a particular community for whom the Gospel was intended, and it is proposed that all of the Gospels were written for "all Christians." Even if this is so, it is still the case that the author belonged to a particular community and must have been influenced to some extent by its nature and needs.

3. There have been attempts to uncover earlier material in the letter (such as series of antithetical statements) and, even more, to identify stages in composition (Bultmann), but these have been largely abandoned.

Hearing the Message of 1 John

First John begins with a stately introduction (1:1–4) reminiscent of the prologue to the Gospel, with its focus on the Word of life that was from the beginning, has been revealed, and has been experienced by believers. The Word as Jesus, as the Christian message, and as itself the life that it promises—all three are bound up together in this expression. The writer aligns himself with the original witnesses and servants of the word, whether or not he is an apostle, sharing the message with a wider group who presumably had not the same firsthand experience.

He wants to promote fellowship between his readers and himself that is simultaneously fellowship with the Father and the Son (1:5–2:17). Therefore, the problem of sin must be dealt with by living in the light and seeking forgiveness provided through the atoning death of Christ. Belonging to Christ is seen in keeping his commandments, which appear to be concrete instances of the basic command to love fellow believers. Not loving the world means not being tempted by worldly temptations rather than not loving nonbelievers (although this point lies outside the writer's horizon).

Another danger to the readers is the risk of false belief, which denies that Jesus is the Son of God (2:18–25). The line of thought here is not completely clear. Plainly, the writer believes that if a person does this, they are no longer in fellowship with God, just as a believer may suggest to a Jew that apart from acceptance of Christ they cannot count God as their Father since God has now revealed Jesus as his Son. The belief in the coming of a final adversary of God, an anti-Messiah, before the End (and the second coming of the true Messiah), as reflected in 2 Thess. 2:8–12 and Revelation, is here picked up, with the claim that anybody who denies that Jesus is the Messiah is in effect a manifestation or anticipation of this final foe.

Nevertheless, the readers should not succumb to this deceit because they have been anointed by God (with a gift of discernment from the Spirit or with the knowledge of the gospel). Furthermore, they can look forward to the coming of Jesus and to their consequent sharing in his glory (2:26–27).

The next part of the letter deals again with the question of sin (2:28–3:10). It emphasizes that the readers should be free from sin because they have a close relationship with Christ and have received a new birth from God; such people do not sin. This leads directly into a reminder that instead of sinning, their positive calling is to love one another, and not to "hate" one another by failing to show genuine, practical love (3:11–24). As they do this, their confidence in prayer will increase.

Yet comes another comment on false teachers, and how to discern the reality or otherwise of messages allegedly given by spiritual inspiration, this time with an assurance that those who are of the truth will not be overcome by false teachings (4:1–6). The rest of chapter 4 reiterates much of what has already been said about the love of God as the pattern for human love, and the confident assurance that God gives to those who love in this way (vv. 7–21). Believers will overcome the world with all its falsity and evil.

Once again, the nature of true belief is spelled out (5:1–12). It is belief in Jesus as the one who came by water (a reference either to his birth or his baptism) and by blood (a reference to his death). This strange expression may be intended to rule out any suggestion that the Son of God had departed from Jesus before his death or simply to emphasize the importance of his atoning death alongside his earlier life.

Finally, there is yet more assurance for the readers (5:13–21). But now specifically they are told that God will hear their prayers for sinful fellow-Christians, except where mortal sin has been committed. "Mortal sin" is generally identified as apostasy.

1 John and the Canon

The letters of John are important testimony to the existence of a major stream in early Christianity alongside the Pauline tradition. Together with the Fourth Gospel, they constitute a closely related set of documents with distinctive vocabulary and theology different from that of the Synoptic Gospels and Paul. The book of Revelation is related more closely to this stream than to any other, and it was traditionally thought to be by the same author. This should not be ruled out as entirely impossible, since the apocalyptic genre could have dictated a distinct style of writing, but it is not widely held. It may be safer to see Revelation simply as another witness to Johannine Christianity in a broad sense.

The similarities between 2 and 3 John and 1 John are clear; the shorter pieces, being real letters, help to relate 1 John to the day-to-day life of actual communities.

The relationship to the Gospel is more complex. A large part of the Gospel is concerned with the relationship of Jesus to nonbelieving Jews, and hence the questions of his messiahship and authority to speak from God are prominent. First John, however, is concerned with problems arising within the Christian community, and the christological error is more concerned with denial of the reality of the incarnation by persons who previously believed in it. There is more stress on the death of Jesus as atonement. It has been argued that this contrasts with the teaching in the Gospel, where (it is claimed) the death of Jesus has significance only as part of the revelation of God in Jesus and not as the means of atonement for sin. But attempts to identify a discontinuity here are fatally flawed by the opening emphasis in the Gospel on Jesus as the Lamb of God who bears sin (John 1:29, 36; cf. 1 John 3:5). The description of the Spirit in the Gospel as "another Comforter" (John 14:16 KJV) is clarified in the light of 1 John 2:1. Within the Gospel the second part especially (John 13–21) is concerned with the disciples after Jesus has left them, and in this part there are closer links with the epistle. As with the other NT letters, there is virtually no reference to the earthly Jesus and his teaching, and this strengthens the hypothesis that the writers leave the straight citation of Jesus almost entirely to the Evangelists. Nor does the letter directly refer to the resurrection and exaltation of Jesus, although the references to abiding in him and to his future coming clearly imply belief in this.

1 John and Theology

Within the history of theology, 1 John has occupied an important place in the debate over freedom from sin and Christian perfection. John Wesley is the best-known advocate of the view that there is a call upon believers to perfection (cf. Matt. 5:48) and that it is possible for them to attain it.

He was careful to fence his doctrine negatively by insisting that (1) it was freedom from known, deliberate sin; (2) a person might fall away from perfection and regain it; and (3) we should be quite cautious in recognizing examples of it. Positively, he preferred to speak not of sinless perfection but of perfect love that drives out sin. Wesley was largely indebted to 1 John for this doctrine, and he insisted that the promises or declarations in 3:4–10 were to be taken seriously. But his related belief that perfection was a state perhaps attained instantly by faith (rather like baptism with the Spirit in the Pentecostal tradition) would appear to come from elsewhere. His teaching has been largely forgotten in the mainstream Methodist churches but has been cultivated and preserved in the Nazarene tradition.

The crucial teaching in 1 John 3 has been variously interpreted, not least in light of the clear recognition that no believers can say, "We have no sin" (1:8, 10). Part of the problem lies in the juxtaposition of these apparently contradictory teachings. Some think that the "impossible sin" in chapter 3 (esp. v. 9) is solely the sin of apostasy (Griffith), but 3:10 might be thought to suggest otherwise. Most argue, in one way or another, that John is describing an ideal or an eschatological state that believers may claim in this sinful world; the paradox of "already . . . not yet . . ." that characterizes Pauline teaching is also valid here. It is also likely that John is addressing two different tendencies in the congregation, one that claimed sinlessness while not loving their fellow believers, and the other that was content with a low level of Christian living and did not grasp at the higher level promised to them.

The truth is probably that different NT writers use different pictures of the Christian life, including traveling toward a future goal, living by the Spirit, living in love, wrestling with temptation, and so on. These all contain an appeal to progress in Christian living. The danger of not taking 1 John 3 on board is that believers may comfortably resign themselves to mediocrity and fail to realize promises of, and provision for, a life free from sin. In reality, John does not put the point any more strongly than Paul does with his: "sin will have no dominion over you" (Rom. 6:14 NRSV).

Possibly the major, lasting contribution of the letter is its identification of love as the quality shown by God in the self-giving of his Son to atone for human sin and in the call for believers to show a like love for one another, demonstrated in action and not just in words (3:16–17). The letter is silent about loving nonbelievers, possibly because lack of love within the Christian community was a more pressing issue, but the readers are faced with the example of a God who first loved us (before we loved him), and the implication of that is surely clear enough.

Bibliography

Bogart, J. *Orthodox and Heretical Perfectionism in the Johannine Community as Evident in the First Epistle of John.* SBLDS. Scholars Press, 1977.

Brown, R. *The Epistles of John.* AB. Doubleday, 1982.

Bultmann, R. *The Johannine Epistles.* Hermeneia. Fortress, 1973.

Edwards, R. *The Johannine Epistles.* NTG. Sheffield Academic Press, 1996.

Griffith, T. *Keep Yourselves from Idols.* JSNTSup. Continuum, 2002.

—————. "A Non-polemical Reading of 1 John: Sin, Christology and the Limits of Johannine Christianity." *TynBul* 49, no. 2 (1998): 253–76.

Klauck, H.-J. *Der erste Johannesbrief.* EKKNT. Benziger/Neukirchener Verlag, 1991.

Lieu, J. *The Theology of the Johannine Epistles.* NTT. Cambridge University Press, 1991.

Marshall, I. H. *The Epistles of John.* NICNT. Eerdmans, 1978.

Schnackenburg, R. *The Johannine Epistles.* Crossroad, 1992.

Smalley, S. *1, 2, 3 John.* WBC. Word, 1984.

Strecker, G. *The Johannine Letters.* Hermeneia. Fortress, 1996.

Wesley, J. *A Plain Account of Christian Perfection.* Reprint, Epworth, 1952.

24

Jude

The challenge of Jude for theological interpretation is not so much its theology as its ethics: what is the ethical evaluation of such a prophetic denunciation? The second challenge is Jude's use of noncanonical literature and its meaning for our view of the canon.

History of Interpretation

The interpretation of Jude begins with 2 Peter, who edits and adapts Jude, such as removing the direct references to the Pseudepigrapha, to form his second chapter. Unlike 2 Peter, Jude was cited relatively early and included in the early canon lists, only to go through a period of questioning due to his citation of Pseudepigrapha. By the end of the fourth century, most of the church had decided for the canonicity of Jude and thus were using the letter. In the contemporary period Jude again fell out of favor, not because of his use of the Pseudepigrapha, but because of his prophetic denunciation that was viewed as ethically sub-Christian. Normally the work was dated late in the first century or in the first half of the second. Thus it was only after a century and more of neglect that the last thirty years have seen a revival of interest in the letter, as it began to be viewed by

229

some as a representative of Jewish Christianity and appreciated by many for its rhetorical skill.

The Message of Jude

Jude's message is relatively straightforward. He is concerned about traveling teachers who are subverting the local church. His concern is not about doctrinal deviation, but about a rejection of the practical rule of Jesus over Christians in that his teachings were being rejected in the name of grace, which was being used to justify licentiousness. Jude denounces this moral deviation and pronounces a sentence of doom on these teachers, a doom based on illustrations drawn from his understanding of narratives that we find in the OT. Because these teachers also appear to have rejected angelic authority (as well as the authority of the established leaders in the church)— whether of fallen or holy angels is not clear—Jude also accuses them of rebellion, adding to this a third charge of greed. Thus, deviation from the teaching and character of Jesus, in the realms of money, power, and sex, he condemns as practices that doom these Christian teachers to hell.

The response that Jude teaches is twofold. First, the believers are themselves to focus more on growing in their Christian life (prayer in the Spirit, love, Christian practice, and eschatological expectancy). Second, they are to reach out to those caught in the teaching of these teachers, extricate such, and receive them. There is nothing said about dealing with the teachers (no sentence of excommunication or instruction to have nothing to do with them), but instead they are left to the judgment of "the Lord," who is coming soon.

Jude and the Canon

It is well known that Jude refers to both *1 En.* 1:9 and probably the lost ending of the *Testament of Moses* (known to us from references in the writings of the fathers). What is not as clearly seen is that most of Jude's references to OT narratives reflect the recontextualization of those narratives in Jewish literature. This means that he makes no differentiation between OT texts and *1 Enoch*, nor a differentiation between the canonical form of a story and how that story was told in later Jewish literature. Thus, Jude demonstrates a stage in the development of canon consciousness in which narratives have authority because they are related to the canon, not because they are the canonical form of a narrative. This reminds us that the questions Jews asked about OT works (whether they could be given up to be burned in situations of persecution) were different than later Christian questions about NT works (whether they were to be read in and thereby endorsed by the church).

As Jude's second contribution to the canon, he makes his twin points that ethical deviations are deviations from the faith as much as or more than doctrinal deviations, and that eschatological expectation determines and enforces ethics. Furthermore, he demonstrates in his treatment of those who have followed the intruding teachers his awareness of the present as a time of grace before judgment.

Finally, Jude also demonstrates that the genre of prophetic denunciation was alive and well throughout the first century.

Theological Significance of Jude

Theologically, Jude reveals that neither post-fourth-century concepts of canon nor modern models of biblical interpretation are absolute. His narrative method, which relies on the later development of the biblical narratives, and his loose sense of canonical boundaries show this.

Furthermore, Jude contributes to our understanding of the importance of eschatological, even apocalyptic, expectation. It is the lively expectation of final judgment that for Jude sanctions present ethical behavior.

Jude also shows us the practical application of the doctrine of grace. Upon repentance alone, people are freely received back into the orthodox camp.

Finally, Jude demonstrates the centrality of the concept that Jesus is Lord to the early church. Those who deny his authority in their lives ethically (no matter what their doctrinal confession) are apostate and under sentence of eternal judgment. Heresy for Jude is primarily ethical.

In none of these is Jude unique, but his contribution nonetheless is real.

Bibliography

Bauckham, R. *Jude, 2 Peter*. WBC 50. Word, 1983.

———. *Jude and the Relatives of Jesus in the Early Church*. T&T Clark, 1990.

Bray, G., ed. *James, 1–2 Peter, 1–3 John, Jude*. ACCSNT 11. InterVarsity, 2000.

Charles, J. D. *Literary Strategy in the Epistle of Jude*. University of Scranton Press, 1993.

Chester, A., and R. Martin. *The Theology of the Letters of James, Peter, and Jude*. NTT. Cambridge University Press, 1994.

Kelly, J. N. D. *A Commentary on the Epistles of Peter and Jude*. BNTC. Baker, 1981.

Kraftchick, S. *Jude, 2 Peter*. Abingdon, 2002.

Neyrey, J. *2 Peter, Jude*. AB 37C. Doubleday, 1993.

Vögtle, A. *Der Judasbrief, der 2. Petrusbrief*. EKKNT 22. Benziger/Neukirchener Verlag, 1994.

Watson, D. *Invention, Arrangement, and Style*. SBLDS 104. Scholars Press, 1988.

25

Revelation ("The Apocalypse of Saint John the Divine")

FRANCESCA ARAN MURPHY

Revelation and the Canon

The Christian Bible concludes with an apocalypse, but like Waterloo, the victory of this "last battle" was a close run. The vicissitudes of the canonization of John's Apocalypse were related to three linked factors, (1) its authorship, (2) its tendency to inspire millennialist fervor, and (3) the question of how this strange vision fits into the NT. The Apocalypse is atypical in that, having achieved recognition as Sacred Scripture, it did not retain it, remaining peripheral to the Western canon until the late fourth century and being ejected from the Eastern canon until the fourteenth century.

An early-second-century bishop of Hieropolis, Papias, thought the apostle John wrote the Fourth Gospel, (First) Epistle (of John), and Revelation. Irenaeus believed Papias to have been a "hearer of John and a friend of Polycarp," who had also known John. On Papias's say-so, Irenaeus considered Revelation and John's Gospel as artifacts of the same personality. Justin Martyr (ca. 100–ca. 165) also thought Revelation was apostolic. The primitive church used two other apocalypses, the Shepherd of Hermas and the *Apocalypse of Peter*. The *Muratorian Canon/Fragment* (ca. 170) describes the author of Revelation as Paul's "predecessor," identifying him with the "eyewitness and hearer" who wrote the Gospel. It rejects the Shepherd as written "recently" and accepts "the apocalypses of John and Peter, though some of us are not willing that the latter be read in church."

Thirty years later, when Montanists turned to the Apocalypse for scriptural legitimation, their opponents discredited the apocalypticism of this Phrygian sect by disparaging the authorship of their favored text. In about 200, a Roman presbyter named Gaius attributed the Apocalypse to the Gnostic Cerinthus because of its teaching a "millennial" (thousand-year) worldly kingdom. Writing around 247, Dionysius, bishop of Alexandria, contended that its stylistic differences from the Fourth Gospel, and its bad Greek, indicate that John the Presbyter wrote it, not John the Evangelist. Eusebius of Caesarea (ca. 260–ca. 339) quotes Dionysius's queries in salacious detail. Eusebius undermines the evidence for Papias's acquaintance with John the Evangelist-Apostle. He describes Papias as "a man of very little intelligence," who taught that "there will be a millennium after the resurrection of the dead, when the kingdom of Christ will be set up in material form on this earth" (*Hist. eccl.* 3.39).

The notion of an earthly millennial kingdom derives from Rev. 20:1–6, in which an angel seized the dragon/devil and "bound him for a thousand years. He threw him into the Abyss, and locked and sealed it over him. . . . After that, he must be set free for a short time. I saw thrones on which were seated those who had been given authority to judge. And I saw the souls of those who had been beheaded because of their testimony to Jesus. . . . They came to life and reigned with Jesus for a thousand years. . . . This is the first resurrection." Those who share in the first resurrection "will be priests of God and of Christ and will reign with him for a thousand years." Like his Montanist adversaries, Gaius the Presbyter read Revelation literally, but he found the implication that Christ will return to set up an earthly kingdom of a thousand years' duration ridiculous.

The manuscript of the Codex Sinaiticus, contemporary with Eusebius, contains Revelation. Cataloging the texts aspiring to canonical status under three headings—"Recognized," "Disputed," and "Spurious"—Eusebius puts Revelation into both first and second categories: "For, as I said, some reject it, but others count it among the Recognized Books" (*Hist. eccl.* 3.25). Eusebius's empiricism binds him to recording that Revelation was widely read in churches; the rationalist in him deprecated millennial enthusiasm.

Eusebius speaks highly of Gaius's reasoning powers. Gaius had asked rhetorically: What "good does" Revelation "do me when it tells me of seven angels and seven trumpets, or of four angels who are to be let loose at the river Euphrates?" Theologians made sense of such images by allegorizing them. The Egyptian bishop Nepos wrote a *Refutation of the Allegorists*, which claimed, according to his critical friend, Dionysius of Alexandria, "that there will be a kind of millennium on this earth devoted to bodily indulgence." Dionysius did not follow those who "rejected and altogether impugned" Revelation because of its literalist interpreters. He "should not dare to reject the book, since many brethren hold it in estimation. . . . For although I do not understand it, yet I suspect that some deeper meaning underlies the words."

The Apocalypse fell under a cloud in the East. It was rejected by Cyril of Jerusalem and Gregory of Nazianzus, and accepted by other bishops, including Athanasius, whose Festival Letter of 367 lists the canonical books. Jerome observed in 414 that "if the usage of the Latins does not receive [Hebrews] among the canonical Scriptures, neither indeed by the same liberty do the churches of the Greeks receive the Revelation of John. And yet we receive both in that we follow . . . the authority of ancient writers, who for the most part quote each of them . . . as canonical and churchly."

The author of Revelation insists on his work's inspired character. He claims that "the Spirit" speaks through him to the church (2:7, 11, 17, 29; 3:6, 13, 22; cf. 22:6; etc.), and concludes with an anathema seldom matched by any framer of canonical lists. "I warn everyone who hears the words of the prophecy of this book: If anyone adds to them, God will add to him the plagues described in this book. And if anyone takes words away from this book of prophecy, God will take from him his share in the tree of life and in the holy city, which are described in this book. He who testifies to these things says, 'Yes, I am coming soon.' Amen. Come, Lord Jesus!" (22:18–20; cf. the injunctions in Deuteronomy, last book in the Torah: 4:2; 12:32). As the only apocalypse to overcome ecclesiastical resistance to apocalypticism, Revelation must have resonated with ecclesiastical needs. Who wrote it mattered to primitive and patristic Christians because John-the-Gospel-writer stood foursquare within the church. Revelation was canonized once exegetes were able to read it synoptically with the rest of Sacred Scripture. Theologians analyzed Revelation alongside apocalyptic sayings in other NT books and in Daniel. So, for example, although "antichrist" does not figure in the Apocalypse, its dragon (12:3), sea beast (13:1), and earth beast (13:11) have been cross-identified with the figure of the Johannine Epistles. Irenaeus, Augustine of Hippo, and Bede understood the lion, calf, man-faced beast, and eagle (4:7) to represent the authors of the four Gospels: conversely, the church sees itself in the Apocalypse when finding it to inform the whole Christian drama. It is "like an onion," said Mr. Tumnus, "except that as you go in and in, each circle is larger than the last" (Lewis 169). Western medieval manuscripts of the Apocalypse were often prefaced by a pictorial biography of John, emphasizing its ecclesial origin. Although the linguistic asymmetries are an obstacle to joint authorship of Gospel and Apocalypse, the uncovering of realized eschatology in both texts harmonizes the Apocalypse with the Johannine corpus.

History of Interpretation

Distinguishing Eschatology and Apocalyptic

A fourth-century scribe wrote "A Revelation of John" at the head of his page, and added in the margin, *tou theologou*, "the theologian." A successor copyist moved the words to center page; ever since, the author has been known as "John the theologian," or "John the Divine" in the Authorized Version (KJV). Today, most scholars see both Gospel and Apocalypse as works of theology. The theology of Revelation flows into *two* elements of Christian thought, eschatological historiography and apocalyptic. Do the two overlap? To what extent should the promises and threats of the Apocalypse be taken as *predicting* history-like events? Is the End datable, and will the world to come have a chronology?

Irenaeus's *Against Heresies* concludes with an apocalyptic vision of the kingdom of Christ on earth. The Irenaean apocalyptic is pictorial and "millennial": "It is fitting," he writes, "that the creation itself, being restored to its primeval condition, should without qualification be under the dominion of the righteous." During Diocletian's persecution, Victorinus read the Apocalypse in a historical and millenary sense, and took its "things that must *shortly* come to pass" (1:1 KJV) to show that the End was imminent. Commenting on Daniel, Jerome forswore a *historical* eschaton: "The saints will in no wise have an earthly kingdom, but only a celestial one; thus must cease the fable of one thousand years." In his Isaiah commentary, Jerome indicated why there was "much difference . . . among men . . . about the way in which John's Apocalypse is to be understood": "To take it according to the letter is to Judaize. If we treat it in a spiritual fashion, as it was written, we seem to contradict the views of many older authorities: Latins such as Tertullian, Victorinus, and Lactantius; Greeks such as Irenaeus, to pass over the others." Jerome rewrote Victorinus's commentary, saving Victorinus's insight that the Apocalypse's eschatology is realized recurrently throughout the history of the church. As Victorinus and Jerome have it, Revelation's seven trumpets blew over the Babylonian Empire and will sound again; its dragon/antichrist depicts Roman emperors and emperors yet to come. The eternity seen in Revelation becomes *always* when it is reflected back into history.

Eusebius of Caesarea compared Constantine's construction of the church of the Holy Sepulchre in Jerusalem to the promise of 21:2 that the heavenly Jerusalem will come down to earth. Did he contradict his own aversion to apocalyptic when he noted God's historical design in the Christianizing of the Roman Empire? Only if we fail to distinguish eschatology, or the philosophy of history, from apocalypse, the ending of time. To do so, one must grapple with the fact that Revelation is a dualistic text. Steeped in OT prophecy, the author summed up his book's symbolic battle in the two cities: Babylon, whoring after power, and Jerusalem, the eternal city. Augustine (354–430) interpreted Babylon and Jerusalem as the city of man and the city of God. He traced their passage through biblical, extrabiblical, and postbiblical history. Stating that "the kingdoms of men are established by divine providence," Augustine saw God's benevolent plan in the reigns of Constantine and Theodosius (5, preface; 25; 26). Postbiblical history is no emptier of theological design for Augustine than for Eusebius. But Augustine is able to put the eschatological philosophy of history that he draws out of Revelation, and its apocalyptic, on different planes. The first is concerned with the "six days" of creation, the ages of history from its origins to the end of time. Christ's Incarnation inaugurated the sixth day in which humanity will live until the end of time. The second coming of Christ, which brings with it the "seventh day," the "eternal Sabbath," ruptures the temporal, numbered series. All history is eschatological, but the Apocalypse is transhistorical.

Augustine stigmatizes the millenarians' pictorialization of the kingdom as a round of "material feasts in which there will be so much to eat and drink that not only will those supplies keep within no bounds of moderation but will also exceed the limits even of incredibility" (20.7). The uncharacteristic stylistic clumsiness indicates that millennialist literalism affected the bishop of Hippo's digestion much as it did that of the bishop of Caesarea.

The Donatist Tyconius (330–90) devised a *Book of Rules* for interpreting Scripture. These exegetical principles enabled him to demillennialize Donatist proof texts. Rule 1 says that Scripture references to "the Lord" sometimes indicate Christ, sometimes his *ekklēsia*-body. Tyconius argues that biblical references to the "coming of the Lord" can mean the advent of the church. Rule 4 states that references to individuals sometimes have a wider application. Augustine used Tyconius's *Rules*. Applying rule 4 to the binding of the devil in Rev. 20, he finds that the devil will not be "thrown into the Abyss" just once, but is constantly driven into the "Abyss" of the hearts of the impious. Rule 5 regulates for a nonarithmetical reading of biblical statements about time. Tyconius had used it against a literal-temporal reading of the thousand-year kingdom. Augustine likewise advised against taking the "thousand years" as a countable series: he took them to symbolize "totality," since multiples of ten produce a "solid figure," such as a "cube" (ibid.).

Augustine takes the "first resurrection" of Rev. 20 to refer to baptism. He distinguishes this from the resurrection to judgment that will occur after the end of time. "It follows," he says, "that the Church even now is the kingdom of Christ and the kingdom of heaven. And so even now his saints reign with him, though not in the same way as they will then reign; and yet the tares do not reign with him, although they are growing in the Church side by side with the wheat. . . . Ultimately, those people reign with him who are in his kingdom in such a way that they themselves *are* his kingdom" (20.9). The "city of God" is not in the temporal future: the eternal Jerusalem is folded into the past and present church on earth. Nor is the kingdom a cosmic "place," but rather a state of being: "they themselves *are* his kingdom." By detaching apocalyptic from chronology, Augustine deterred Christians from seeing *endings*, such as that of the Roman Empire, as signs of the End. Apocalyptic is more elusive than the philosophy of history, for Augustine: Constantine *is* part of God's providence; the present-day church *is and is not* the kingdom of the saints.

Both the North African bishop of Justiniapolis, Primasius (540s), who knew Victorinus-Jerome's commentary, and the Spanish Beatus of Liébanus (c. 780) treat Revelation as a book about Christ and the church. Where Primasius relates the woman giving birth (12:2) to the Virgin Mary, Beatus identifies her with a feminine *Ekklēsia*. Beatus initiates a line of commentarial cross-reference of Revelation to the Song of Songs. Drawing on *The Book of Rules* and the commentaries of Jerome and Primasius, the Venerable Bede uses Tyconius's rule 1 to interleave Revelation and the Song. In his eighth-century *Explanatio Apocalypsis*, Bede states that it is the church that says, "I am dark and comely" (Song 1:5). For Bede, both the Song and Revelation are allegories of the church's mission. The woman in labor is "the Church, in a spiritual sense, bring[ing] forth those with whom it travails"; "she brought forth a man child" (12:5 KJV) means the church "ever" giving birth to Christ.

Bede notes that Tyconius's rule 6 concerns "recapitulation." Chronological *"sequence"* sometimes enfolds flashbacks to earlier events. Revelation does not progress in a straight line. After the seventh seal has been opened (8:1), Bede finds that "now he recapitulates from the beginning, as he is about to say the same things in another manner"; the "sequence" cycles around to begin again with the first of the seven trumpets (8:2).

Primasius had broken the text down into sections: (1) seven churches; (2) seven seals; (3) seven trumpets and the woman of Rev. 12; (4) beasts of land and sea, and seven bowls with seven plagues; (5) new heaven and earth. Such sectional divisions became standard. Bede read Revelation as the recurrent story of the "seven days" of history. He created *seven* sections within Revelation, adding two to Primasius's five by giving the woman's labor and conflict with the dragon its own section, and separating the fate of Babylon (Rev. 17:1–20:5; sec. 6) from the wedding of Jerusalem and the Lamb (chs. 21–22; sec. 7). For Bede, the sections of the book of Revelation are isomorphic with the divisions of time. He organizes the apocalypse into the sevenfold division of history. Although he quotes Augustine verbatim on Rev. 20, Bede smoothes the transition from eschatology to apocalypse. The Revelation commentaries of Charlemagne's court theologian, Alcuin (ca. 800), and Haimo (ca. 840) adopt Bede's septilinear periodization of history. Augustine's *City of God* inspired Charlemagne's desire that his empire would reflect the new Jerusalem. Medieval theologians were in line with Augustine when Revelation informed their perception of history, as with Bede observing bad monks, heretics, and Arians in the four horses of Rev. 6:1–8. Reading the signs of the times providentially, or eschatologically, is Augustinian; reading history apocalyptically is not.

The Benedictine Berengaudus (840–92) builds on the sense of optimism that had accumulated within Western commentaries on Revelation. His *Expositio super septem visiones libri Apocalypsis* connects the Lamb of Rev. 5–7 and 21:9 with John the Baptist's "Behold, the Lamb of God" in John 1:29 (RSV). John continues, "Happy are those who are called to his supper" (Rev. 19:9 AT). For Berengaudus, Revelation is a vision of the marriage feast of the Lamb and his *Ekklēsia*. He downplays its conflictual element to the extent of reading the four horses of Rev. 6 as figures of "the Lord," rather than harbingers of the devil. Writing in the reign of Charles the Bald, Berengaudus positions the "persecutions" of Rev. 16 in the past; nowadays, he notes, emperors promote true worship.

A tenth-century Spanish illuminated copy of Beatus of Liébanus's commentary states: "I have depicted the wonderful words of the story in sequence, so that those who know of them will be terrified by the events of the future judgment." Revelation 3:12 promises, "Him who overcomes I will make a pillar in the temple of my God." Following Bede, Berengaudus read Rev. 3:12 as a reminder that "the heavenly [city], . . . unlike the old, is not built of stones but is daily constructed by the saints." He found that promise *fulfilled* in the *present*, in the Saint-City of Rev. 21. Medieval Christians walked into church under the statue of *Christ in Judgment* in the west porch, where the damned departed to the left, the saved to the right; thus, the worshipper entered paradise. Bernard Guinée remarked that "Paradise was the Christian's country in the Middle Ages." Their ecclesiastical interpretation of Revelation came quite naturally. The number of surviving illuminated copies of Berengaudus's commentary shows how popular it was. Illustrated versions of his commentary on Revelation influenced the churches on the pilgrimage route to Compostella. Romanesque sculptures represent John's elders in burlesque postures, in which scholars struggle to find Christian value. In the choir frieze at Marignac, the elders of Rev. 4 frolic naked with domesticated dragons. Derk Visser suggests that this is the expression of Revelation as read beside the Song of Songs, indicating a "medieval mind-set which saw *salvation promised* as *reality believed*," and which "therefore focussed less on the *Last Judgement* than on the blessed life that came after." Revelation's marriage feast, already enjoyed at Mass, was the basis not of fearful predictions of antichrist, but of "utopian expectation" (Visser 182–83).

Apocalypse as History

Joachim of Fiore (1135–1202) described the Apocalypse as "the key of things past, the knowledge of things to come; the opening of what is sealed, the uncovering of what is hidden." Joachim's *Expositio in Apocalysism* is the most influential work of biblical exegesis of all time. Historians of ideas have traced its spore from the Spiritual Franciscans to Hitler's Third Reich. The Calabrian hermit's long lineage is paradoxical, in that he retrenched himself against the intellectual developments of his time. He was a visualizer of Scripture when the figural syntheses of the patristic era were giving way to the discursive analyses of the scholastic *Summae*.

At Easter of 1183, Joachim's efforts to penetrate Revelation were rewarded: "Suddenly something of the fullness of this book and of the entire harmony of the Old and New Testaments was perceived with clarity of understanding in my mind's eye" (*Expositio*). For Joachim, Revelation is the wheel within the wheels of history, as mapped out by the two Testaments. The "seven times" that Joachim discerned in OT and NT are recapitulated in the seven epochs he pictured in the Apocalypse. These "epochs" correspond to a linear sequence of events in world history, down to his own time. Most earlier exegetes had seen correspondences between past or present events and those described in Revelation. Joachim made a *science* of theological historiography, using Revelation to predict future events and persons: the Apocalypse "embraces the fullness of history" (*Expositio*). The seven epochs of Joachim's Apocalypse depict three sequential "states": the Status of the Father (Rev. 1:1–11:18), the Status of the Son (Rev. 11:19–19:21), and the Status of the Spirit (Rev. 20:1–10). The third age of grace would commence around 1200–1260. It will be an age of "Spiritual men," in which the "everlasting gospel" (Rev. 14:6) shall be preached by a suprainstitutional church. The Sabbath will come on this earth, after the defeat of antichrist, anticipating the descent of the new Jerusalem. Joachim's eighth era, eternity, melts into the seventh temporal epoch; eschatology and apocalyptic are effectively equated. The "third Status of the Spirit" will not last a thousand years; Joachim was not technically a "millennialist."

Joachim related Revelation's twin cities to Scripture scholars, the Babylonian, bestial-*carnal* exegetes, and Jerusalem's *spiritual* interpreters. The first wave of Joachimism, from the thirteenth to the sixteenth century, addressed itself to separating the carnal and the spiritual within the church. In his 1297 Apocalypse commentary, the Spiritual Franciscan Peter Olivi enlarged upon Joachim, adding a fiercer conception of antichrist, with whom Revelation's true witnesses would soon be embattled. Olivi spoke of "spiritual" and "carnal" churches. A cult of Spiritual Franciscanism, with a special devotion to Olivi, emerged in Languedoc. In 1326, Pope John XXII had Olivi's commentary condemned. After studying Olivi and the Apocalypse, the Franciscan John of Rupescissa predicted the coming of antichrist in 1366, followed by a thousand-year kingdom. He claimed the right to reject Augustinian amillennialism on the basis of an "intellectual vision," revealing to him the meaning of Rev. 16–20. Thomas Aquinas observed: "Although the state [*status*] of the New Testament in general is foreshadowed by the state of the Old, it does not follow that individuals correspond to individuals. . . . [This] would seem applicable to the statements of the Abbot Joachim" (*Summa theologiae* III, Q. 77, Art. 2, Reply Obj. 3). Yet Aquinas's comment did not deter the spread of Pseudo-Joachimite prophecies, identifying antichrist with this and that emperor.

Joachimism inspired the fifteenth-century Bohemian Taborites, who rose in rebellion against the church's leaders. The Taborites were the first "Rapturists," expecting that, once the earth had been cleansed by massacre, the elect would soar into the earth to greet their Christ, whereupon the third age of grace would dawn on earth. Thomas Müntzer (1488–1525) picked up Joachimite apocalypticism on his travels in Bohemia. Preaching on Daniel before Duke John of Saxony, he advised: "Drive Christ's enemies out from among the Elect. . . . The sword is necessary to exterminate them. . . . At the harvest-time one must pluck the weeds out of God's vineyard. . . . The angels who are sharpening their sickles for that work are . . . the . . . servants of God." In response to Luther's *Letter to the Princes of Saxony*, Müntzer denoted the author as the beast and Babylonian whore of Revelation. Luther reserved such appellations for the pope—not necessarily a mark of apocalypticism, since "antichrist" had become a general term of abuse. The Anabaptist Hans Hut identified Müntzer and Heinrich Pfeiffer as the two witnesses of Rev. 11. Hut used Revelation as a calendar to date the last judgment (Pentecost, 1528). The Anabaptist "calendarizer" Melchior Hoffmann applied Revelation to the events of 1520–30. Faced with the millennialism of Thomas Müntzer and the Münster Anabaptists, Luther relegated Revelation to the outskirts of his German NT, complaining that "this writer recommends his own book much too highly and does not show Christ clearly." Seventeenth-century Protestant theologians like Cocceius nonetheless understood prophecy, like that of Revelation, as future-related historiography. The "innocently licentious" English Ranters and Muggletonians inherited the myth of the Apocalypse as predicting a third age of the Spirit (Kermode).

Joachim of Fiore entrenched history in sacral patterns at a time when the human sciences were gaining a measure of secularity. His was an evolutionist history, conceiving the three "states" as three trees growing from one root. His Apocalypse exegesis flowered in the secular utopias of the Enlightenment. Joachim's "three ages," culminating in earthly fulfillment, return in Comte's theological, metaphysical, and positivist "states"; in Hegel's idea of a growth of freedom from oriental despotism, through the aristocratic Middle Ages, to modernity, in which all are free; and in the Marxist-Leninist triad of primitive communism, bourgeois society, and the classless Jerusalem of communism. Gaius the Roman Presbyter might feel that his hypothesis of the Gnostic Cerinthus fathering the Apocalypse has been verified by its ideological progeny.

Time Shall Be No More?

In *The End of All Things* (1794), Kant commented aversely on the angel's pronouncement "that there shall be time no longer" (Rev. 10:6). "If we are to assume that this angel . . . was crying nonsense, he must have meant that there shall be change no longer." This, Kant felt, is "a contradictory notion that revolts the imagination." Notwithstanding his pessimistic conception of human nature, Kant translated the Joachimite Apocalypse tradition into a "rational" belief in humanity's *temporal* progress. One strand of contemporary Apocalypse commentary shares the pessimism of the German philosopher, and the sense that Revelation must be about *time*. In the 1830s, John Nelson Darby created a premillennial, "dispensationalist" theology. Dispensationalist Apocalypse interpreters were in the late twentieth and early twenty-first century as widely consulted as astrologers, identifying modern politicians with the agents of Revelation, as in Hal Lindsey's *The Late Great Planet Earth* (1970). With the Gnostics, and in some sense with Revelation, Darby had divided humanity in twain. He believed that once having been beamed up into heaven, the "heavenly church" would reign over the "earthly people"—left behind after the rapture. Tim LaHaye's Left Behind series is a fictional account of events occurring during the rapture/ millennium; with forty million volumes in print, these are the best-selling Christian novels in history.

Some contemporary biblical scholars employ the notion of recapitulation to make sense of Revelation's nonsequential "narrative." David Barr finds "three one-act plays" in the text: (1) Christ's dictation of seven letters, (2) the Lamb's opening of the sealed book, and (3) the war between the dragon and the faithful, culminating in the triumph of bride over whore. This manifests the "three dimensions" of Christ's work—(1) the salvific/ judgmental, (2) the enabling of worship, and (3) the overthrow of evil— "not three consecutive actions" (Barr, "Transformation").

The Message of Revelation

Pictorializers and Hearers

Historically, Revelation exegetes have tended either to pictorialize the text or to listen to it. Jacques Ellul claimed, "The apocalypticist is first of all a seer while the prophet is a hearer. . . . The apocalypticist also receives words, but he is first of all the one who sees the personages, the scenes, the scenario, the events" (21). Most narrative "pictorializers" see John's visions as weaving God's design for history down to its conclusion, thereby providing a "sense of an ending," the rounded rationale of history. On the other hand, there are those for whom the "*orality* of the book is an essential element of its hermeneutic" (Barr, "Enactment"). This takes account of the fact that Revelation is more like a dream than a progressive story. Its agents and objects are not set on a single visual plane; it builds up expectations of order by taking the reader through numbered sequences, and then abruptly spins off rhythm into nightmare. The nonrepresentationalists receive the book as primarily a rendition of *eternity*, in which created past, present, and future are heard *simultaneously*, or polyphonically, in the voices of the liturgy before the throne of God. In the *Messiah*, Handel's librettist integrated Revelation with the resurrection themes of biblical prophecy. Treated as a self-standing lyric, Revelation is a popular source of Christian rock music. Are its choral hymns the home key of the Apocalypse? Somewhere in the middle, between pictoralizations and hearings, stand nonrepresentational picturings, such as the surreal features of the medieval Last Judgments, or the conception of Rev. 14 in Jan van Eyck's *Adoration of the Lamb* (1420s), its horizon of seven church buildings indicating past, present, and future time. When painters view *eternity* scenically, they eschew visual *narrative*. Is Revelation analogous to a *movie*, a visual narrative of *time* and its close, or is it using quasi-*musical* modes to render *timelessness*?

Since the eighteenth century the techniques of Western music have expressed temporal progression. The French composer Olivier Messiaen (1908–92) abandoned them, replacing counterpoint with heterophony, progressive development with symmetry, ordered change with repetition, and resolved diatonic chords with tritones. His first organ work, *Le banquet céleste*, opens with a chord of seven seconds' duration. Messiaen inscribed the score: "He that eateth my flesh and drinketh my blood, dwelleth in me, and I in him" (John 6:56). The piece evokes the participation of Christ's eternity in time, in what the Catholic Messiaen believed to be the supratemporal sacrifice of the Mass. Messiaen's *Quartet for the End of Time* (first performed in a German prison camp in 1941) is dedicated "in homage to the Angel of the Apocalypse, who raises his hand heavenwards saying: 'There will be no more Time.'" The effects of this musical exegesis of the Apocalyse work against unilinear clock time, and in favor of multitemporality or timelessness. It lets us hear eternity as stasis and as playfulness.

Resurrection

Revelation teaches that the end point of history is cosmic catastrophe. In his first words to the narrator, Christ announces that he has defeated death (1:18). Each of the promises made by the resurrected Christ to the seven churches in Rev. 2–3 is about eternal life. The message of Revelation is resurrection. From the seven days of Gen. 1, createdness in the Bible signifies temporality. With the "new heaven and new earth" of Rev. 21, the created cosmos is lifted into eternity. Resurrection to eternal life is the transposition of temporal-created life into eternal-created life. Revelation's apocalyptic fulfills rather than overthrows its eschatological philosophy of history. According to Aquinas, "The being of the creature cannot wholly come to an end"; "even if it is transient, the creature will never fall back into nothingness." Revelation's "new Jerusalem" is made from the precious stones of paradise; resurrection is the regaining to eternity of what was given in the Garden of Gen. 1–3. The "kings of the earth" will bring "their glory into" the new Jerusalem (21:24 RSV). Christ says, "Behold, I make all things new" (21:5 RSV), not "Behold, I make a new set of things" (von Balthasar, 5:200). "Our faith tells us that this 'new' reality was already present in the 'old,' in our drama," the old Narnia present in the new (Lewis 170).

Fire

Exegetes from Augustine to the present have thought it appropriate that the Apocalypse brings history to a close in *fire*. "The Apocalypse, convulsed with lightning, blazing with conflagration, provides us only with final, perpendicular excerpts of the last stages of dramatic action between heaven and earth, God and his creation. There is no other way of portraying this final act. This drama, in which God's absoluteness (understood as power of love) touches the sphere of the fragile creature, can only be a fiery event, a history of fire, made up either of devouring or of healing flames" (von Balthasar, 4:59).

Revelation and Theology

God

A 1422 Sienese antiphonal illustrates "[God] will wipe every tear from their eyes" (Rev. 21:4) with a picture of the Lord bending to wipe a pilgrim's eye. The warmth of such depictions comes from their comicality. Revelation does not contain anthropomorphic images of God. But it does show God. The narrator sees, not only the throne of God, but also "one seated on the throne," a multicolored being around whom is wrapped "a rainbow . . . like an emerald" (4:2–3 RSV).

The Trinity

Revelation's salutation makes reference to God ("who is, and who was, and who is to come"; cf. Isa. 44:6; 48:12), to "the seven spirits before his throne," and to "Jesus Christ, . . . the faithful witness" (Rev. 1:4b–5). It thus is the most "trinitarian" book in the Bible. In Rev. 22:13 Christ says, "I am the Alpha and the Omega, the First and the Last, the Beginning and the End" (cf. 1:8; 1:17; 21:6; etc.). As divine self-designations, "Alpha and Omega," "the First and the Last," and "the Beginning and the End" occur seven times, a number that signifies completeness for the author. Primasius and Beatus of Liébanus used Revelation against the christological heresies of Arianism and Adoptionism. The angel of Rev. 19:10 refuses the narrator's prostration, telling him to worship Christ alone. In his Revelation commentaries and *God Crucified*, Richard Bauckham contends that Revelation is pragmatically "trinitarian," in that Christ is included in the "monotheistic liturgy" of the heavenly agents. In practice, Christ is worshipped as God.

Worship of the Lamb

Revelation was probably composed for oral reading at a Christian service of worship. Each of the three scrolls in Revelation mentions true worship of God. The "last battle" is not between good and evil as abstractly conceived but between worshippers of the beast and worshippers of God. The leitmotif of the Apocalypse is worship combined with judgment. The one who is thus worshipped is not simply a conquering hero, a symbol of power, but "a Lamb standing, as though it had been slain" (5:6 RSV). The "true witnesses" who participate in this triumphal paean are those who have "conquered [the devil] by the blood of the Lamb and by the word of their testimony, for they loved not their lives even unto death" (12:11 RSV). The judgment of the world is the sacrifice of the Lamb.

Bibliography

Augustine. *Concerning the City of God against the Pagans,* trans. H. Bettenson. Penguin, 1972.

Balthasar, H. U. von. *Theo-Drama.* Vol. 4, *The Action.* Ignatius, 1994. Vol. 5, *The Last Act.* Ignatius, 1998.

Barr, D. "The Apocalypse as a Symbolic Transformation of the World: A Literary Analysis." *Int* 38, no. 1 (1984): 39–50.

———. "The Apocalypse of John as Oral Enactment." *Int* 40 (1986): 243–56.

Bauckham, R. *The Climax of Prophecy*. T&T Clark, 1993.

———. *God Crucified*. Paternoster, 1998.

———. *The Theology of the Book of Revelation*. Cambridge University Press, 1993.

Bede. *The Explanation of the Apocalypse,* trans. E. Marshall. J. Parker, 1878.

Campenhausen, H. von. *The Formation of the Christian Bible*. Black, 1968.

Carey, F., ed. *The Apocalypse and the Shape of Things to Come*. British Museum Press, 1999.

Cohn, N. *The Pursuit of the Millennium*. Secker & Warburg, 1957.

Collins, A. Y. *The Combat Myth in the Book of Revelation*. Scholars Press, 1976.

Ellul, J. *Apocalypse*. Seabury, 1977.

Emmerson, R., and B. McGinn, eds. *The Apocalypse in the Middle Ages*. Cornell University Press, 1992.

Eusebius of Caesarea. *The Ecclesiastical History,* trans. K. Lake. LCL. Heinemann, 1926.

Griffiths, P. *Olivier Messiaen and the Music of Time*. Faber & Faber, 1985.

Kermode, F. "Millennium and Apocalypse." Pages 11–27 in *The Apocalypse and the Shape of Things to Come,* ed. F. Carey. British Museum Press, 1999.

Lewis, C. S. *The Last Battle*. Bodley Head, 1956.

Metzger, B. *The Canon of the New Testament*. Clarendon, 1987.

Olson, C. "No End in Sight." *First Things* 127 (November 2002).

Peterson, E. *Reversed Thunder*. Harper, 1988.

Pieper, J. *The End of Time,* trans. M. Bullock. Faber & Faber, 1954.

Thomas Aquinas. *Summa theologiae*. Vol. IIIa, qq. 79–90.

Visser, D. *Apocalypse as Utopian Expectation (800–1500)*. Brill, 1996.

Voegelin, E. *Science, Politics and Gnosticism*. H. Regnery, 1968.

Scripture Index

Subject Index

theology of, 159–60
1 Thessalonians and, 155, 156
Third Reich, 240
Thomas Aquinas, 63, 109, 117,
119, 120, 241, 245
time, end of, 242–43
timelessness, 244
Timothy
childhood of, 171
in Philippians, 138
as successor to Paul, 170
1 Timothy, Epistle of
authenticity of, 162–63
canonical context of, 165
congregational life in, 164–65
dating of, 162–63
interpretation of, 162–63
message of, 163–65
theology of, 165–68
women in, 166–67
2 Timothy, Epistle of
authenticity of, 169–70
canonical context of, 172–73
dating of, 170
interpretation of, 169–70
message of, 170–72
style of, 170
theology of, 173–74
Titelmans, François, 63
Titus, Epistle to
authenticity of, 175
authorship of, 176, 177
canonical context of, 179
dating of, 176
emphasis on sound doctrine,
178
interpretation of, 175–77

message of, 177–79
theology of, 177, 180
tomb, empty, 69
Torah, the, 113
torah-observance, 77–78
Tractates on the Gospel of John
(Augustine), 62
tradition, 17
Trajan, 210
transfiguration, the, 43, 217
transformation, 101, 110
Triads, The (Palamas), 109
tribalism, 81
Trinity, 30, 47, 246
Tübingen School, 64, 202
two-source theory, 40
Tyconius, 237–39
Tyndale, 202

underprivileged, 99, 104

Valentinus, 97
van Eyck, Jan, 244
Venerable Bede, the. *See* Bede,
the Venerable
vengeance, 158–59
Victorinus, 236, 237
vindication, 164
violence, 94, 144
virgin birth, 52, 55
virginity, exaltation of, 120
Visser, Derk, 240
"Voice of an Eagle, The" (Eriugena), 63
Vorlage, 189
Vulgate, the, 187

water baptism, 77
way, the, 44
wealth, 168
Wesley, Charles, 109
Wesley, John, 91, 226–27
Westcott, B. F., 64
Western music, 244
Winter, S., 183
wisdom, 100, 142
Wisdom literature, 204
Wisdom of Solomon, 89
Witherington, Ben, 110
witness, 78
woman with issue of blood, 31
women, 167
and authority, 165
clothing of, 103–4, 165
in Colossians, 141
in contemporary society, 167
in 1 Corinthians, 103–4
as deacons, 164
gender heirarchy and, 103
in Luke, 55
ministry and, 166–67
status of, 144
Word, the, 66, 71, 72, 198, 224
words of institution, 35
worship, 103–4, 128, 246
wrath, 152–53
Wright, N. T., 211

Yahweh, 142, 143, 144, 151
yetser (inclination), 218

Zacchaeus, 54
Zechariah, 53
Zwingli, 202